AF698704

PRINCIPLES OF Economics

AN INCENTIVES- AND EXAMPLES-BASED APPROACH TO THE CONSEQUENCES OF ECONOMIC DECISIONS

Bassim Hamadeh, CEO and Publisher
John Remington, Senior Field Acquisitions Editor
Gem Rabanera, Project Editor
Alia Bales, Production Editor
Miguel Macias, Senior Graphic Designer
Stephanie Kohl, Licensing Coordinator
Don Kesner, Interior Designer
Natalie Piccotti, Senior Marketing Manager
Kassie Graves, Director of Acquisitions and Sales
Jamie Giganti, Senior Managing Editor

Copyright © 2019 by Cognella, Inc. All rights reserved. No part of this publication may be reprinted, reproduced, transmitted, or utilized in any form or by any electronic, mechanical, or other means, now known or hereafter invented, including photocopying, microfilming, and recording, or in any information retrieval system without the written permission of Cognella, Inc. For inquiries regarding permissions, translations, foreign rights, audio rights, and any other forms of reproduction, please contact the Cognella Licensing Department at rights@cognella.com.

Trademark Notice: Product or corporate names may be trademarks or registered trademarks, and are used only for identification and explanation without intent to infringe.

Cover image copyright© 2017 iStockphoto LP/MF3d.

Printed in the United States of America.

ISBN: 978-1-5165-3475-3 (pbk) / 978-1-5165-3476-0 (br)

cognella® | ACADEMIC PUBLISHING

PRINCIPLES OF Economics

AN INCENTIVES- AND EXAMPLES-BASED APPROACH TO THE CONSEQUENCES OF ECONOMIC DECISIONS

First Edition

Anthony Noce, Ph.D

cognella® | ACADEMIC PUBLISHING

Contents

Preface

There are three primary reasons for which I undertook this initiative to create an incentives-based approach to principles of economics. The first is that there are many students who are not business or economics majors but who would like to take an introductory economics course either as a general education elective or simply to increase their knowledge of how the economy around them functions, how government works to influence the economy, or even how to dispel the jargon that is presented to them by politicians during elections. In such cases, it is best not to present students with selected chapters from introductory microeconomics and introductory macroeconomic texts and then call it a "principles" or "survey" course. Rather, a more thoughtful approach to the understanding of economics and its applicability to everyday life would be better appreciated by such students. It would be more beneficial for the general student to have much of the mathematical sections of micro and macro texts, which are absolutely necessary and beneficial to the economics and business majors, rewritten in more accessible terms. Thus, this text is not just a collection of micro and macro chapters. It is a text that uses specifically chosen examples to illustrate the power of economic thinking and the consequences it has on everyday life.

The second reason for this undertaking was inspired by an anonymous student who wrote in their assessment of my course that the Principles of Economics class is delivered exactly as it should be—solely on the basics—nothing more, nothing less—and that it was kept lively and interesting with many examples. In this vein, I use examples in this text that are relevant and thought-provoking and I limit the text to a set of chapters that can actually be covered in one semester. Rather than overwhelm a text with extra material that will never be covered in a principles course, this book focuses on developing a finite amount of material so that students do not feel overwhelmed but yet get a good grounding in the basics of economic theory and application.

The third reason follows from the second. There are many extraordinary microeconomics and macroeconomics texts on the market available to students, which are well written and wholly appropriate for students in business and economics. However, using these texts for a principles course may be a zealous attempt to gourmandize a principles course, but an unnecessary one. In addition, it is difficult to justify textbook price ranges for a principles course. So, in an effort to moderate costs for students, this text presents material that is truly for one semester of teaching, and should there be additional material that a particular instructor feels is relevant or important, then the instructor has the flexibility to add such material to his or her course.

This book is intended primarily for nonmajors to meet specific general education learning outcomes, but economics and business students can find it a useful reference. The material in this book can also easily be adapted for seniors in high school for the general economics course or for AP economics courses. I truly hope the reader enjoys the many examples and the approach used herein.

Pedagogical Note to Instructors and Students

The treatment of economics throughout each chapter includes application or thought questions that allow students to pause and evaluate their understanding of the knowledge they have just acquired. However, unlike other texts, the chapters do not have end-of-chapter questions. Rather, the book has been divided into three sections, each section grouping three or four similarly themed chapters, and at the end of each section, students will find a test, which would be similar to an in-class test lasting about 75 minutes. Each test will cover information found within the section and includes a combination of multiple-choice questions, short-answer essay-type questions, mathematical calculations, and/or analytical questions. The purpose of testing by section is to allow the student to evaluate his or her ***comprehensive*** knowledge of each economic theme. Solutions to each test are provided at the end of each test.

About the Author

Anthony Noce has been a professor in the Department of Economics and Finance since the 2014–2015 academic year. In 2017, after only three years of teaching at SUNY Plattsburgh, Dr. Noce was honored with SUNY Plattsburgh's prestigious Teacher Excellence Award.

Dr. Noce joined SUNY Plattsburgh after working as a senior economist for the Government of Canada. He spent 12 years working for three federal government departments—Health, Industry and Fisheries and Oceans—where he was responsible for a variety of economic and policy files. He also served as a delegate for the Canadian government at the Organization for Cooperation and Development (OECD), Paris, France, participating in the development of the first surveys on information and communication technologies. Dr. Noce has also taught at Castleton University, Vermont, USA; Concordia University and Marianopolis College, Quebec, Canada; and Algonquin College, Ontario, Canada.

Dr. Noce holds degrees in both chemistry and economics and teaches in the following areas:

Principles of Economics
Introductory Micro- and Macro-Economics
Intermediate Macroeconomic Theory
Intermediate Business Statistics
Environmental and Ecological Economics
Sustainability
Econometrics and Multivariate Statistics

Dr. Noce's research focuses on the following topics:

Economic growth and environmental/ecological interactions
The role of energy and technology in economic growth
Incentives
Deuterated hydrogen-ozone radical reaction kinetics using quantum chemistry computational methods

SECTION 1

CHAPTERS 1–4

The Foundational Knowledge

ANCIENT GREEK STREET VENDOR: Street vendor offering fruits and pastries stacked in a great basket.

Source: *https://commons.wikimedia.org/wiki/File:Street_vendor_Pan_Painter_MAN.jpg.*

CHAPTER 1

Incentives and Scarcity

LEARNING EXPECTATIONS

- To understand and apply the main themes of economics
- To critically relate the concept of efficiency to scarcity
- To relate scarcity to opportunity cost and determine opportunity cost using production possibility frontier graphs

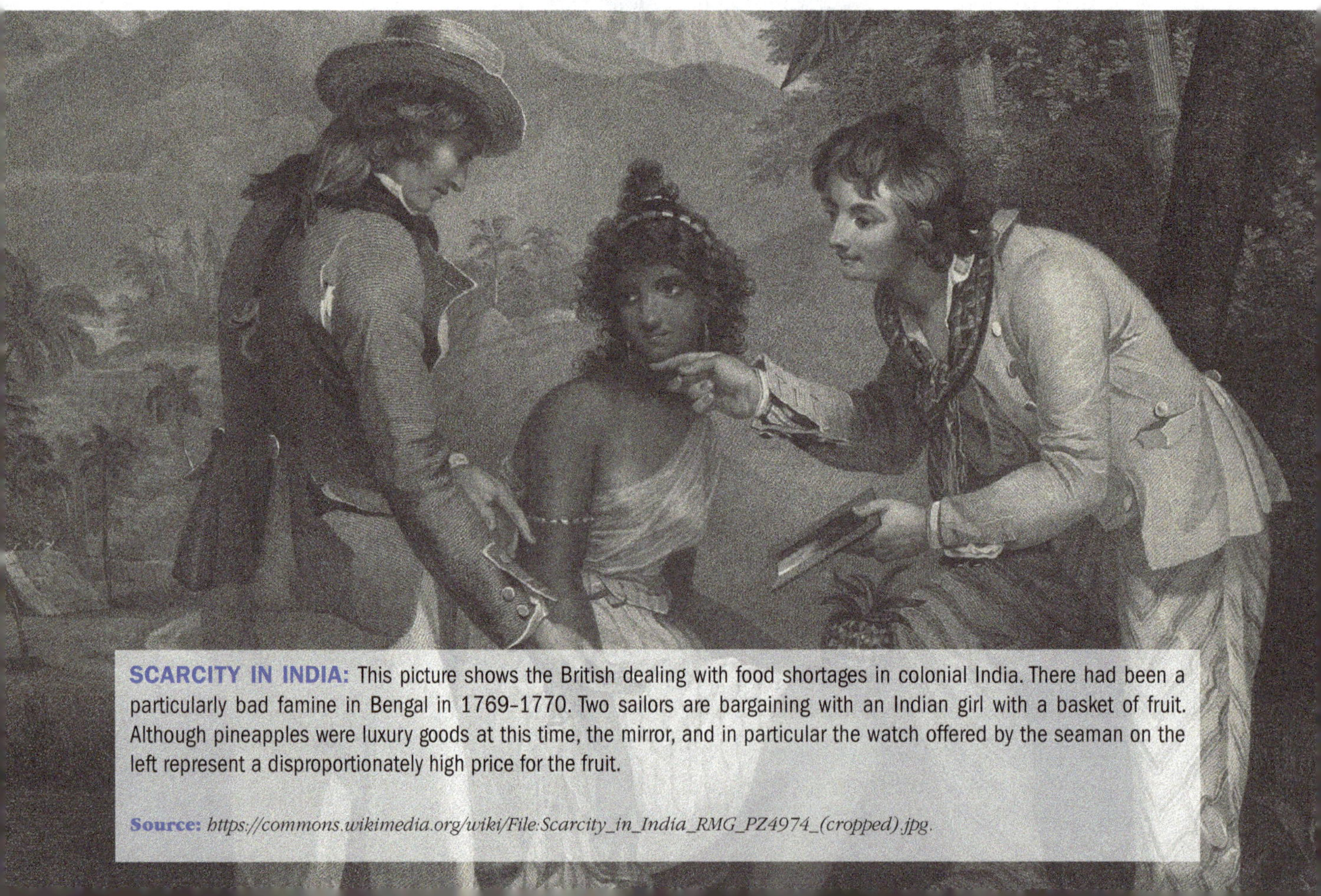

SCARCITY IN INDIA: This picture shows the British dealing with food shortages in colonial India. There had been a particularly bad famine in Bengal in 1769-1770. Two sailors are bargaining with an Indian girl with a basket of fruit. Although pineapples were luxury goods at this time, the mirror, and in particular the watch offered by the seaman on the left represent a disproportionately high price for the fruit.

Source: *https://commons.wikimedia.org/wiki/File:Scarcity_in_India_RMG_PZ4974_(cropped).jpg.*

The Definition

Many people have had mixed ideas of what economics is really about. In one sense, it is similar to psychology. That is, it is about the study of human behavior. But unlike psychology, economics is not the study of only human behavior, but the interaction of human behavior with different environments. Interactions can occur between individuals (or households), or between individuals and firms, or firms and government, or firms and the natural environment, and so forth. All these players—firms, households, and governments—are referred to as **agents** in the language of economics. What we tend to do in economics is try to predict the behavior of agents.

There are two aspects to economics. Introductory textbooks usually focus on economics as the study of the allocation of **scarce resources.** We all face limited resources—be they human or labor resources, natural resources such as land, capital (machinery, infrastructure) resources, technological resources, or even time. Economics, in part, then is the study of how we should allocate these limited resources efficiently. However, there is another aspect to economics. Economics is also about incentives and behavior. The classic definition of economics comes from the English economist Lionel Robbins when, in 1935, he described economics as a science in which we study human behavior as a relationship between ends and scarce means that have alternative uses. That is a fine definition, but economics is also about how individuals, firms, different markets, and governments respond to incentives. So let us begin with a definition of incentives, what are they, and some interesting stories of how incentives work and how they backfire. We will then move on to the more classic definition and application of economics, which is the allocation of scarce resources.

Theme 1: Incentives

Let us consider the first theme: responding to incentives. So, what are incentives? Well, first, what they are not are motivations. Rather,

- **Incentives** are inducements to act in a particular way. They are **extrinsic** or external awards or benefits "offered" contingent upon an outcome (e.g., tax credit for fuel-efficient cars).
- Incentives can also appear in the form of costs (e.g., sin taxes).
- Incentives are simply a way to communicate to agents that you would like them to alter their behavior. The agent still has the choice to accept the guidance—or not.
- Incentives do not necessarily change motivation, and the two ideas are not the same. Consider the following questions:
    - Who gets stronger in the face of failure? Answer: motivated people.
    - Who shies away from failure? Answer: incentivized people.

Studies[1] have shown that **intrinsic** (internal or self-generated) motivation will decrease over time if extrinsic incentives are introduced for behaviors that an individual already found motivating. Thus, while incentives are not motivations, they are inducements for one to alter one's behavior. Incentives are there because an individual, a firm, a government, or even oneself wants some alteration in one's behavior.

Incentives are offered contingent upon some outcome. Take sin taxes as an example. A **sin tax** is a special tax on goods or services that are deemed undesirable or harmful to an individual or society, such as alcohol or tobacco. Some states and local governments are imposing or considering imposing sin taxes on soda. The sin tax is meant to discourage (i.e., a disincentive or negative incentive) one from smoking and drinking. So the incentive there is that if you have to pay more, then you actually curtail your activity.

Another example of a (positive) incentive is a tax credit for fuel-efficient cars. So if you are in the market to buy a new car, the government may reduce the price by providing a rebate on it via credit. You, the purchaser, would have an incentive to buy a more fuel-efficient car than you would otherwise. Of course, the agent can accept or not accept the incentive. There is always a free choice.

The Two Types of Economic Incentives

While there may be many different types of incentives, such as moral or natural incentives, economists are generally interested in the following two:

1. **Monetary or remunerative:** incentives that come in the form of material reward, such as bribes, pay bonuses, and the like, for behaving in a particular manner—especially money in exchange for acting in a particular way. Wages, prices, and bribery are all examples of remunerative incentives.
2. **Threatening or coercive: incentives that** engage the agent in punishment for behaving incorrectly.

Incentives Example 1: Terrorism, Drugs, and Remunerative Incentives

Let us take a look at the Afghan mujahideen. They were initially Islamic, Afghan opposition groups to the government of the pro-Soviet Democratic Republic of Afghanistan during the late 1970s. The Soviet war in Afghanistan, which lasted from 1979 to 1989, saw the mujahideen fight against both the Soviet forces in Afghanistan and the Afghan government. Their operations were funded by collecting taxes from peasant farmers that were growing opium poppies.

The United States had interests in blocking expansionary ideas of the Soviet Union and thus supported the mujahideen through the CIA's Afghan operation. The CIA recommended that the mujahideen levy high taxes on the land used by Afghan poppy farmers in order to finance the resistance against the Soviet Union.[2] Imposing a tax on poppy farmers would lead one to think that this is a disincentive to the production of opium poppy, somewhat akin to a sin tax.

If you are an opium poppy farmer and I tax you, what happens? You will grow less of the crop, right? That would be the normal response, but opium poppy production is very lucrative, and farmers would not switch to growing another less profitable crop. Therefore, the opposite occurred, just as the CIA had envisioned. The land tax forced (i.e., incentivised) farmers to intensify opium production enough to afford the tax increases.[2] In fact, in the fertile Helmand valley, which was once the breadbasket of southern Afghanistan, CIA arms were transported into that region via Pakistan for the resistance against the Soviets, and the caravans that carried those arms more often than not returned to Pakistan filled with opium. Once the opium crossed the border into Pakistan, it was sold to one or more of the 100 to 200 Pakistani heroin refiners operating in the country's covert war zone administered by the CIA's close ally, General Fazle Haq,[3] a high-ranking general in the Pakistan Army and the former martial law administrator of Khyber Pakhtunkhwa Province in Pakistan.

This tax incentive to grow more, not less opium poppy, had disastrous effects on Afganistan's agricultural sector. Instead of growing other crops, almost all of the fertile land was used to grow opium poppy. It also had disastrous effects on the rest of the world, as much of the heroin produced in Pakistan found its way to European and American youths.

Incentives Example 2: Low Birthrates

Most of the developed world is facing very low birthrates, with replacement levels falling below that which is required to keep a population size stable. The replacement level for most industrialized countries is 2.0 to 2.1 children per woman but can be as high as 3.3 in developing countries where there is a high mortality rate. Globally, a replacement level of 2.33 children per woman would keep the world's population growth rate at zero.

One particular European country, Estonia, was facing extremely low birthrates of 1.2 to 1.3 children per woman in the mid-1990s. The Estonian government started to worry, because at replacement levels of 1.2 children per woman, the country faced a decreasing population in which millions of Estonians would not be replaced over the next 40 to 50 years. With the threat of losing half of its population, the Estonian government decided in the late 1990s to pay women to have more children. Thus, they offered a remunerative incentive of paying working women who take time off after having a baby their entire salary for up to 15 months. Will this incentive convince you to have one more baby than you had otherwise planned? Do you think Estonian women said, "Yeah, I'll sign up for this"?

The result of this government incentive proved to be disappointing (see figure 1.1). Birthrates increased from a low of 1.28 children in the late 1990s to about 1.72 in 2010 and started to fall again after 2010. The birthrates have since never reached replacement levels.

FIGURE 1.1 Total Fertility Rates for Estonia, 1960–2014

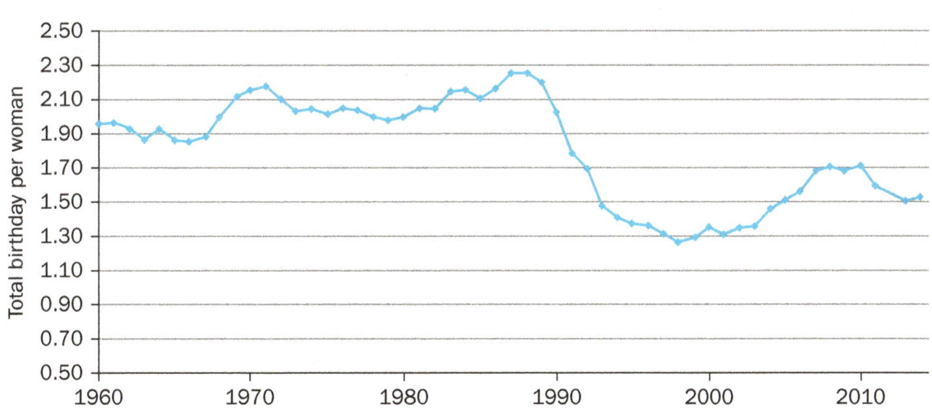

Incentives Example 3: High Birthrates and the Case for Condoms

Unlike many developed countries, developing and underdeveloped nations sometimes have the opposite problem of not enough children—too many babies. Some in developed countries hold the view that developing nations have too many children and that is what holds back their economic growth. Many nonprofit organizations and famous speakers such as Bono and Bill and Hillary Clinton advocate that developed nations should help developing countries reduce their birthrates. The theory and reason are put as follows: A lot of individuals in developing nations do not have access to birth control or cannot afford birth control. Therefore, developed nations should help provide free birth control. One way to do this is to provide free condoms.

This idea to control exponential population growth is not new to economics. In the early 19th century, Thomas Malthus also warned about exponential population growth outstripping food production, which would lead to widespread famine. Today, this concern is more about exponential population growth outpacing economic growth. While most economists find that there is no evidence that population growth affects either negatively or positively per capita economic growth, some have taken to the belief that affordability of contraceptives is the main cause of unchecked population growth and, by extension, the main cause of low economic growth. Some countries such as the United Kingdom have in the past contributed millions of dollars to supply the developing world with both male and female condoms.

The World Bank also maintained efforts to contain population growth in some underdeveloped countries. The World Bank's so-called cash for condoms program is heavily criticized in renowned economist William Easterly's book *The Elusive Quest for Growth*, in which he argues that condoms could never prevent unwanted babies because babies cost more than condoms; thus, if it were a question of affordability, couples would simply elect not to have babies. This has not happened, because the incentives for having children are quite numerous. In some villages, having many children, especially boys, is very important because they work on the farm. So, one would ask, "Why would I use condoms if I need seven boys to help me out on the farm?" In some places, having girls can help generate funds for a family. Some girls can be sold to older, rich men as brides, thus benefiting the remaining members of the household. In other villages, people tend to have a lot of children because many of them die during the first few years of childhood due to a prevalence of disease and bad health care. So, a household may decide on having twice as many children as they would otherwise need in order to create their own form of child insurance.

In sum, it is the lack of economic growth that does not provide the incentive to reduce fertility rates, and not the lack of contraceptives that reduces economic growth rates.

Incentives Can Backfire

There are instances in which rewarding self-interest with economic incentives can backfire. First articulated by Adam Smith, an 18th-century Scottish moral philosopher and pioneer of political economy, incentives that go against one's "moral sentiments" are counterproductive.[4] In fact, experimental economists have found evidence that supports *The Theory of Moral Sentiments*' suggestion that incentives that contradict one's moral sentiment would likely backfire. For example, in one experiment, offering a reward for donating blood decreased the number of people willing to donate by about half. Yet allowing blood donors to contribute the reward to charity reversed the effect. In this experiment, it seems that the reward or incentive backfired because it likely makes the blood donor feel like he or she is interested in profit rather than being altruistic. In another experiment conducted in Haifa, Israel, six day care centers implemented fines for late pickups. The disincentive backfired such that the number of late parents doubled. The fine may have reduced the parents' ethical obligation of not inconveniencing the day care employees. The fine transformed "lateness" into a simple commodity (service) that parents could now buy.[4]

Incentives can backfire even if morals are not involved. Take, for example, a book published by Ralph Nader (1965), entitled *Unsafe at Any Speed*, which called attention to various design elements that made cars more dangerous than necessary. The federal government responded with "a wide range of automobile safety legislation, mandating the use of seat belts, padded dashboards, collapsible steering columns, dual braking systems, and penetration-resistant windshields."[5] Economists, of course, would have been happy to point out that they could have predicted the consequence of such regulations: an increase in the number of car accidents. What? Why? Well, a relatively high risk of dying in a car accident is quite a strong incentive to drive carefully. However, a driver with safety features such as a seat belt and padded dashboard is less at risk for death. Responding to incentives, drivers drove less carefully. The result was more accidents.[5]

Theme 2: Scarcity

We will now explore theme 2, the classic theme in economics: the study of the allocation of scarce resources. We broadly group resources in the world into four categories:

1. Land and other natural resources
2. Labor resources (technical/nontechnical)
3. Capital (buildings, machinery, and technology)
4. Time

So, what makes a resource scarce? Too much demand for it? Not exactly a demand issue. Rather, any good or service that, if priced at zero, would be in short supply is defined as a **scarce** good or service.

Let us ask the following question: *Is moon dust scarce?*

The supply of moon dust is fixed, but there is no foreseeable human need for it. Thus, it is not "scarce."

Let us ask another question: *Is the first bucket of herring caught scarce?*

To answer this question, it would be helpful to know that it is referring to Vlaggetjesdag (Flag Day), which is the event that heralds the arrival of the New Dutch herring every year. The herring from the first basket is auctioned off for many thousands of euros. The inexpensive fish commands such a high price because the first bucket has traditionally been held as symbol of good harvest, and because there is only one "first" bucket, it can be deemed as scarce.

One can also create an artificial kind of scarcity to increase a good's or service's value. Music artists do this when they announce their "last concert" tour, only to then have another a few years later.

Example of Resource Scarcity—Water: Lesotho and South Africa's Military Coup

The South African province of Transvaal is quite dry; the arid conditions sometimes lead to critical water shortages. To alleviate the problem, South Africa tried in vain to negotiate with Lesotho, a landlocked country within the borders of South Africa, for 30 years to divert water from Lesotho's mountains to Transvaal. At one point, a military coup against Lesotho's tribal government took place, and in 1986, South Africa gave its support to Lesotho's military, which eventually was successful in its coup. South Africa admitted to providing its support for the coup for one reason only—South Africa claimed that Lesotho had been providing sanctuary to guerrillas of the African National Congress, which were fighting the South African government at that time. Although the reason provided is a legitimate one, interestingly, within months the governments of both countries concluded an agreement, the huge Highlands Water Project, that provided South Africa with the water it required. The need for water was likely an ulterior motive for South Africa's assistance to Lesotho's military coup.[6] Research suggests that the renewable resource most likely to stimulate interstate resource war is river water.[6]

Scarcity Leads to Choice or Trade-Offs

If we have scarce resources, we have to make choices in the use of something that is in short supply. We have to use scarce resources in the most efficient manner possible. So what are the choices societies, individuals, and governments have to make?

Scarcity leads to the following choices:

1. What goods and services will be produced?
   (e.g., more day care centers or more football stadiums; more hospitals or more schools; more heart surgeries or more cancer treatments)
2. How will the goods and services be produced?
   (e.g., more labor or more machines; in the United States or offshore)
3. For whom will the goods and services be produced?
   (e.g., are the goods and services for a particular group or class of society?)

These are all questions that need to be asked and answered, given scarce resources. If these were not issues of concern, one would not need to concern oneself with the study of economics. The way in which a society answers these questions is in the manner in which it votes for particular types of governments or leaders. Political parties and leaders often have different views on how resources should be allocated, and the way the choices are made is a direct result of which political party is governing a country.

One should note that scarcity is not the same thing as poverty. Scarcity can occur among the rich. Low incomes do not create more scarcity, and high income levels do not create less scarcity.

Example of Trade-Offs: The Avahan Project (India)

Assume you are presented with the following choices (trade-off) in effective prevention of deaths (in the developing world) from AIDS:

1. spend money on educating prostitutes, OR
2. spend (the same amount of money) on retroviral treatments

Which do you think is most effective? According to the World Health Organization, money spent on educating prostitutes saves at least 100 times more lives than the same amount of money spent on retroviral treatment. An example of such education comes from the Avahan project (India). This project works to reduce HIV transmission among sex workers. The project accomplishes its aims through sexual education, promotion of condoms, promotion of behavioral change, and community advocacy. The Avahan project has been quite effective. From 2003 to 2013, the Avahan project prevented 57% of HIV infections in southern India. As a result, this particular project has been internationally recognized as a cost-effective and successful HIV prevention program.[7]

Efficiency and Scarcity

If one wants to achieve a maximum amount of output when faced with limited resources, then it is imperative that one employs the resources in the most efficient manner possible. An **efficient process** is one that uses the minimum amount of resources to achieve the desired result.

How does the concept of efficiency relate to scarcity? Think about whether your time is scarce. How do you use it differently during exam week versus a vacation period?

If a resource is not regarded as scarce, then one does not need to care much about how to use it efficiently. For instance, there is plenty of air around us, and for most of us, it is clean, safe air to breathe. It is easily considered not to be scare. However, when more burdens are put on a resource such as clean air, then the importance of efficiency escalates.

Let us examine the ownership of scarce resources, and which society uses them most efficiently. There are three types of economic systems, summarized in Figure 1.2, where the ownership of scarce resources differs:

1. **Capitalism:** A type of economic system in which ownership of productive resources is privately held. Resource allocation decisions are made mostly through free markets. What to produce and what to buy is decided by consumers and private firms. Capitalism is part of what is called **classical liberalism**—a system that relies on open elections and on markets. Most of the time, but not always, capitalism is the more efficient and less egalitarian of the three types of economic systems. It produces more wealth but suffers from unequal distribution of the wealth.

2. **Socialism:** A type of economic system in which ownership of productive resources is held by the government. Resource allocation decisions are made through public agencies. These agencies could be accountable to the populace and subject to political control through elections, but they also could be simply coordinated by government.

   Socialism doesn't necessarily imply one kind of political system over another. Socialism is sometimes less efficient but more egalitarian in the distribution of wealth that it generates. It may, however, not generate as much wealth as capitalism. To some extent, this may be a result of socialism's focus on providing jobs for the masses rather than on providing goods and services.

   In a pure form of socialism, ownership of resources is transferred to the workers. This means that the United States is not a country that operates under the banner of socialism. However, it is, in part, a social democracy because of social programs such as Social Security, Medicare and Medicaid, unemployment insurance, and food stamps. Bernie Sanders, for example, who campaigned for the 2016 Democratic presidential nomination, would have likely moved the United States toward a purer form of socialism with his 12-point proposal for the country. His 12-point proposal encouraged workers to set up worker-owned cooperatives. He is a supporter of a social democratic, Scandinavian-style welfare state in that he advocates better and free state education, health care, and social service provisions for the general population. He did not, however, advocate the appropriation of private-sector firms.[8]

3. **Communism:** Similar to socialism, communism is a type of economic system in which ownership of productive resources is held by the government. However, resource allocation decisions and government ownership of productive resources are enforced via a one-party state (referred to as a **central planner**). The level of public ownership is the highest of all three economic systems. Communism generates less wealth than capitalism or socialism, and it is generally the least efficient system, but it is the most egalitarian system (although under communism, dictators and high-ranking party officials live in a better socioeconomic state than do common citizens).

FIGURE 1.2 Summary of Efficiency and Egalitarian Ratings

	Least Efficient	Moderately Efficient	Most Efficient
least Egalitarian			Capitalism
Moderately Egalitarian		Socialism	
Most Egalitarian	Communism		

Ownership of Scarce Resources: Accountability Matters

In terms of efficiency, the party that is accountable for the use of scarce resources usually takes efficiency seriously. However, when accountability is unclear, so are the outcomes. Let us look to foreign aid as an example. In foreign aid, the traditional approach is to announce good intentions and allocate a lot of money. However, some have asked, maybe somewhat rhetorically, why in the past 50 years—in which the West spent $2.3 trillion on foreign aid—has the West not been able to deliver $4 bed nets to poor families and $0.12 medicines to children to prevent half of all malaria deaths, but in a single day, July 16, 2005, the American and British economies delivered 9 million copies of the newest Harry Potter book to its fans? This is a question of accountability.

When it is clear who is accountable, then efficiency reigns. For example, the Washington, DC, nonprofit organization Population Services International (PSI) is funded based on outcomes. When outcomes are desirable, it is able to attract more funding. PSI is accountable for the outcome. In one instance, the organization was able to deliver insecticide-treated bed nets to the poor in Malawi. PSI created a two-tiered system by selling nets to poor mothers and to health clinics in the Malawian countryside for $0.50, and to richer, urban Malawians through private markets for $5 per net. Note that nurses who distribute the nets get rewarded $0.09 per net, which provides them with the incentive to always keep the nets in stock.[9]

Opportunity Cost

Every time scarcity forces one to make a choice, one is incurring an **opportunity cost**—the cost incurred of giving up the *next best* alternative choice. Opportunity costs are measured in terms of *forgone alternatives*: a decision to have more of one thing requires a decision to have less of something else. If you decide to do one more heart surgery and you have to give up one cancer treatment, then your forgone alternative is a cancer treatment. If the cancer treatment is your next best alternative choice to a heart surgery, then the opportunity cost of one heart surgery is one cancer treatment. Countries and governments incur opportunity costs as well as firms and individuals. When you need to decide whether you would rather study for a course or go out to the local bar, you are faced with a choice. If you decide to go to the bar and your next best alternative is to study, then your opportunity cost is the three hours of study time. If your next best choice happens to be going to the movies, then that is your opportunity cost.

Example: North Korea Faces Opportunity Costs as Well

North Korea, like any other country, makes choices when deciding what resources to use to produce goods and services. Of course, if the North Koreans decide to put all their efforts into producing military goods and use their tractors to pull servicemen and missile launchers instead of using the tractors for wheat production, then their opportunity cost is the X amount of wheat that they could have produced had they used the tractors for agricultural instead of military purposes.

North Korea has also made the choice to start brewing Taedonggang beer. Beer production requires barley and/or wheat, which are scarce resources that can be used for other purposes such as feeding animals and humans. North Korea has very scarce resources, so it tends to have bouts of famines and many undernourished or malnourished citizens. Thus, whatever barley or wheat that is being used to produce beer could have been used to feed the poor. From 1994 to 1998, 3 million people died of malnutrition, but during that time, the government decided that it was going to import expensive but used brewing equipment from England and pay millions of dollars for it to start producing this special North Korean beer. The opportunity cost of Taedonggang beer is the 3 million people that died during the same time period.

Opportunity Cost Application Questions

1. In 2014, the National Security Agency (NSA) in the United States was criticized for monitoring individuals' cell phone calls, e-mails, and so forth. If one is going to put resources into monitoring communications, then there is an opportunity cost of having people monitoring the calls and of creating the infrastructure and the technology. Can you discuss what those trade-offs would have been or could have been?

   One possible answer is that the big trade-off is between the right to privacy (which is a benefit we all enjoy) and greater security—particularly protection from terrorist threats (from which we also benefit). Another possible answer is that if the best alternative of use for the billions of dollars spent on monitoring could have been for health care research, then the opportunity cost of NSA surveillance is less progress in cancer or childhood diseases research.

2. Assume now that a popular music video was viewed by many different people. That is, the total viewings are 2,039,916,167. Also, assume that the video is 4 minutes and 12 seconds long. If we are considering the construction of the Empire State Building as the best forgone alternative, what would be the opportunity cost of watching the music video in its entirety? Note that the Empire State Building took 7 million labor hours to build. What is the opportunity cost of watching the music video in terms of Empire State Buildings?

   Answer: Viewers have spent about 8,567,647,901 minutes watching the video (2,039,916,167 × 4.2 minutes). That's equivalent to about 142,794,132 hours. If the Empire State Building took about 7,000,000 hours to complete, then the opportunity cost of the music video is 142,794,132 ÷ 7,000,000, or 20.4 Empire State Buildings.

Depicting Opportunity Cost Graphically

We can depict opportunity costs and trade-offs graphically using a two-dimensional graph called a **production possibility curve (PPC)**, sometimes referred to as a **production possibility frontier.** We illustrate opportunity costs using two aggregate goods (i.e., goods measured in grouped category such as "food" or "military goods") so that each aggregate good is placed on a corresponding axis. A PPC illustrates the different combinations of goods and/or services (called bundles) that can be produced with a given amount of resources in the most efficient way. Any point or bundle below a PPC implies that the bundle is attainable, but scarce resources are not being utilized efficiently. Any point or bundle outside a PPC suggests that the bundle is unattainable given the current level of scarce resources. A bundle of goods that lies on the PPC suggests that the bundle of goods is attainable and that resources are being utilized most efficiently. Thus, in figure 1.3, bundles A are unattainable with the given resource levels; bundles B and C are attainable and efficiently produced; and bundles D are attainable but not produced efficiently.

Note that a PPC can be drawn as a linear (straight) line, as in panel B in figure 1.3, which implies **constant opportunity costs** between two goods or services. That is, increasing output of good Y from 10 units to 20 units (moving from bundle C to bundle B) incurs an opportunity cost of 15 units (50 – 35), and that cost will always be the same along the entire curve.

In contrast, a PPC can be drawn, more realistically, as a concave function, as in panel A in figure 1.3, which implies **increasing or decreasing opportunity costs** between two goods or services. That is, increasing output of good Y by moving from bundle C to bundle B incurs an opportunity cost of only 5 units (50 – 45), but this cost is not the same along the entire curve. For concave curves, opportunity costs always increase as we give up more and more of one good for the other.

FIGURE 1.3 Possible PPCs

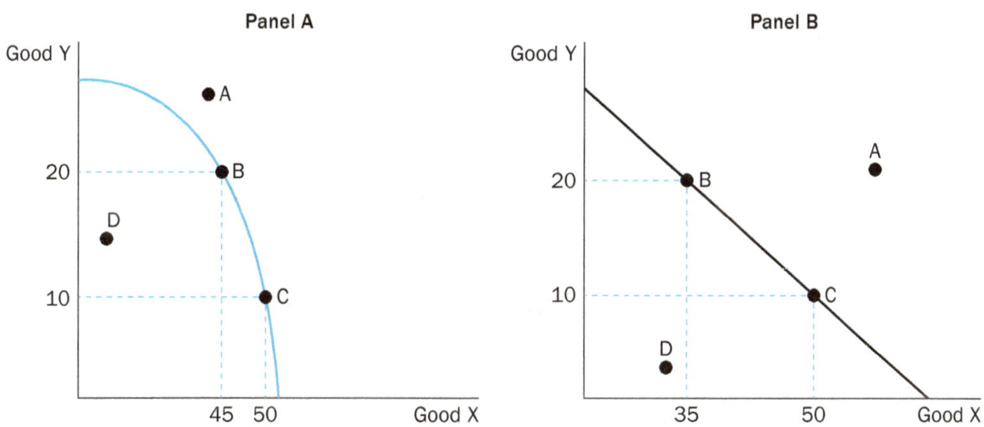

Let us proceed to explain the phenomenon of changing marginal opportunity cost using Portugal as an example (see figure 1.4). Assume that Portugal produces only two aggregate goods: wine and soccer players. As the economy moves down along its PPC, there are *increasing marginal opportunity costs* because increasing wine production by a given quantity requires ever larger decreases in the production of soccer players. For instance, if one were to increase wine production from 0 to 200 units, then the economy has to part with only 50 soccer players. This is illustrated by moving from point A to point B. However, if one were to scale up production further, by another 200 units, then the economy has to part with 150 soccer players. This is illustrated by moving from point B to point C.

Increasing opportunity cost is a universal phenomenon because resources are not all equally efficient in all production applications.

FIGURE 1.4 Portugal's PPC

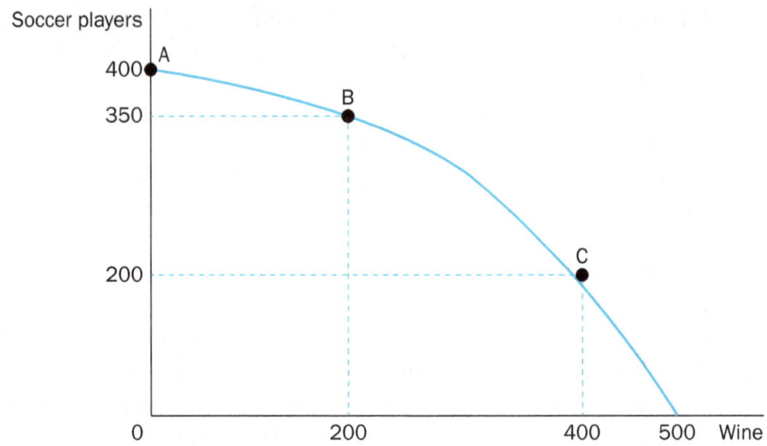

Shifts in the PPC

The PPC will shift outward when there are:

1. Improvements in productivity and efficiency (e.g., new technology or techniques of production); or
2. Increases in availability or exploitation of factor resources (e.g., increase in the size of the workforce, more capital equipment available for businesses, new energy resources).

The PPC will shift inward when there is:

1. A reduction in a country's, individual's, or firm's ability to produce any given good or service. This may be a result of war, bad management, loss of natural resources, and so forth; or
2. A loss of technology due to economic decline.

Figure 1.5 illustrates the case of improved production capacity in a given country, which leads to economic growth due to technological changes in either one or both production sectors. Panel A illustrates that increases in the availability of resources and new, more efficient technologies allow the economy to move from point A (using technology or resources available in, say, 1987) to point B, producing more computer chips and more beef (using technology or resources available in, say, 2017).

Panel B illustrates how technological change in beef production increases the quantity of meat farmers can produce per year, but a lack of technological improvements in the computer sector leaves the maximum quantity of computer chips that can be produced unchanged. Both of the panels show shifts in the production possibilities curve that represent **economic growth.**

FIGURE 1.5 PPCs Shifts and Economic Growth

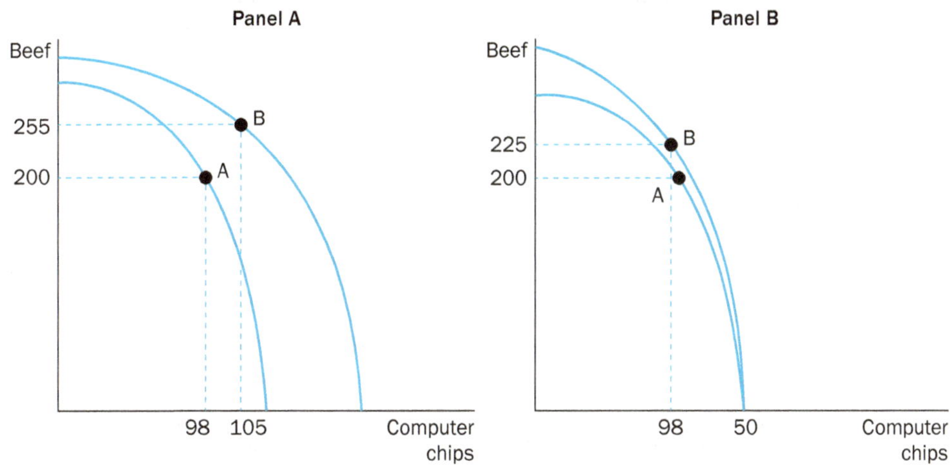

A SOLVED PPC APPLICATION EXERCISE[10]

A student can study (or, in economic terminology, produce/acquire knowledge) using the following combination of semester study hours for psychology and biology.

Alternative	Semester Hours Devoted to Psychology	Semester Hours Devoted to Biology
A	50	0
B	40	10
C	30	18
D	20	24
E	10	28
F	0	30

a. Draw the PPC. Place biology hours on the x-axis.

b. Is it possible and/or efficient for this society to produce 25 psychology study hours and 25 biology study hours?

c. Is it possible and/or efficient for this society to produce 42 psychology study hours and 1 biology study hour?

d. If the society is currently producing alternative B, then the opportunity cost of moving to alternative A is ______ biology study hours.

e. Is the opportunity cost of producing psychology study hours higher or lower moving from alternative F to E than moving from B to A? Why?

f. Draw a new PPC if you improve the efficiency in resources used for increasing both psychology study hours and biology study hours.

Answers:

a.

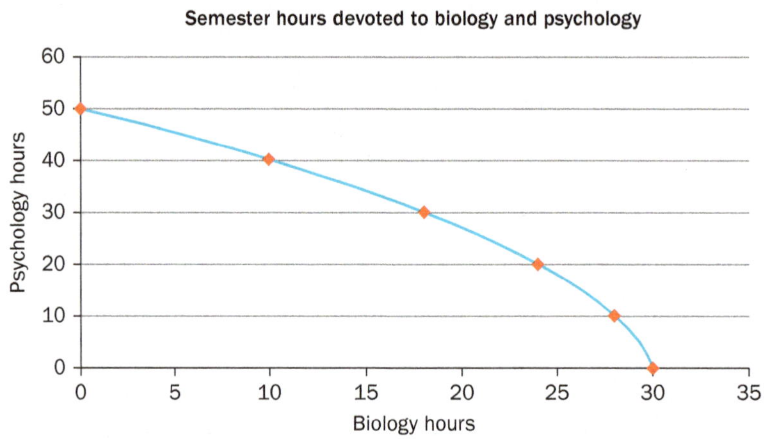

b. Not possible—would require MORE than an efficient use of resources

c. Possible, but inefficient

d. 10

e. Lower (only 2 biology study hours are forgone). Producing the first few psychology study hours likely uses resources that are not well suited for biology study.

f.

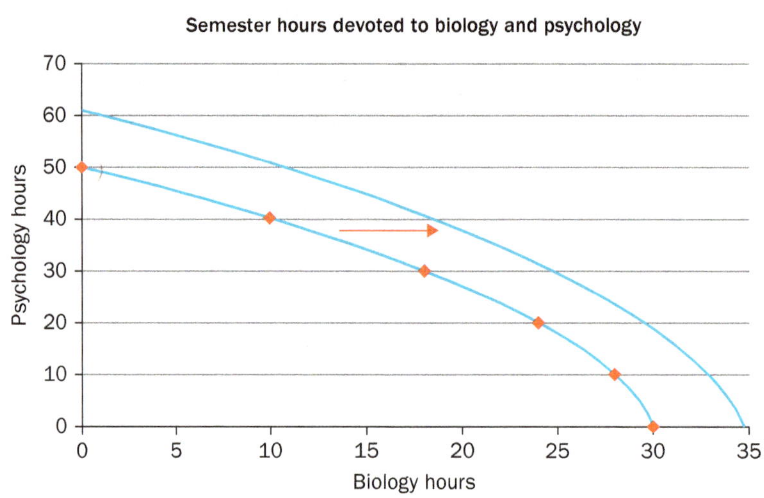

Chapter Summary

In this chapter, we noted that economics is the scientific study of relationships between various agents. These agents—individuals or households, governments, firms, and even the environment—continuously interact with each other. The economic study of these complex interactions among the various agents is not unlike psychology. Economists engage in the study of human behavior in which humans make economic decisions concerning the allocation of scarce resources. Both psychologists and economists know well that humans respond to incentives, and the form in which an incentive exists can provide one with the ability to alter an agent's behavior. Furthermore, choices, scarcity and opportunity cost are prominent in all societies. The way in which societies make the choices always implies the existence of cost. A production possibility curve is a graphical manner in which one can illustrate the attainable combinations of two goods or services, given a set of scarce resources. Ownership of those resources can be divided among private or public interests, depending on a country's economic system.

CHAPTER 2

Economics Is Not a Belief System

FACTS VERSUS OPINIONS

LEARNING EXPECTATIONS

- To differentiate between a belief system and one based on scientific inquiry
- To understand and recognize different types of economic statements
- To understand the role of experimental data versus observational data

Source: *Copyright © Andreas Schwarzkopf (CC BY-SA 3.0) at https://commons.wikimedia.org/wiki/File:2017-04-22,_March_for_Science_in_Freiburg,_Plakat_Science_is_not_belief_system_auf_dem_Augustinerplatz.jpg.*

It is unfortunate that some hold the view that economics as a discipline requires a token amount of faith in its theories and laws. Perhaps it is the continuous exposure to political debates that espouse "belief" in an economic approach versus another. Too often, politicians or even laypersons state, "I believe that system or approach X is better than approach Y." Well, there is no need to "believe" in one type of economics or another; economics is not a religious-based discipline. Rather, economics is an extremely empirically-based system in which conclusions are based on rigorous statistical and mathematical analyses. Economists require extensive training, at the graduate level, in modeling, simulation, statistical analysis, and cognitive reasoning. While it is true that economists have views, such as *having more goods and services is better than having fewer* or *eradicating the world of material poverty is an ultimate goal*, these views in and of themselves are not true belief systems. Rather, they are formed as part of an exploration and understanding of data and other observations of economic phenomena.

Although economics as a discipline is not a belief system, economists can sometimes be guilty of imposing their own value systems on the goal of economics as a discipline. As Robert H. Nelson has written, "Richard Ely, who helped found the American Economic Association in 1885, believed that economics would provide the scientific knowledge to sustain 'a never-ceasing attack on every wrong institution, until the earth becomes a new earth, and all its cities, cities of God.'"[11] Economics—or more correctly, economists—have an enthusiasm for economic progress, and one may argue that holding the view that economic progress is the only way to eliminate poverty is somewhat akin to having a religious devotion to a strongly held belief. For instance, are we absolutely certain that the use of free markets, which are most effective in maximizing total available goods and service in any one country, also results in net social gains for, say, the United States when the United States moves toward markets with concentrated power in retail (e.g., Walmart, Target, Costco) and agrochemicals (Bayer, Monsanto, and a few others) that can supress wages (via trade), cause thousands of smaller business to close their doors, and undermine the vitality of some communities?

Like any other scientist, economists can disagree on any one conclusion or theory that is grounded in incomplete data. Economists are sometimes unable to carry out true experiments. In contrast to many laboratory experiments, in which the effect of one factor on some dependent variable can be isolated from others, much of the data collected for the purpose of economic analysis are observational data, in which one cannot control for extraneous influencing factors. Conclusions based on such observational data can lead economists to disagree. Think about a well-designed chemical experiment wherein one is interested in the effect of pressure on the rate of a chemical reaction. In the laboratory, one can control for the effect of temperature on the rate of the chemical reaction by keeping temperature constant and varying only the pressure, thus isolating the effect of pressure on the rate of reaction. With observational data, one is simply collecting measurements on movements in the values of two or more variables without controlling for any other variable that may influence the outcome of what is being measured. So, it will be difficult to ever establish a causal relationship. In economics, when using observational data, economists can, at best, only establish correlations between two or more variables.

The One-Handed Economist

"What this country needs are some one-armed economists."
—Harry Truman

Economics as a social science has changed over time, based on new ideas, empirical and historical evidence, and society's subjective values. Therefore, it is important to be able to distinguish between what is opinion and what is fact in the realm of economics. The need to be aware of the difference between a statement of fact, a value judgement, and an analytical deduction in economics cannot be stressed more strongly.

For the reasons described above, economists speak using two types of statements:

1. ***Normative:*** statements that value judgements which cannot be evaluated solely by recourse to facts.
2. ***Positive:*** statements that are matters of fact, wherein disagreements can appeal to evidence.

Distinguishing what is true from what one would like to be true requires distinguishing between positive and normative statements, and, in addition, the use of analytical statements.

Characteristics of Positive Statements

- Concerned with what is, was, or will be.
- Can be simple or complex, but are basically matters of fact.
- Positive statements, if testable, can be proved wrong by empirical evidence.
- Disagreements over positive statements are appropriately handled by an appeal to the facts.

Examples:

- "It is possible to break up an atom."
- "The price of gasoline is $4.35 per gallon."
- "Raising interest rates encourages people to save."

Characteristics of Normative Statements

- Concerned with what one believes something ought to be.
- Makes or is based on a value judgement.
- Is not a testable statement.
- Disagreements over normative statements cannot be handled merely by an appeal to facts.

Examples:

- "It is wrong to steal."
- "We should lower income taxes."
- "Health care is more important than Social Security."

Analytical Statements

One must also be aware of analytical statements. These statements are true by definition and are generally self-explanatory. Analytical statements often have little to no informative value but are used in debates to win arguments that would otherwise not be completely valid.

Examples of analytic sentences include:

- "Frozen water is ice."
- "Bachelors are unmarried men."
- "Two halves make up a whole."

Notice that in the statements above, no additional knowledge is contained in the ***predicate*** (what is being said about it) that is not already given in the ***subject*** (what is being talked about). Analytical sentences are redundant statements whose explanation relies wholly on a definition. Although they do not give consequential information about the world, analytical statements inform one about logic.

One can use analytical statements to win debates *even though they may be based on inaccuracies*. Here is an example:

(1) With capitalism, market forces determine how resources are allocated.
(2) It is more efficient to allocate resources through market forces than central planning.
(3) An efficient system is superior to an inefficient system.
(4) Therefore, capitalism is superior to socialism.

These four statements form a logically strong argument. However, are statements (2) and (3) true? Statement (2) and (3) become analytical, that is, true by definition if we define the premises as such. Once one has set, by definition, that an efficient system is superior (always), then statement (4) follows easily, and one falls into the trap of losing the counter debate.

Application Questions

WHICH OF THE FOLLOWING ARE ANALYTICAL, POSITIVE, AND NORMATIVE STATEMENTS?

1. Pollution is the most serious economic problem.
2. What policies can lower unemployment?

3. It is better to have low unemployment rather than low inflation.
4. No unmarried man is married.
5. The earth is less than 5,000 years old.
6. Extraterrestrials frequently visit the earth in human form.
7. A full deck of playing cards contains 52 cards.
8. A meter is longer than a centimeter.
9. The government should enforce minimum prices for tobacco in a bid to control its consumption.
10. A decrease in average temperatures will increase the demand for heavy coats.
11. The government is right to introduce a ban on drinking alcohol in public places.
12. Lower alcohol prices have increased the demand for alcohol among teenagers.
13. Frozen water is ice.

SOLUTIONS

1. Pollution is the most serious economic problem
   Normative
2. What policies can lower unemployment?
   Positive
3. It is better to have low unemployment rather than low inflation.
   Normative
4. No unmarried man is married.
   Analytical
5. The earth is less than 5,000 years old.
   Positive
6. Extraterrestrials frequently visit the earth in human form.
   Normative/Positive?
7. A full deck of playing cards contains 52 cards.
   Analytical
8. A meter is longer than a centimeter.
   Analytical
9. The government should enforce minimum prices for tobacco in a bid to control its consumption.
   Normative
10. A decrease in average temperatures will increase the demand for heavy coats.
    Positive
11. The government is right to introduce a ban on drinking alcohol in public places.
    Normative
12. Lower alcohol prices have increased the demand for alcohol among teenagers.
    Positive
13. Frozen water is ice.
    Analytical

Chapter Summary

In this chapter, we made a distinction between a belief system and a system in which the scientific approach is employed. The study of economics falls in the latter category. Although economics is a scientific discipline, it unfortunately must rely on incomplete data at times. Reliance on incomplete data or even observational rather than experimental data leads economists to make best educated guesses. Thus, when data are lacking, economists can utter normative statements. However, when data are complete, economists will turn to positive statements. One can also use analytical statements, which are true by definition. However, analytical statements usually have little to no informative value. They are usually used in debates to win arguments that may or may not necessarily be valid arguments.

CHAPTER 3

Why So Much Government Cheese?

SUPPLY AND DEMAND AND MARKET CONTROLS

LEARNING EXPECTATIONS

- To understand how prices are determined in a market-based system
- To apply the laws of supply and demand for price determination in a variety of contexts
- To explain why surpluses or shortages occur using the tools and laws of supply and demand

ADAM SMITH (1723–1790) was a Scottish economist, a moral philosopher, and is best known for two classic works: The Theory of Moral Sentiments (1759) and An Inquiry into the Nature and Causes of the Wealth of Nations (1776). Adam Smith is said to have laid down the foundations of classical free market economic theory.

Source: *https://commons.wikimedia.org/wiki/Adam_Smith#/media/File:AdamSmith1790.jpg.*

KARL MARX (1818–1883) is one of the most influential figures in human history. His work in socialist economic thought has been lauded and heavily critized.

Source: *https://commons.wikimedia.org/wiki/File:Karl_Marx.jpg.*

From Where Prices Come

> *"As values, all commodities are only definite masses of congealed labour time."* —Karl Marx

The price of a good or service is a temporary phenomenon. That is, prices may rise and fall based on a list of factors that are also in flux. Understanding from where prices come also allows one to understand from where profits originate. Historically, profits have been an area of study that generated much philosophical debate; perhaps they still do. In general terms, a firm generates profits when the good or service it is selling is priced above its cost of production (more about this in chapters 5 and 6). The question for many economic philosophers then is how much profit is "normal" and how much profit "exploits" the consumer or laborer? To be "normal," profits and thus prices should reflect the inherent value of a good or service. If so, then one needs to now define *value*.

There are many classical theories of value, but one in particular has been, in part, responsible for economic revolutions around the world. That theory is the **labor theory of value.** The labor theory of value is the foundation of traditional Marxian economics, which is discussed in Karl Marx's 1867 book, *Das Kapital* (Capital). In short, the theory postulated that the value of a good can quantitatively be measured by the average number of labor hours required to produce that good. This theory was not specific to Marxism, although Marx used it to exploit the vices of capitalism. The idea that a good should be valued more than another if it required more labor to produce it than the other good was entertained by Adam Smith in his piece *The Wealth of Nations* (1776) and David Ricardo in his *Principles of Political Economy* (1817). As an example of the application of this theory, if a chair usually takes twice as long to produce as a bench, then chairs are twice as valuable as benches. Over time, the price of chairs will be two times the price of benches, irrespective of the value of the physical (nonlabor) inputs. We can see, however, the inherent flaw in this argument if we consider an antique chair. At the point of initial production, the chair is valued (priced) in terms of the labor hours used to produce it. Yet, many years later, as the chair then becomes an antique, it carries a higher value than its initial price. This is true of many antiques, including paintings (especially those of dead artists). In all these cases, no additional labor hours were employed to produce or alter the good, so why is this viewed to be worth more over time?

Marx did not address this issue. He did argue that the labor theory of value can be extended to describe the value of all goods, including labor itself, which Max called "labor power." This good called labor power is what workers sell to capitalists in return for wages. Marx went on to ask a very poignant question about profits. He queried that if goods are priced such that they reflect or equate to the true value of the labor that was necessary to produce them, then how would it be possible to generate any profit? Marx answered his own question by stating that capitalists, because of their position of power and ownership of the means of production, must be exploiting workers. We now understand that prices and thus profits not only include labor hours, they also reflect scarcity or perceived scarcity of a good or service. Thus, markups and profits reward entrepreneurial capitalists who take risk (i.e., a risk premium) and organize production.

The Market

As the previous section illustrates, labor hours—or more generally, production costs—are not the only determinants of price. Prices should also carry perceptions related to scarcity, not only scarcity of resources, but of substitutes, and the preferences of the buyer(s). Thus, the two essential elements for price determinations are the activities of the seller (or producer) and the wants and desires of the buyer (or consumer). This agreement on price can occur between one buyer and one seller, or many buyers and many sellers, or any combination of buyers and sellers. The place, whether real or virtual, where this "negotiation" occurs is called a **market.** Formally, a market is any place where goods and services are bought and sold, and where buyers and sellers are in free intercourse with one another such that the prices of identical goods tend to equate easily and quickly. In a **market system** (capitalism), consumers ultimately determine which goods and services will be produced.

We will consider a particular market—the **perfectly competitive market.** Such a market exists if the following four assumptions hold:

1. There are many buyers and sellers (everyone is a **price taker**).
2. All goods and services are identical/homogeneous (no product differentiation, no brands, and no consumer loyalties).
3. Everyone has perfect information about prices (no information asymmetries, and price or cost information is easily available).
4. Anyone can enter and leave the market with ease (which provides for an even degree of competition).

Consumers and the Law of Demand

The law of demand: *Ceteris paribus* (Latin phrase meaning "other things remaining the same"), the higher the price of a good, the lower the quantity demanded.

WHAT THE LAW OF DEMAND EXPLAINS:

Substitution effect: This effect occurs due to a change in the quantity demanded of a good that results from a change in price such that the good becomes more or less expensive *relative* to other goods that are deemed to be its substitutes.

Income effect: This effect occurs due to a consumer's ability to purchase more or less of a good or service when the good's or service's price changes.

We will describe these two effects in detail in the next section. First, let us look at a graphical representation of prices and the quantity demanded of any good or services, given various prices.

The data that describe prices and quantities demanded are placed in a table called a **demand schedule** (see figure 3.1). Note that a demand schedule is a list of all quantities demanded at each price. In this case, we have a demand schedule that lists the price of a bottle of beauty cream and the quantity demanded by all consumers for each price level. In order to arrive at the total consumer demand for each price level, we simply add each (individual) consumer's quantity demanded of beauty cream for each price level.

FIGURE 3.1 A Demand Schedule for Beauty Cream

Price ($/bottle)	Quantity Demanded (millions of bottles)
1.50	9.10
2.25	6.55
3.75	3.75
4.19	3.10
5.23	1.90

We can now plot the data found in the demand schedule in order to view the demand for beauty cream graphically. Figure 3.2 presents the same data graphically. For historical reasons, price is always placed on the y-axis and quantity demanded on the x-axis. Also, **inverse demand curves** for almost every possible good and service are downward sloping (i.e., they have a negative slope). Notice that as the price of the beauty cream increases, the quantity demanded of the beauty cream falls. For example, when the price of the beauty cream is $3.75, consumers are willing to buy 3.75 million bottles per day. When the price drops to $1.50, consumers are willing to buy 9.1 million bottles.

FIGURE 3.2 An Inverse Demand Curve for Beauty Cream

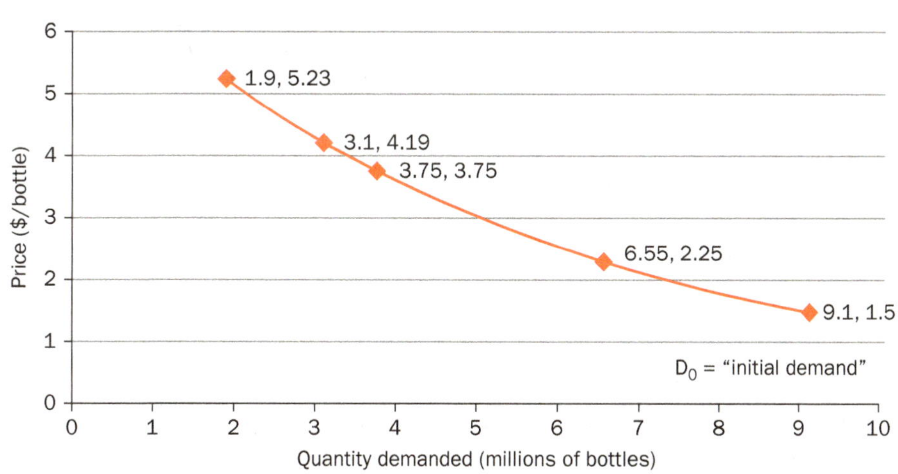

IMPORTANT THINGS TO NOTE

1. The change in price moves our quantity demanded (bought) up and down (i.e., *along*) the demand curve.
2. The change in quantity as a result of a change in price is referred to as a change in quantity demand***ed***, but not a change in demand. A change in demand, as we will see in the next section, is a shift of the demand curve either to the right or to the left, and it is **NOT** a result of changes in price.

Shifts in the Demand Curve

The demand curve or line is a graphical representation of a mathematical equation or function. Just like any equation or relationship, the demand for a good or service is a function of (i.e., depends on) a variety of factors, not including price. A demand curve is drawn with the assumption that everything *except the product's own price is held constant*. A change in the following five factors, which are sometimes referred to as buying plans, will shift a demand curve to the right or to the left, as illustrated in figure 3.3.

1. The price of related goods and services
2. Income levels
3. Expected future price
4. Preferences/tastes
5. Population size

FIGURE 3.3 Illustrating Shifts in the Demand Curve

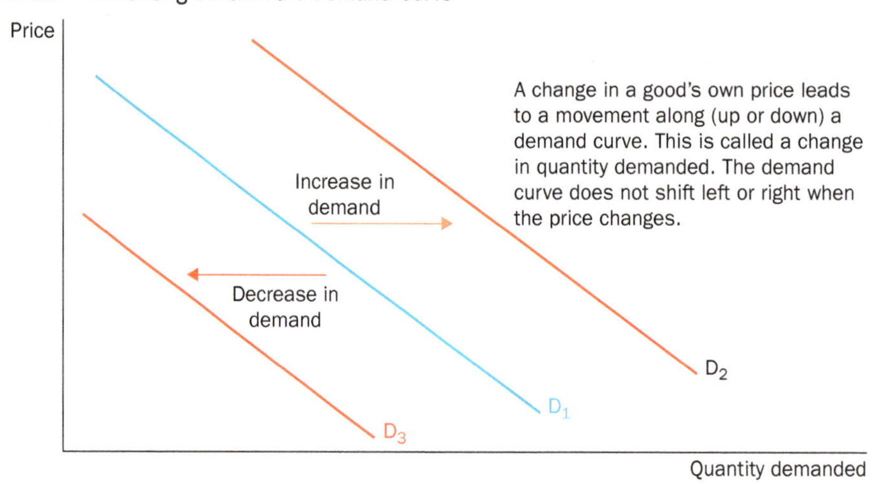

Let us now appreciate why each of the five factors listed earlier has an effect on the positioning of the demand curve.

1. THE PRICE OF RELATED GOODS AND SERVICES

All goods and services can be classified according to their relationship to the good for which we draw the demand curve. So, we may take any good X and then classify another good, Y, relative to X. The other goods relative to X can be (1) **substitutes** for X, (2) **complements** of X, or (3) completely unrelated to X.

If a good, Y, is completely unrelated to good X, then the price of good Y, the unrelated good, has no effect on the demand for X. For example, if we are interested in the demand for cookies and the price of shoes increases, then the increase in the price of shoes will have no effect on the demand for cookies.

If, however, a good, Y, is a **complement** to good X, then it is usually used jointly with good X. For example, coffee and sugar are complements to each other. Other examples include pizza and cheese, peanut butter and jam, and so forth. *In cases of complementary goods, when the price of a complement falls, the demand curve for the other good will shift to the right.* For instance, if we are talking about good X (i.e., coffee), then when the price of sugar, which is a complement to coffee, falls, the demand curve for coffee will shift to the right. This shift occurs because sugar, which is the complementary good, is now less expensive to consume, and therefore more of it will be demanded. Therefore, more of the good coffee will be demanded as well, because it is usually consumed with its complement. This is illustrated in figure 3.4.

FIGURE 3.4 Effect on the Demand for Coffee When the Price of its Complement, Sugar, Falls

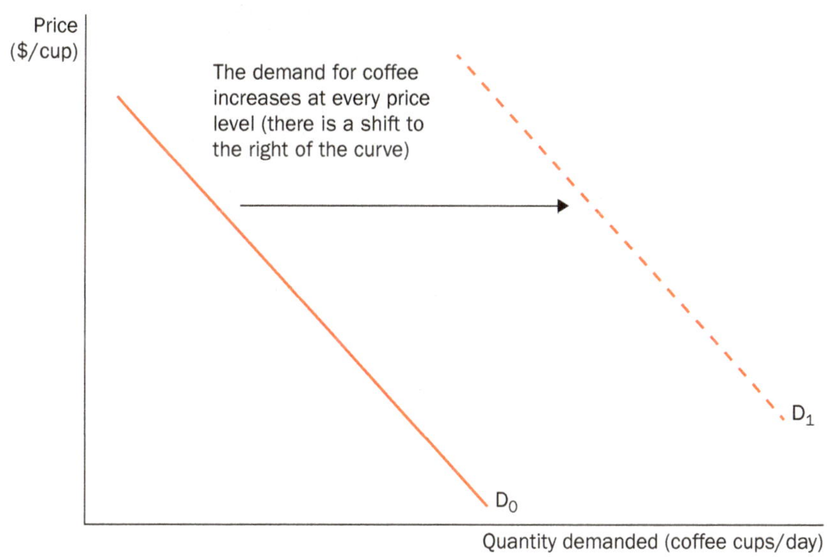

The reverse is also true. If the price of sugar were to increase, then the demand for coffee would decrease. We would see a leftward shift of the demand curve for coffee (see figure 3.5). In general terms, *when the price of a good Y that is complementary to another good, X, increases, the demand curve for good X will shift to the left.* Here, the reasoning is the same as before—given that the complementary good Y is now more expensive to consume, less of it will be demanded. Thus, less of the good in question, say, good X, will also be demanded, because it is used jointly with its complement.

FIGURE 3.5 Effect on the Demand for Coffee When the Price of its Complement, Sugar, Increases

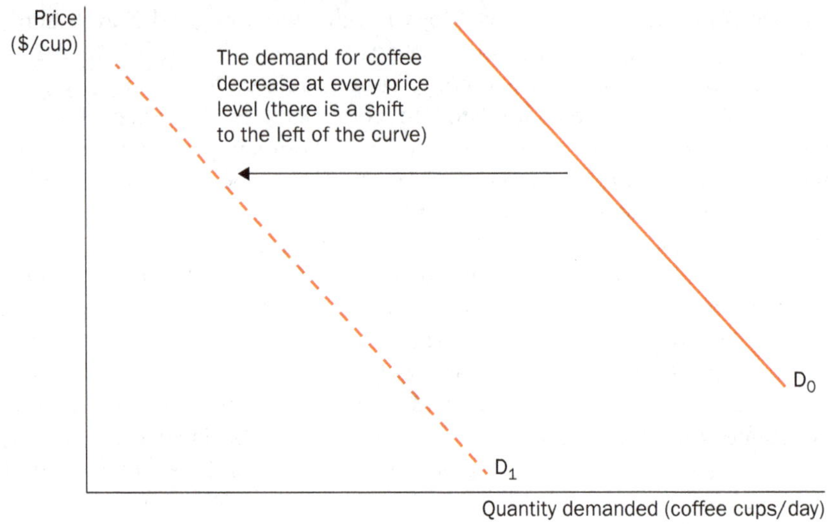

If a good, Y, is a **substitute** to good X, then it is usually used in place of good X. For example, coffee and tea are substitutes for many consumers. Other examples include a vacation in Paris and a vacation in Rome, chicken and turkey, cow's milk and almond milk, and so forth. *In cases of goods that are substitutes, when the price of a substitute falls, the demand curve for the other good will shift to the left.* For instance, if we are talking about good X (i.e., coffee), then when the price of tea, which is a substitute to coffee, falls, the demand curve for coffee will shift to the left. This shift occurs because tea, which is the substitute good, is now less expensive to consume, and therefore more of it will be demanded. Therefore, less of the good coffee will be demanded, because it can be substituted with a less expensive alternative. This is illustrated in figure 3.6.

FIGURE 3.6 Effect on the Demand for Coffee When the Price of its Substitute, Tea, Decreases

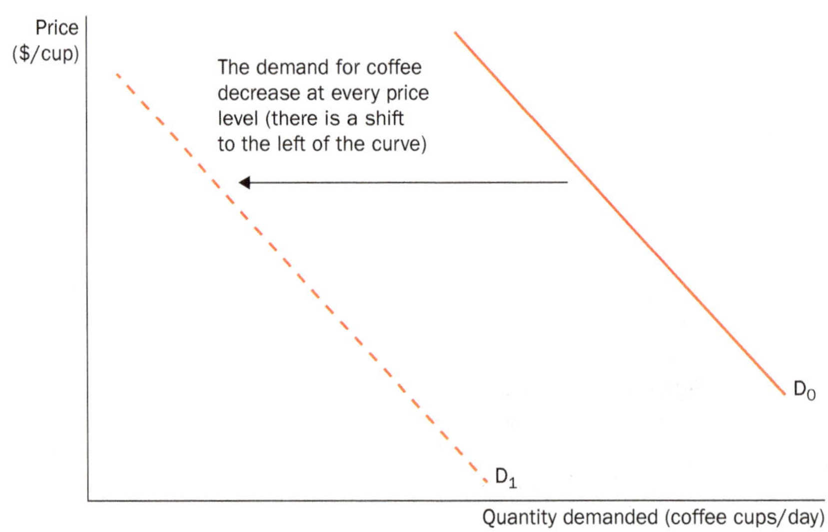

If, however, the price of tea were to increase and tea is viewed as a substitute to coffee, then the demand for coffee would increase because coffee is now less expensive *relative* to tea. Thus, *in cases of goods that are substitutes, when the price of a substitute increases, the demand for the other good will increase. This increase in demand causes the demand curve to shift to the right.* For instance, if we are talking about good X (i.e., coffee), then when the price of tea, which is a substitute for coffee, increases, the demand curve for coffee will shift to the right. This shift occurs because tea, which is the substitute good, is now *relatively* more expensive to consume, and therefore less of it will be demanded. This is illustrated in figure 3.7.

FIGURE 3.7 Effect on the Demand for Coffee When the Price of its Substitute, Tea, Increases

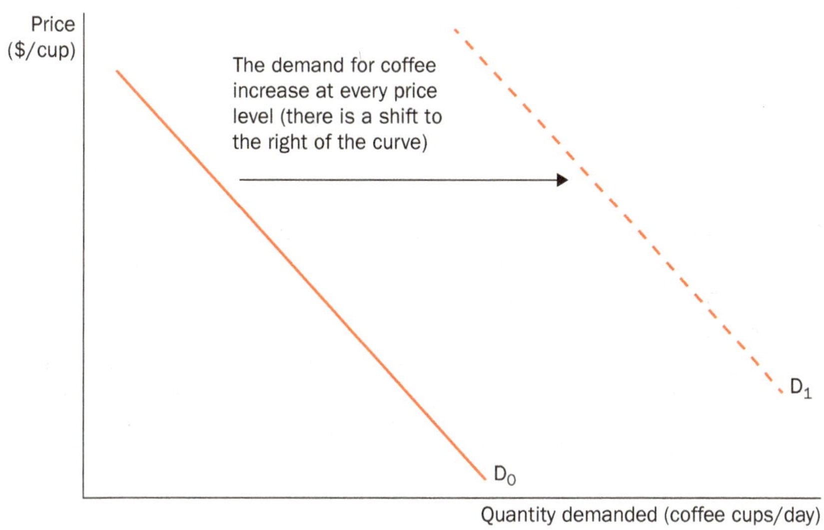

2. INCOME LEVELS

Assume, for example, that all of a sudden, you went from a $50,000-a-year job to a $200,000-a-year job. Your income has increased by a factor of four. Does this mean that you will buy more of everything at any given price? Does the demand curve simply shift to the right? Well, that depends on the type of good or service we wish to consume

When considering the effects of changes in income levels on the demand of a good or service, one must first consider whether the good in question is a **normal good** or an **inferior good.**

- **Normal good:** By definition, a normal good is one whose demand increases when incomes increase. Examples of normal goods and services include lean cuts of meat, travel, medical services, education, household furniture, and the like. When incomes increase, there is an increase in demand for normal goods, resulting in a rightward shift in the demand curve. Conversely, as incomes decline, the demand for normal goods decrease, and this causes their demand curves to shift to the left (see figure 3.8).

FIGURE 3.8 Effect on the Demand For Lean Cuts of Meat, A Normal Good, When Income Levels Increase

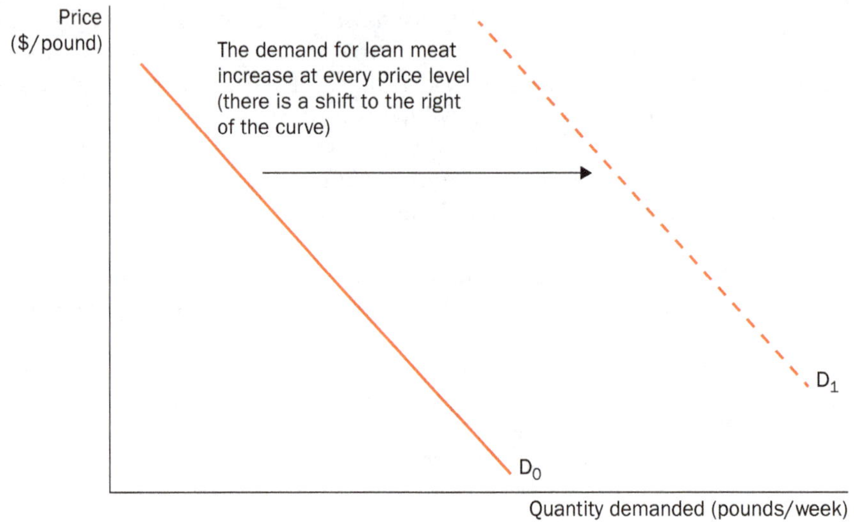

- **Inferior good:** By definition, an inferior good or service is one in which its demand increases when incomes decrease and whose demand decreases when incomes increase. Examples of inferior goods include rice, potatoes, fast-food meals, and the like. Inferior goods are labeled as such not because they are of lesser quality, which they can be, but because of the decline in their demand when incomes increase. For example, some fast-food restaurant chains experienced increased sales during the 2008–2009 Great Recession, despite decreasing income levels (see figure 3.9).

FIGURE 3.9 Effect on the Demand for Fast-Food Meals, An Inferior Good, When Income Levels Increase

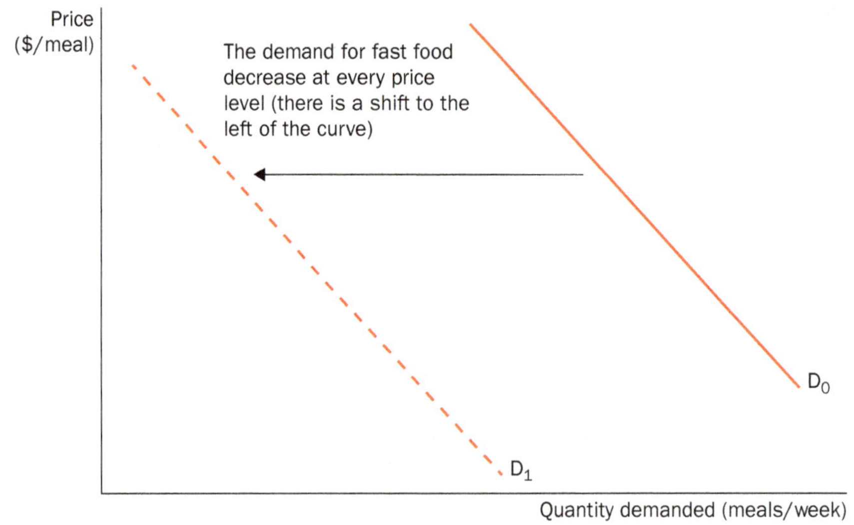

3. EXPECTED FUTURE PRICE

If you expect prices to go up in the future, what will your demand for something do now? Go up or go down? Go up. If you are anticipating a price increase, for say, gasoline, you will fill up your gas tank today because you do not want to pay the higher prices tomorrow. So, the demand for gasoline goes up today, shifting the demand curve for gasoline to the right at every price level. Note that, as has been the case with all the demand changes presented thus far, the prices of the good in question stay the same, yet the demand curve shifts due to some other factor. In this example, gasoline prices today remain unchanged, but the demand for gasoline shifts to the right because one expects prices to increase in the future (see figure 3.10).

Other things held constant, the demand for a good (today) will decrease if it is expected that future prices will decrease.

FIGURE 3.10 Effect on the Current Demand for Gasoline When Future Prices for Gasoline are Expected To Increase

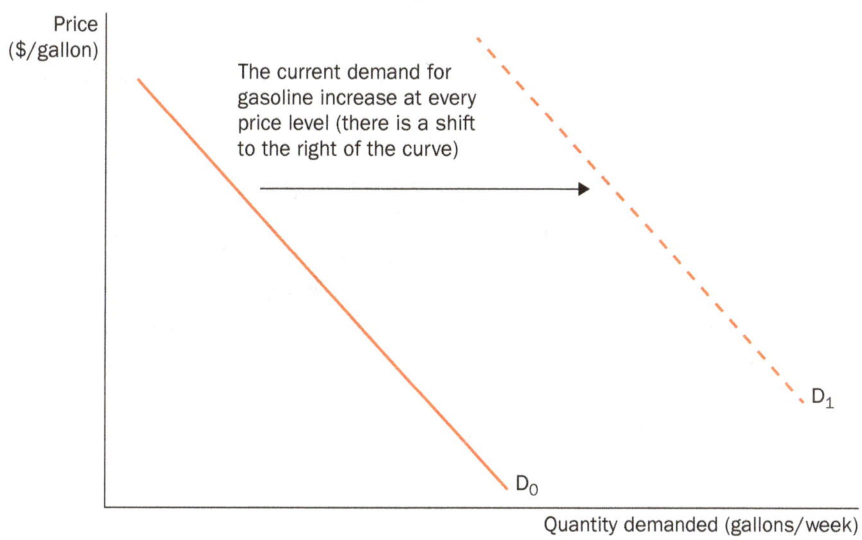

4. CONSUMER PREFERENCES/TASTES

Consumer preferences are assumed to be held constant when one moves up and down (i.e., along) a demand curve. However, over time, consumers may shift their preferences to wanting either more or less of a good or service. Sometimes, preferences change so dramatically that they can actually eliminate a demand curve altogether. Are you familiar with bell bottom jeans? If you are unfamiliar with them, then I will explain. They were a style of jeans that consumers thought were sexy in the 1970s. Thus, the 1970s demand curve for bell bottom jeans lay far to the right. Over the past 40 years, consumer preferences have changed such that bell bottom jeans have become less popular. Thus, the 2016 demand curve for bell bottoms lies far to the left (see figure 3.11).

BELL BOTTOM JEANS.

Source: *Copyright © Mike Powell (CC BY-SA 2.0) at https://commons.wikimedia.org/wiki/File:Bell_bottoms.jpg.*

FIGURE 3.11 Effect on the Demand for Bell Bottom Jeans When Consumers Find Them Less Desirable Over Time

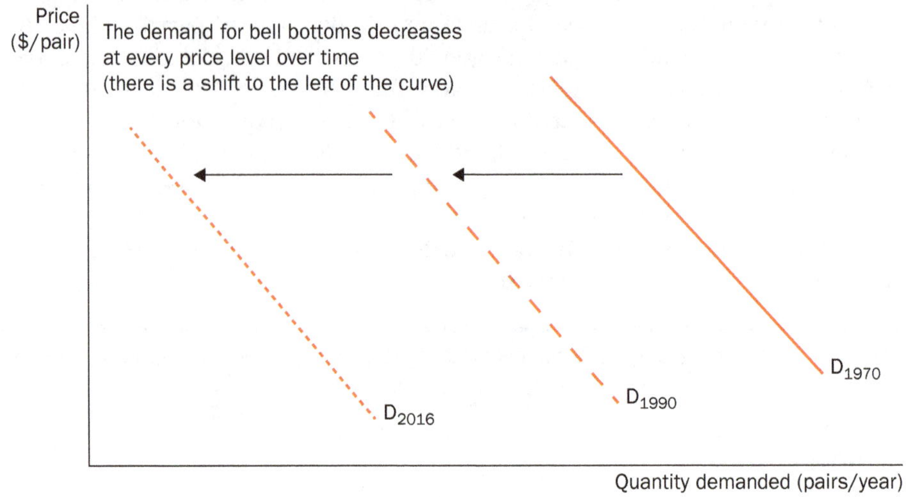

5. POPULATION SIZE

Any demand curve for a good is composed of the sum of demand curves for each individual consumer who buys a good or service. Thus, increasing the number of buyers increases the demand for a particular good or service, shifting the demand curve to the right. Likewise, decreasing the number of buyers decreases the demand for a particular good or service, shifting the demand curve to the left. Figure 3.12 illustrates the effect on demand when an additional consumer enters the market for coffee.

FIGURE 3.12 Effect on the Demand for Coffee When the Number of Consumers Increases

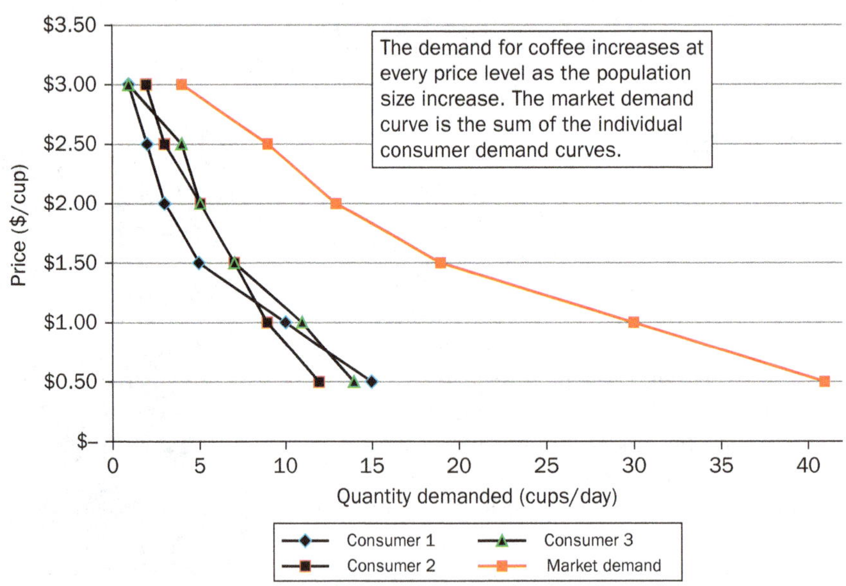

Suppliers and the Law of Supply

The **law of supply** pertains to producers. It is a statement about the relationship between the quantities of a good or service that a supplier is willing to supply at different prices. The law of supply states that, *ceteris paribus, the higher the price of a good, the greater the quantity supplied.* Note that the quantity supplied of a good or service is the amount that producers plan to sell in a given period of time.

Data on the quantity supplied at different price levels are tabulated in a **supply schedule**, and the data can be plotted to derive a **firm's supply curve.** In order to arrive at the **market supply curve**, we add the quantity supplied at each price by every firm in the market selling the same good or service.

We will again consider the market for beauty cream. We will plot the data found in the supply schedule (figure 3.13) in order to view the supply for beauty cream graphically. Figure 3.14 presents the same data graphically. As with demand curves, price is always placed on the y-axis. Quantity supplied is placed on the x-axis. Also, **supply curves** are always upward sloping (i.e., they have a positive slope). Notice that as the price of the beauty cream increases, the quantity supplied of the beauty cream increases. For example, when the price of the beauty cream is $3.75, producers are willing to supply 8.6 million bottles per day. When the price drops to $1.50, producers are willing to supply 3.9 million bottles.

FIGURE 3.13 A Supply Schedule for Beauty Cream

Price ($/bottle)	Quantity Supplied (millions of bottles)
1.50	3.90
2.25	6.55
3.75	8.60
4.19	9.40
5.23	11.50

FIGURE 3.14 A Supply Curve for Beauty Cream

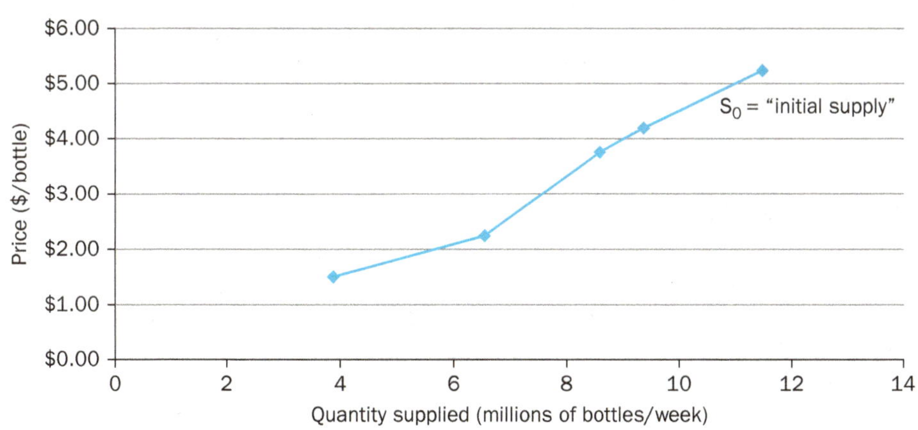

IMPORTANT THINGS TO NOTE

1. The change in price moves our quantity supplied up and down (i.e., *along*) the supply curve.
2. The change in quantity as a result of a change in price is referred to as a change in quantity suppli***ed***, but not a change in supply. A change in supply, as we will see in the next section, is a shift of the supply curve either to the right or to the left, and it is **NOT** a result of changes in price.

Shifts in the Supply Curve

The supply curve or line is a graphical representation of a mathematical equation or function. Just like any equation or relationship, the supply for a good or service is a function of (i.e., depends on) a variety of factors, not including price. A supply curve is drawn with the assumption that everything *except the product's own price is held constant*. A change in the following five factors will shift a supply curve to the right or to the left in the same manner in which a demand curve shifts:

1. Price of factors of production (inputs)
2. Expected future prices
3. The number of suppliers
4. Technology
5. Government taxes and subsidies

We will now discuss each of these five factors in turn.

1. PRICE OF FACTORS OF PRODUCTION (INPUTS)

For any supplier to produce a given good or service, it needs to employ factors of production. These factors of production themselves carry a cost. If the price of one or more of the factors of production for a particular good or service should increase, then the cost of production increases, and the producer is then willing to supply less of its good or services at a given market price. For example, if the wages for coffee growers increase, then the cost of producing coffee increases. Therefore, coffee producers are now willing to supply less coffee at any given market price. As a result, the supply curve shifts to the left (see figure 3.15).

2. EXPECTED FUTURE PRICES

If a supplier expects prices of its good to go up in the future, then it will be more willing to supply its good at the higher future price than supply it at today's lower price. Thus, the current supply curve will shift to the left, and the supply will decrease. For example, if a coffee supplier knows that coffee prices will rise in the next six months, it will reduce supply today, perhaps by increasing inventories, and supply more coffee in the future when it can benefit from higher prices (see figure 3.16).

FIGURE 3.15 Effect on the Supply of Coffee When the Price of Labor, One of its Factors of Production, Increases

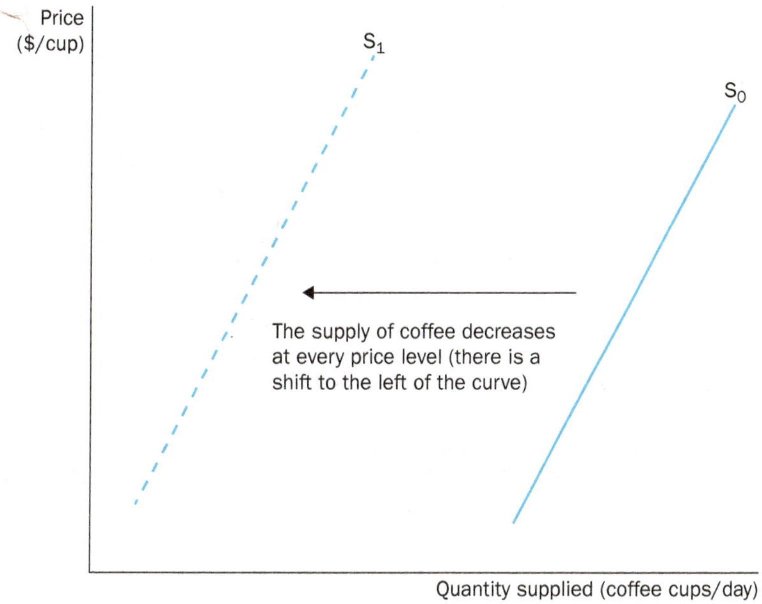

FIGURE 3.16 Effect on the Supply of Coffee When the Expected Future Price of Coffee is Higher Than The Current Price

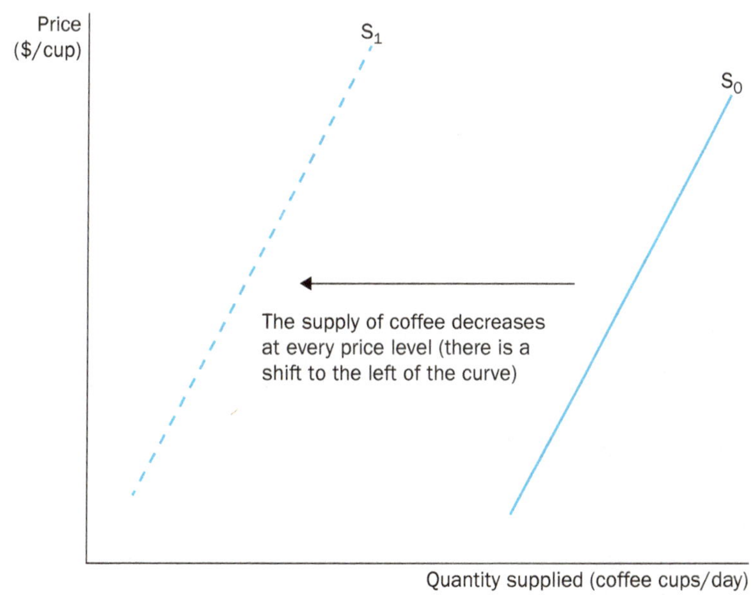

3. THE NUMBER OF SUPPLIERS

A market supply curve for a good is the sum of individual supply curves of all firms operating in the market. Thus, if more firms enter the market, then more of a particular good or service will be produced and supplied at any given price. This increase in the number of firms shifts the supply curve to the right. Likewise, decreasing the number of firms decreases the supply of a particular good or service, shifting the supply curve to the left.

4. TECHNOLOGY

All production processes use technology. **Technology** includes not only computers, robotics, and automated assembly lines but any production method that combines different types of resources to improve the production of a good or service. For example, a shovel would have been considered new technology at the time of its invention because it made the tilling of earth and thus the production of food more efficient. Technological advances increase **productivity**, which is defined as output per labor hour, and as a result lower the costs of production. When the costs of production decrease, firms are more willing to increase the supply of their good or service at any price level. The supply curve will shift to the right (see figure 3.17).

FIGURE 3.17 Effect on the Supply of Coffee When Mechanical Strippers Used for Coffee Fruit Harvesting Were Invented and Then Employed in the Production Process

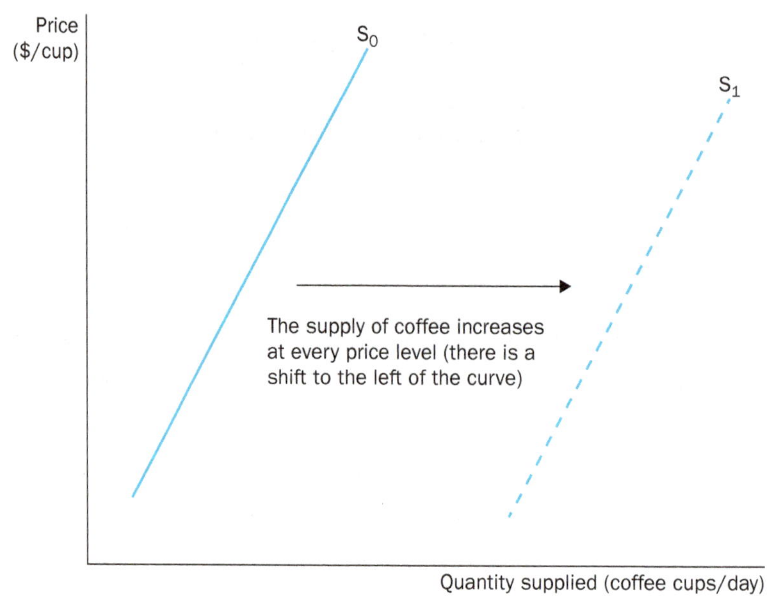

5. GOVERNMENT TAXES AND SUBSIDIES

A government can provide subsidies or tax holidays/rebates to encourage the production of a particular good or service. A subsidy is money provided by the government to producers, and it acts as an incentive to increase production. In essence, subsidies or tax holidays/rebates make production less expensive, thus shifting the supply curve to the right. Let us examine subsidies for coffee in Colombia.

Colombia is the world's second-largest arabica coffee producer, accounting for 15% of global arabica exports.[12] Coffee farming is the main source of income for rural Colombians, but profits from coffee have been shrinking because the costs of production inputs, such as labor and fertilizer, have increased rapidly over the past decade. Rising costs have made Colombia less competitive compared to other arabica coffee producers. In response, in 2013 the Colombian government provided direct cash subsidies to farmers.[12] As a result, farmers' opportunity cost of coffee farming, in terms of land, labor, and time, has decreased. They are now more willing to continue growing coffee beans, and more of them. This governmental action has caused the supply curve for arabica coffee to shift to the right (see figure 3.18).

FIGURE 3.18 Effect on the Supply of Coffee When the Colombian Government Provides Coffee Growers With Subsidies

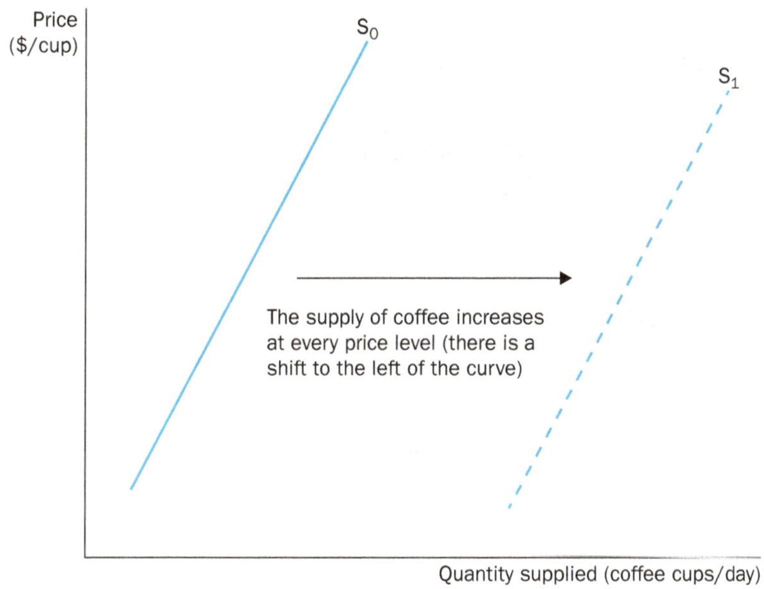

Market Equilibrium: The Interaction of Supply and Demand and the Market-Clearing Price

In a perfectly competitive market, for any good or service we have many buyers, each with their own demand curve, the sum of which constitutes the market demand curve. Likewise, in a perfectly competitive market, for any good or service we have many sellers, each with their own supply curve, the sum of which constitutes the market supply curve. Each player in the market will have a price it is willing to pay or receive for a given quantity of a good or service. The question is then, at what price will the good or service be sold, given the infinite possible prices that a buyer or seller can choose? The final market price will be determined by the intersection of the market supply and market demand curves. This process of price determination in the market is guided, as Adam Smith observed, by an invisible hand. An imperceptible negotiation takes place among the multitude of buyers and sellers to arrive at a price at which the supply of a good exactly equals the demand for a good. This price where supply equals demand is called the **market price**, sometimes referred to as the **equilibrium price** or **market-clearing price, P_e.**

This imperceptible negotiation of price is simply a larger-scale version of negotiations that take place between two people trying to reach a deal on the price of, for example, a used car or selling an antique, as made famous by the series *Pawn Stars*. In a competitive market, the buyer and seller are free to walk away from any deal that does not meet the price the buyer is willing to pay or the seller is willing to accept. We will return to our beauty cream example to determine our market-clearing price. Figure 3.19 plots both the supply and demand curves on the same graph. The point where the two curves intersect represents the price and quantity at which the supply of beauty cream exactly equals the demand for beauty cream.

FIGURE 3.19 The Supply and Demand Schedule and Market-Clearing Price for Beauty Cream

Price ($/bottle)	Quantity Demanded (millions of bottles)	Quantity Supplied (millions of bottles)
1.5	9.1	3.9
2.25	6.55	6.55
3.75	3.75	8.6
4.19	3.1	9.4
5.23	1.9	11.5

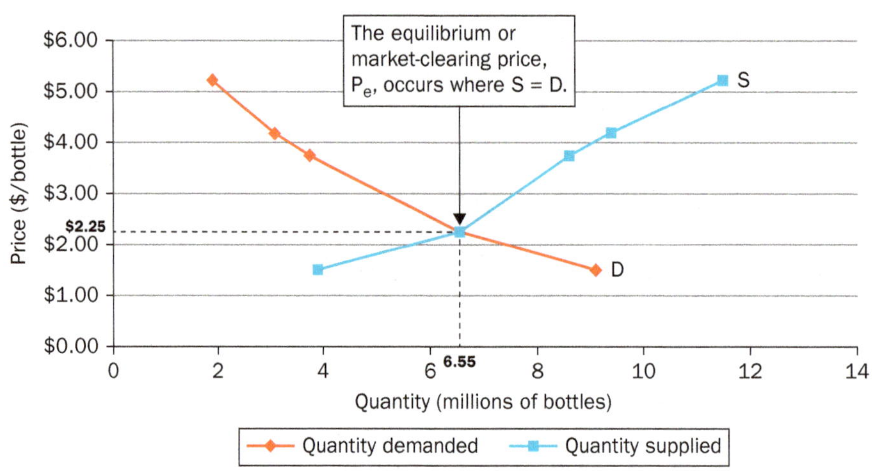

Price Determination When Factors Affect the Supply and Demand Curves

We can now examine the effects on the market-clearing price when "shocks" occurs. The "shocks" are events that affect one or more of the five factors that shift the demand curve or one or more of the five factors that shift the supply curve. We will start with a simple example and then provide two more examples of increasing difficulty.

EXAMPLE 1: THE EQUILIBRIUM PRICE FOR PEPSI

Consider the supply and demand market for Pepsi. What happens to Pepsi's original equilibrium price and quantity, P_o and Q_o, if there is a decrease in the supply of Coke?

SOLUTIONS

1. *Let us first draw the original market for Pepsi. We see in figure 3.20 that the intersection of the original supply and demand curves, S_o and D_o, results in an original equilibrium price and quantity, P_o and Q_o.*

FIGURE 3.20 The Original Market for Pepsi

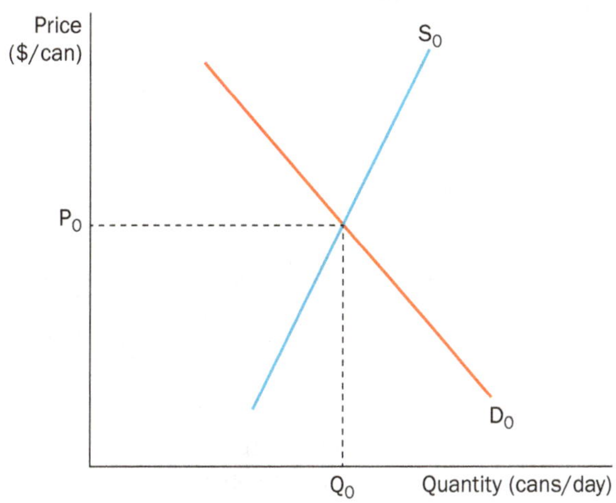

2. *Now, consider the decrease in the supply of Coke. In the separate Coke market (figure 3.21), a decrease in supply causes the supply curve to shift to the left. This causes the price of Coke to increase from P_o to P_1.*

FIGURE 3.21 The Market for Coke

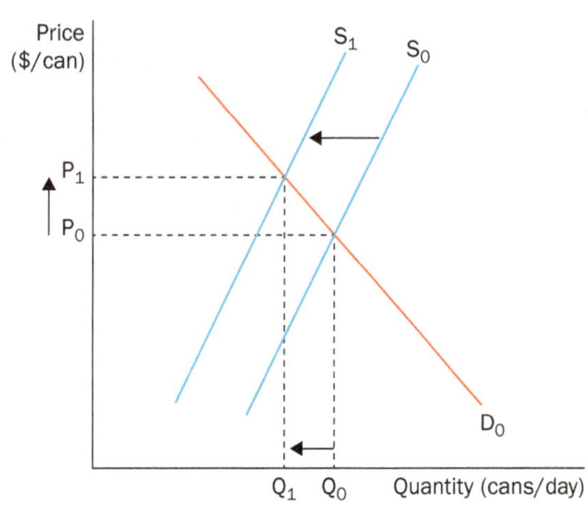

3. *Since Coke and Pepsi are substitutes, then an increase in the price of Coke should cause consumers to demand more of its substitute, Pepsi. This causes Pepsi's demand curve to shift to the right (figure 3.22), which results in an increase in the price of Pepsi (P_1) and an increase in the quantity demanded and supplied, Q_1.*

FIGURE 3.22 The New Market for Pepsi

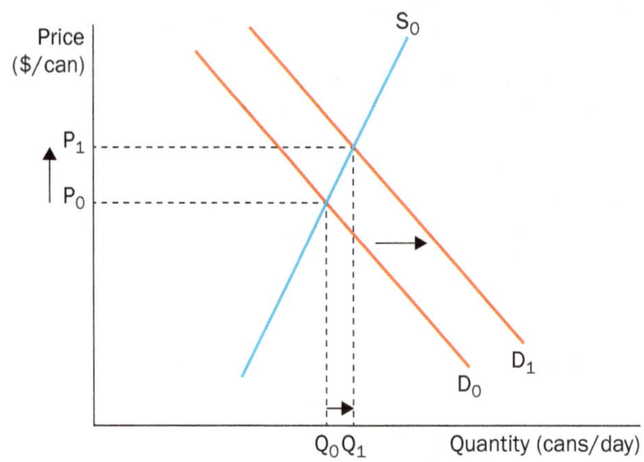

EXAMPLE 2: SWEET AS SUGAR

In 2015, it was reported that the price of sugar fell to a six-year low based on speculation that the global excess of sugar would further increase because of the expected good harvest in Brazil, which is the world's top producer of sugar.

a. Illustrate the supply and/or demand movements on the global sugar market.
b. Illustrate the supply and/or demand movements on the baked goods and candy market.
c. Illustrate the supply and/or demand movements on the artificial sweeteners market.

SOLUTIONS

a. *Good harvests for any crop results in more crop produced. Thus, the supply of the crop, in this case sugar, will increase. This implies a shift to the right of the world's supply curve for sugar, as illustrated in figure 3.23. The shift in supply decreases the equilibrium price and increases the equilibrium quantity.*
b. *We now need to examine the effect of a decrease in the price of sugar that was a result of an increase in its supply. We ask ourselves, "What is sugar to baked goods and candies?" Sugar is an input into the production of baked goods and candies. Therefore, when the price of a factor of production decreases, this implies that production is less costly. Firms will be more willing to increase the supply of their goods. Therefore, in the market for baked goods and candies, the supply curve will shift to the right, which results in lower prices for baked goods and candies (figure 3.24).*

FIGURE 3.23 The World Sugar Market

FIGURE 3.24 The Baked Goods And Candy Market

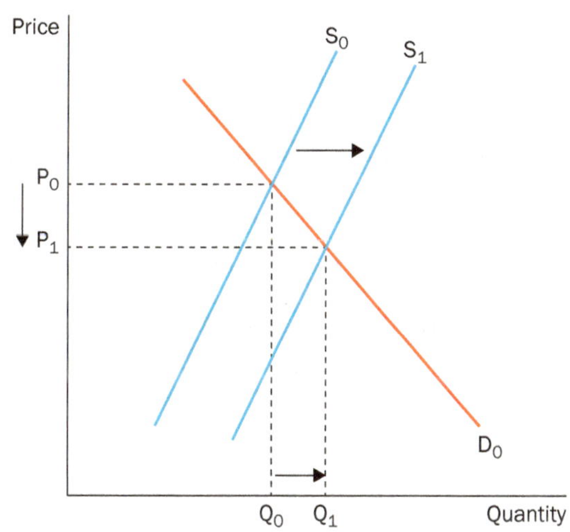

c. *The effect of an increase in the supply of world sugar on the artificial sweeteners market can be deduced by recognizing that sugar and artificial sweeteners are substitutes. Thus, a decrease in the price of sugar will cause consumers to demand less artificial sweeteners. The demand curve in the artificial sweeteners market will decrease (shift to the left). As illustrated in figure 3.25, this results in a lower market-clearing price for artificial sweeteners and less quantity demanded and supplied.*

FIGURE 3.25 The Artificial Sweeteners Market

Application Question

PRICE DETERMINATION (AN AMBIGUOUS EFFECT)

Soft drink companies like Coca-Cola and PepsiCo also manufacture a variety of bottled water drinks (e.g., Dasani by Coca-Cola and Aquafina by PepsiCo). We are interested in determining the final position of price and quantity of bottled water when the following occurs:

- Nightclub patrons who use Ecstasy have now realized that they need to stay hydrated and cooled. Ecstasy is a strong stimulant, and without sufficient water to cool and hydrate the body, a user can easily overheat when dancing. Body temperatures can rise to over 109 degrees Fahrenheit, which leads to organ failure and death.
- Coca-Cola and Pepsi introduce a new line of bottled water for the nightclub scene.

SOLUTION

The introduction of new varieties of bottled water will increase the supply of bottled water. Thus, the supply curve of bottled water will increase, shifting the supply curve to the right. This shift will result in a lower equilibrium price for bottled water.

The realization by Ecstasy users that they need to consume more water increases the demand for bottled water. This increase in demand shifts the demand curve to the right, which pushes the equilibrium price of bottled water up. Figure 3.26 illustrates these two movements. We notice from figure 3.26 that the new equilibrium price, P_1, is higher than the original equilibrium price, P_0. This final increase in price occurred because the *increase in demand for bottled water by Ecstasy users was larger than the increase in the supply of bottled water by the firms producing the bottled water.*

Note carefully that the first movement, marked 1, caused the original demand curve (D_0) to intersect the original supply curve (S_0) at a price that is higher than P_1. The market finally settles at point B when the supply curve shifts to the right as a result of more bottled water being produced and supplied. Nevertheless, movement 2 is less pronounced than movement 1, and thus the final market-clearing price is higher than the original market price.

FIGURE 3.26 The Bottled Water Market When Demand Increases More Than Supply

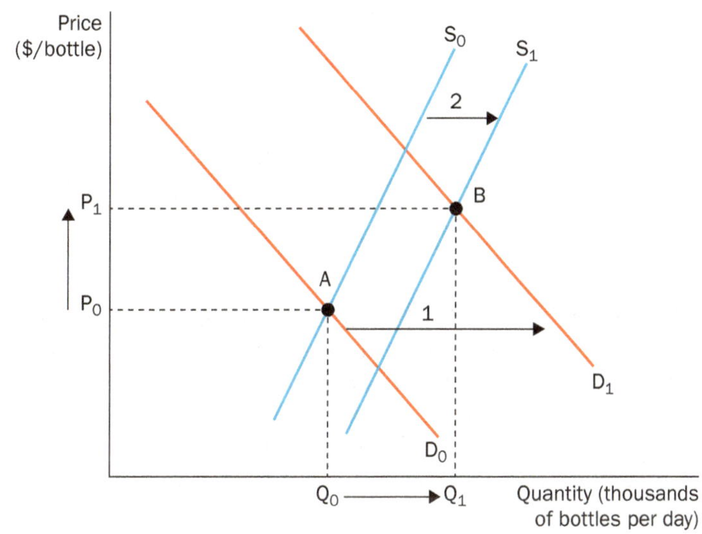

Unless we have more information about the actual magnitudes of the movements for each of the supply and demand curves, the determination of whether the final equilibrium price is higher than, lower than, or equal to the original equilibrium price when both supply and demand curves shift is ambiguous. For instance, we can arrive at a different conclusion for the final positioning of the equilibrium price for the bottled water market if we assume that the increase in supply outstrips the increase in demand for bottled water. As we now see in figure 3.27, the new equilibrium price, P_1, is lower than the original equilibrium price, P_0.

Where Else Can We Stuff Cheese?
The Consequences of Price Floors and Ceilings

The United States produces and stores a lot of cheese—emphasis on "a lot." In 2016, approximately 1.2 billion pounds of surplus cheese was accumulated in commercial storage freezers across the continent, representing the largest stash of cheese in US history. Some of the extra cheese in 2016 was a result of cheaper European imports and

FIGURE 3.27 The Bottled Water Market When Supply Increases More Than Demand

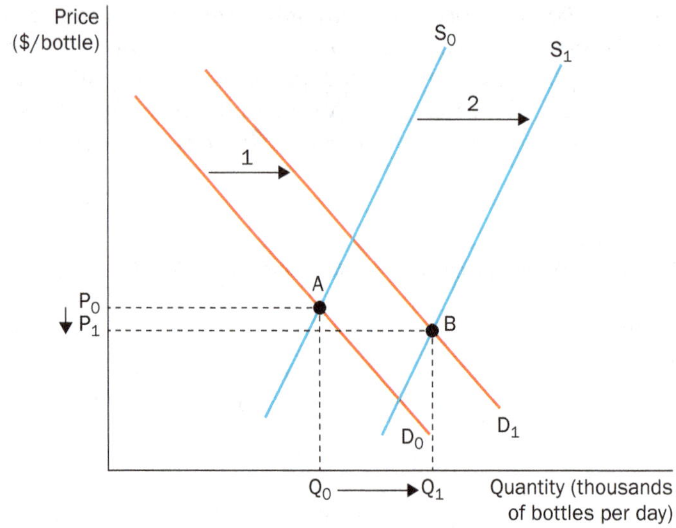

a strong US dollar, but the United States has been storing excess cheese for decades—none of which is a result of cheaper imports or the strength of the US dollar.

The answer to this cheese puzzle is an economic one, of course. However, we need to begin our story as far back as the 1930s because the US government has had a long-standing pro-cheese policy for the better part of the 20th century that still continues to this day. The federal government started regulating farm milk prices as a result of the Great Depression. In 1937, the US Department of Agriculture set forth regulations that established minimum prices for farm milk, which in turn vary based on the type of products that are made from the farm milk. The legislation that provides the US Department of Agriculture with the power to decree minimum prices is the Agricultural Marketing Agreement Act. This act further sets regulations that create geographic marketing areas where all dairy producers receive the same price for their farm milk.

Due to continuing lobbying by milk producers, no other farm product has been regulated as rigidly as milk. Although the Agricultural Marketing Agreement Act of 1937, as amended, was part of President Roosevelt's New Deal to stabilize prices during the Great Depression for small farmers, minimum prices that milk producers must receive are still in effect today. These minimum prices are a result of what are called *marketing orders*, which are binding on all handlers (or milk users). A marketing order may limit the quantity of milk marketed or establish the grade, size, quality, or prices of dairy products. Marketing orders also exist to regulate the sale of fruits and vegetables.

As we will analyze using our supply and demand model, these pricing regulations have led to an overproduction of milk—so much so that the government looks for means to rid itself of the excess. It has done so in many ways over the years:

- The government produces a processed cheese, called government cheese, which is distributed to food charities. Government cheese was used in military kitchens and in schools starting in the 1960s and was provided to welfare beneficiaries, Food Stamp recipients, and the elderly receiving Social Security. This cheese is also distributed to victims of natural disasters.[13]

- In 1981, President Reagan authorized the release of 30 million pounds out of the 560 million pounds of stockpiled excess cheese to states that wished to give it to their underprivileged residents. The cheese (and butter as well) was often from food surpluses stockpiled, in unsliced block form, by the government as part of milk price supports.
- In the 1990s, Dairy Management Inc. was established by the Clinton administration. Its annual funding of $140 million was authorized by Congress. Dairy Management Inc. is a promotional organization for dairy producers that, in part, works in partnership with firms such as McDonald's, Domino's, Taco Bell, and Quaker to create new and innovative products using dairy, such as Pizza Hut's cheese-topped crust and Taco Bell's double steak quesadillas, as well as cheesy pizzas for the federal school lunch program.

Canada has a similar system of tariffs, quotas, and price controls that protect the domestic farming industries of dairy, poultry, and eggs.

We now turn to how government regulations such as setting minimum prices (or in other cases, maximum prices) affect our supply and demand model and ultimately lead to overproduction of cheese.

Price Floors and Price Ceilings

When perfectly competitive markets operate freely, equilibrium prices are determined by the intersection of the supply and demand curves. At the point where they intersect, quantity demanded and quantity supplied are equal to each other; thus, there is no excess and no shortage of the good or service. It is for this reason that we refer to the equilibrium price as the market-clearing price. However, when price controls are placed on the market by governments, then we generate a situation in which the market does not clear.

There are two types of price controls that can be mandated:

- **Price floors:** These are minimum prices at which a good or service must be sold. The price at which a good or service must be sold can be set higher by the supplier than the floor price, but the good or service cannot be sold below the set minimum. The prices set for milk producers are floor prices.
- **Price ceilings:** These are maximum prices at which a good or service must be sold. The price at which a good or service must be sold can be set lower by the supplier than the ceiling price, but the good or service cannot be sold above the set maximum. Rental control is an example of mandated ceiling prices.

Let us examine the effect of floor prices on the cheese market using figure 3.28. Assume first that in the absence of any government regulation the market-clearing price, P_e, is $3.50 per block of cheese (point A). This price is generated when the supply and demand curves intersect. At point A, there is no excess or shortage of cheese because the quantity supplied, Q_e, at $3.50 per block is 5 million blocks, which is exactly equal to the quantity demanded, also Q_e.

Now, assume that the dairy association lobbies the government to impose a price floor of $4.50, which is the minimum price at which a block of cheese can be sold. The black dotted line indicates the price floor. Notice that at the floor price, the quantity of cheese demanded is 2.5 million blocks (point B), while that which is supplied is 15 million blocks (point C). Therefore, the market has a surplus of 12.5 million (i.e., 15 – 2.5) blocks of cheese.

FIGURE 3.28 The Cheese Market with a Price Floor

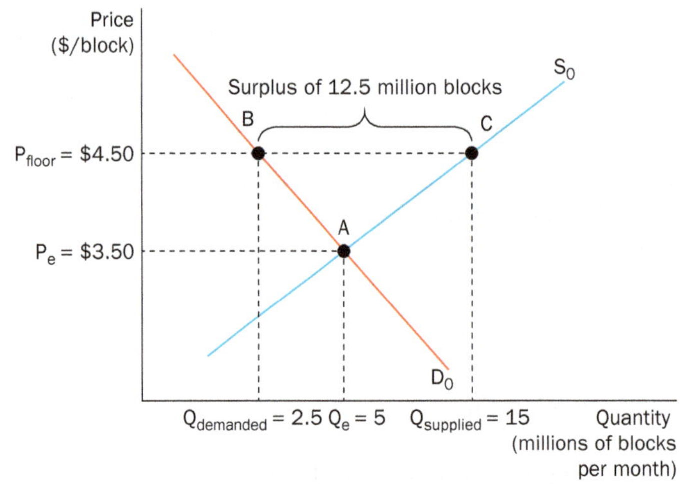

Governments impose not only price floors but price ceilings as well. These price regulations come about from pressure from industry lobbyists, but they may also arise from individuals or politicians who themselves believe that some prices are either "too high" or "too low." As a result, governments, either out of their own beliefs or because of pressure from interest groups, will try to "fix" the "wrong" prices by imposing a price ceiling or price floor. A common example of a price ceiling is rental control, which almost always leads to a shortage of housing units. A common example of a price floor is the minimum wage, which when raised at the wrong time (during a recession) may lead to job losses.

We will look at another example of a price ceiling and how it leads to a shortage using figure 3.29. South American countries like Argentina have continually experimented with price controls for food, with disastrous consequences. Usually, as a response to inflation (that is, rising price levels), some governments set price ceilings for a variety of supermarket goods, including meat, fruits, and vegetables. First, we assume, using figure 3.29, that in the absence of any government price control, the market-clearing price, P_e, is $3.50 per pound of meat (point A). This price is generated when the supply and demand curves intersect. At point A, there is no excess or shortage of meat, because the quantity supplied, Q_e, at $3.50 per block is 5 million pounds of meat per year, which is exactly equal to the quantity demanded, also Q_e.

Now, assume that in response to increasing food prices, the Argentinian government imposes a price ceiling of $2.50, which is the maximum price at which a pound of meat can be sold. The black dotted line indicates the price ceiling. Notice that at the ceiling price, the quantity of meat demanded is 8.5 million pounds (point C), while that which is supplied is 1.5 million pounds (point B). Since the price set by government is lower than the market price, producers will be willing to produce less than they were before the price fix, and some may drop out of the market altogether. Therefore, the market has a shortage of 6 million (i.e., 8.5 – 1.5) pounds of meat.

This pricing strategy will harm not only the producers but also consumers, who will have difficulty finding the products they want or need. Shortages caused by these types of price controls have led to increases in crime as a result of **black market** operations. A black market, also called an **underground market,** is simply a venue whereby goods or services are exchanged illegally. Black markets tend to appear when goods and services cannot be exchanged freely at market prices. Black markets cater to those who are usually desperate in acquiring some good or service—whether it is drugs or food. In some South American countries with food shortages that were brought about by price ceilings, consumers who bought meat on the black market had to pay 5 to 10 times the market price.

FIGURE 3.29 The Meat Market with a Price Ceiling

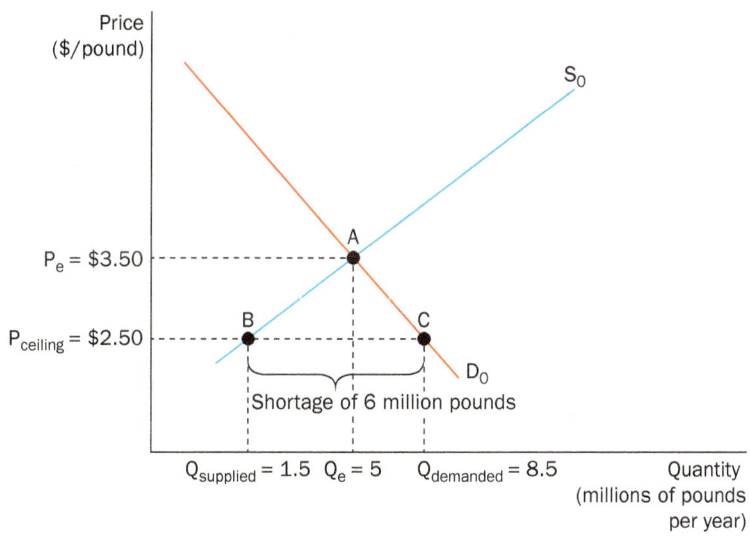

Chapter Summary

In this chapter, we noted that the price of a good or service is determined by the intersection of the supply and demand curves for that good or service. The equilibrium price, which is based on the intersection of supply and demand, is one in which many factors play a defining role. These factors are shifters of the demand and supply curves, and together they determine the value of a good or service. This price value is not equivalent to the Marxist theory, the labor theory of value.

When there is a shortage of a good or service, price is assumed to rise. When there is a surplus of a good or service, price is assumed to fall. The actual market price is always in flux, but it will tend to move to equilibrium; when the equilibrium price is reached, one does not expect to have either a shortage or a surplus of a good or service. However, if a government imposes, on the perfectly competitive market, a price that is above what would otherwise be the equilibrium price, then this price floor will lead to surpluses. If a government imposes, on the perfectly competitive market, a price that is below what would otherwise be the equilibrium price, then this price ceiling will lead to shortages.

CHAPTER 4

Why Do I Always Bear the Burden of the Sales Tax?

ELASTICITY, REVENUE, AND TAX BURDEN

LEARNING EXPECTATIONS

- To understand and calculate various price elasticities
- To apply the concept of price elasticity for the determination of revenue
- To use price elasticities to determine tax burden

JOHN BULL, BAITED BY THE DOGS OF EXCISE: A British satire on efforts by William Pitt, George Rose, and some members of Parliament to impose new "Excise" duties on tobacco (cf. Tobacco Excise Bill). The additional tax burden on British citizens is implied by the image of a bull, muzzled and blindfolded, with legs chained to a stump, being harassed by dogs (depicted with heads of members of Parliament). Edward Thurlow, also shown as a dog, registers his opposition to these "New Excise Fetters for John Bull" by urinating on tobacco leaves. Among the members of Parliament depicted are: William Wyndam Grenville, Henry Dundas, Charles Lennox Richmond, Charles Jenkinson, Richard Pepper Arden, Sir Charles Pratt Camden, and possibly Francis Osborne Carmarthen.

Source: *https://commons.wikimedia.org/wiki/File:John_Bull,_baited_by_the_dogs_of_excise_LCCN2004682250.jpg.*

Price Elasticity of Demand, E_{p1}

The laws of supply and demand predict the direction of price and quantity change but not the magnitude of the changes. For example, when there is a price increase, we know that the law of demand predicts a movement along the demand curve such that quantity demanded decreases. But, do we know by how much it decreases? If the price increase is $1, by what amount will quantity demanded decrease in millions of beer bottles per day or thousands of pounds per year of meat? To answer these questions, we need to introduce the concept of **elasticity.** Let us begin with an example—marijuana since its legalization is growing in many jurisdictions.

Let us assume that the demand for marijuana is described by demand curve A in jurisdiction A and described by demand curve B in jurisdiction B (see figure 4.1). The supply curve for marijuana is the same in both jurisdictions. Now, assume that the supply of marijuana decreases. The supply curve shifts to the left, leading to a drop in price in both jurisdictions. However, notice that in panel A (demand curve A), the same shift in the supply curve results in a bigger price increase than in panel B, but the change (or decrease) in quantity demanded is smaller than the decrease in quantity demanded in panel B.

With a *flatter demand curve*, D_B, the price change is *smaller*, but the change in quantity demanded is *larger*.

A small change in price that is accompanied by a large change in quantity demanded means that a good or service is quite responsive to changes in price. When a good or service is very responsive to changes in its price, we label its demand as **elastic.** Relatively unresponsive changes in quantity demanded when prices change is referred to as **inelastic demand.** This concept is no different than the elasticity of elastic bands. The pull on an elastic band is analogous to a price change. By applying a small force or pull, some elastic bands will stretch more than others. Those that stretch more are more responsive (i.e., more elastic) than those that stretch less (less responsive; therefore, they are inelastic).

FIGURE 4.1 Different Responses to the Same Shift in Supply

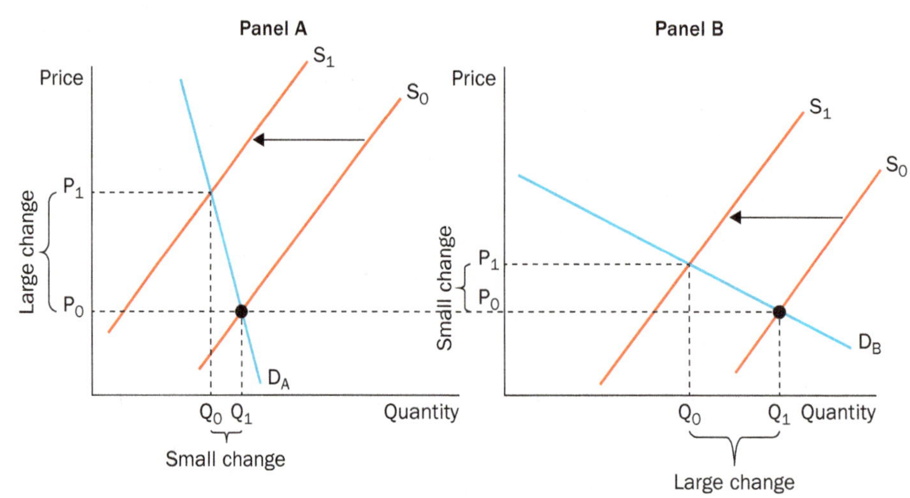

Calculating Elasticities

In order to arrive at a quantitative value for elasticities, we use the arc elasticity formula, E_p, which is the absolute value of the ratio of the average percentage change in quantity demanded and the average percentage change in price:

$$E_p = \left| \frac{\Delta Q}{Average\ quantity} \div \frac{\Delta P}{Average\ price} \right| = \left| \frac{Q_2 - Q_1}{\frac{(Q_2+Q_1)}{2}} \div \frac{P_2 - P_1}{\frac{(P_2+P_1)}{2}} \right|$$

The formula above will give us a value for E_p that ranges from 0 to positive infinity.

- If E_p for a good or service is between 0 and 1 ($0 < E_p < 1$), we label the good as having an **inelastic** price elasticity of demand.
- If E_p for a good or service is equal to one ($E_p = 1$), we label the good as having **unit** price elasticity of demand.
- If E_p for a good or service is greater than one ($E_p > 1$), we label the good as having an **elastic** price elasticity of demand.

Application Question

CALCULATING ELASTICITY

Assume that the quantity demanded for high-quality marijuana is 10 ounces per week when its price is $280 per ounce. When the price increases to $320 per ounce, the quantity demand falls to 8 ounces per week. Is the arc price elasticity of demand for marijuana elastic or inelastic?

SOLUTION

List the given values:

$Q_1 = 10$
$Q_2 = 8$
$P_1 = 280$
$P_2 = 320$

Calculate the following:

$Q_2 - Q_1 = 8 - 10 = -2$
$P_2 - P_1 = 320 - 280 = 40$
$(P_2 + P_1)/2 = (320 + 280)/2 = 300$
$(Q_2 + Q_1)/2 = (8 + 10)/2 = 9$
$(Q_2 - Q_1)/[(Q_2 + Q_1)/2] = -2/9 = -0.222$
$(P_2 - P_1)/[(P_2 + P_1)/2] = 40/300 = 0.133$
$E_p = |(-0.222)/0.133)| = 1.65$

Thus, the price elasticity of demand for marijuana is elastic.

INTERPRETING ELASTICITY VALUES

In the example above, we found that the price elasticity of demand for marijuana is 1.65. We know that this implies elastic demand, but what does this really mean? How does one interpret this number? Elasticities tell us the amount, in percentage terms, by which quantity demanded changes when there is a percentage change in price. For this reason, there are no units attached to elasticity measurements. We would thus interpret or state an elasticity value of 1.65 in any of the following, equivalent ways:

- "A 1% increase in the price of marijuana leads to a 1.65% decrease in the quantity demanded of marijuana," or
- "A 10% increase in the price of marijuana leads to a 16.5% decrease in the quantity demanded of marijuana," or
- "A 100% increase in the price of marijuana leads to a 165% decrease in the quantity demanded of marijuana," or
- "A 5% increase in the price of marijuana leads to an 8.25% (i.e., 5 × 1.65%) decrease in the quantity demanded of marijuana," or any other equivalent manner.

The Relationship of Elasticity to the Slope of the Demand Curve

One can easily determine whether a good or service has an inelastic, elastic, or unit elastic demand by simply examining the slope or steepness of the product's demand curve. We will describe the shape and elasticity of five curves and provide example for each type.

1. Perfectly inelastic demand, $E_p = 0$

Perfectly inelastic demand implies that a change in price leads to no change in quantity demanded. This occurrence is rare but not impossible. Life-saving drugs have price elasticities of demand that are virtually zero. If one were to increase the price of a life-saving drug, such as insulin or epinephrine, the patient is likely to buy the same amount; otherwise, he or she will suffer fatal consequences.

Other examples:

- Table salt, $E_p = 0.10$ (because it has no real substitutes and it makes up a very small portion of a household's overall budget)
- Food as general category, $E_p = 0.21$

The demand curve for a good or service with perfectly inelastic demand is vertical (see figure 4.2).

FIGURE 4.2 The Demand Curve for a Good or Service with Perfectly Inelastic Demand

2. **Perfectly elastic** demand, E_p = infinity

At the other extreme, we have perfectly elastic demand, which implies that a change in price leads to an infinite change in quantity demand. While there is no good or service that has a perfectly elastic demand, one can think of momentary occurrences of perfectly elastic demand of goods or services that have perfect substitutes. You may have two hairdressers located side by side on the same street and feel indifferent about cutting your hair at either salon. If one of them were to increase its price, even by a little, you would completely stop your patronage.

The demand curve for a good or service with perfectly elastic demand is horizontal (see figure 4.3).

FIGURE 4.3 The Demand Curve for a Good or Service with Perfectly Elastic Demand

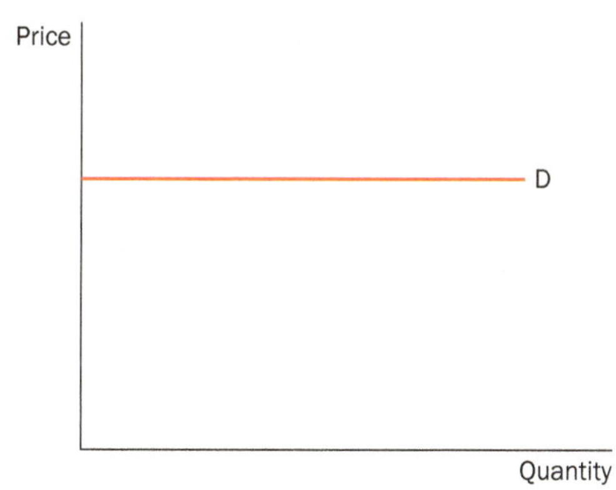

3. Inelastic demand, $0 < E_p < 1$

Inelastic demand implies that a change in price leads to smaller percentage change in quantity demand.

Examples:
Beer, $E_p = 0.29$ (interpret as: "A 1% increase in the price of beer leads to a 0.29% decrease in the quantity demanded of beer.")

Coffee, $E_p = 0.25$
Cigarettes, $E_p = 0.45$

The demand curve for a good or service with inelastic demand is relatively steep (see figure 4.4).

FIGURE 4.4 The Demand Curve for a Good or Service with Inelastic Demand

4. Elastic demand, $E_p > 1$

Elastic demand implies that a change in price leads to larger percentage change in quantity demand.

Examples:
Restaurant meals, $E_p = 2.3$ (interpret as: "A 1% increase in the price of restaurant meals leads to a 2.3% decrease in the quantity demanded of restaurant meals.")

Fresh green peas, $E_p = 2.8$
Automobiles, $E_p = 4.0$
Foreign air travel, $E_p = 4.0$

The demand curve for a good or service with elastic demand is relatively flat (see figure 4.5).

FIGURE 4.5 The Demand Curve for a Good or Service with Inelastic Demand

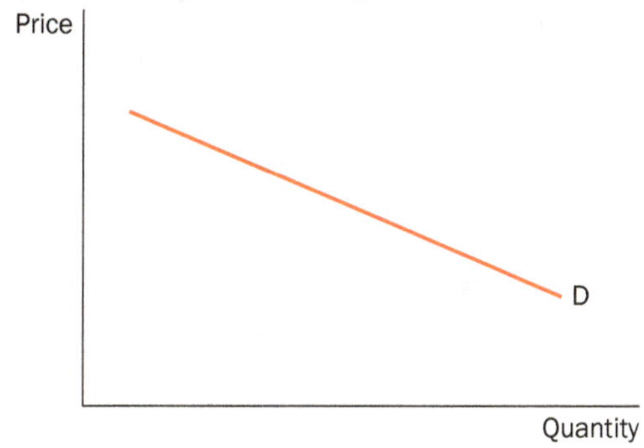

5. Unit elastic demand, $E_p = 1$

Unit elastic demand implies that a change in price leads to an equal percentage change in quantity demand.

Examples:

Breakfast cereals, $E_p = 1.0$ (interpret as: "A 1% increase in the price of breakfast cereals leads to a 1% decrease in the quantity demanded of breakfast cereals.")

The demand curve for a good or service with unit elastic demand is a hyperbola (inverse function), as figure 4.6 illustrates.

FIGURE 4.6 The Demand Curve for a Good or Service with Unit Elastic Demand

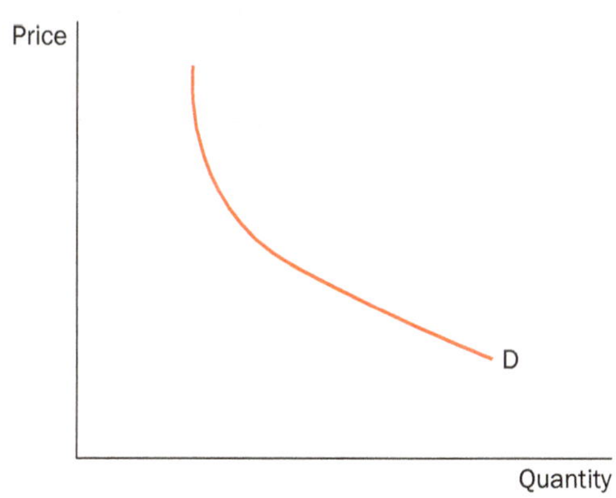

Determinants of Elasticities of Demand

There are some common characteristics of goods and services that determine whether they will have elastic or inelastic price elasticities of demand. We explore four such determinants.

1. ***Availability of substitutes***

   Commodities with close substitutes tend to have an elasticity greater than 1 (e.g. lamb, butter, broccoli, GM cars).

2. ***Category size***
   Defining categories broadly reduces the elasticity because it reduces the number of available substitutes (e.g., toothpaste versus Colgate toothpaste).

3. ***Portion of overall budget***
   If the portion of the overall household budget spent on a particular good is small, then the elasticity will tend to be small (e.g., table salt, toothpicks).

4. ***Time period***
   In the short run, elasticities tend to be small (not easy to find substitutes). Demand becomes more elastic in the long run (e.g., OPEC price increases in 1973).

Note that for some goods, there is no distinction between long and short runs because the response by consumers is immediate.

The Relationship between Price Elasticities of Demand and Revenue

Firms care about their products' elasticities because, once known, elasticities can answer the following questions for a firm:

1. Does revenue always increase after a price increase?
2. Does revenue always decrease after a price decrease?

The answer to both is no. Let us examine why. First, a firm's revenue, R, is defined as the price, P, of a good or service times the quantity sold, Q, of that good or service:

$$R = P \times Q$$

Second, as we have seen from our discussion of elasticities, the percentage change in quantity demanded does not always equal the percentage change in price, unless elasticity is unitary (equal to 1).

CASE 1: A STEEP DEMAND CURVE, $E_p > 1$

Let us examine fresh green peas, which have an $E_p = 2.8$. This implies that a 10% increase in the price of peas leads to a 28% decrease in the quantity demanded of peas. So, assume that at \$1 per bag, 3 bags are demanded. The total revenue for the firm is:

$$R_o = P \times Q = (\$1) \times (3 \text{ bags}) = \$3$$

Now, let us increase the price by \$0.10, which is an increase of 10% from the original price. With $E_p = 2.8$, the quantity demanded of peas decreases by 28%, or (0.28) × (3 bags) = 0.84 bags.

Now, the firm's total revenue is:

$$R_1 = P \times Q = (\$1.10) \times (2.16 \text{ bags}) = \$2.38$$

Thus, in cases where price elasticities of demand are elastic, total revenue decreases when there is a price increase.

CASE 2: A RELATIVELY FLAT DEMAND CURVE, $0 < E_p < 1$

Let us examine coffee, which has an $E_p = 0.25$. This implies that a 10% increase in the price of coffee leads to a 2.5% decrease in the quantity demanded of coffee. So, assume that at \$1 per cup, 3 cups are demanded. The total revenue for the firm is:

$$R_o = P \times Q = (\$1) \times (3 \text{ cups}) = \$3$$

Now, let us increase the price by \$0.10, which is an increase of 10% from the original price. With $E_p = 0.25$, the quantity demanded of coffee decreases by 2.5%, or (0.025) × (3 cups) = 0.075 cups.

Now, the firm's total revenue is:

$$R_1 = P \times Q = (\$1.10) \times (2.925 \text{ bags}) = \$3.22$$

Thus, in cases where price elasticities of demand are inelastic, total revenue increases when there is a price increase.

CASE 3: A UNIT ELASTIC DEMAND CURVE, $E_p = 1$

Let us examine grapes, which have an $E_p = 1$. This implies that a 10% increase in the price of grapes leads to a 10% decrease in the quantity demanded of grapes. So, assume that at \$1 per pound, 3 pounds are demanded. The total revenue for the firm is:

$$R_o = P \times Q = (\$1) \times (3 \text{ pounds}) = \$3$$

Now, let us increase the price by \$0.10, which is an increase of 10% from the original price. With $E_p = 1$, the quantity demanded of grapes decreases by 10%, or (0.1) × (3 pounds) = 0.3 pounds.

Now, the firm's total revenue is:

$$R_1 = P \times Q = (\$1.10) \times (2.70 \text{ pounds}) = \$2.97$$

Thus, in cases where price elasticities of demand are unit elastic, total revenue remains approximately unchanged.

Income Elasticity of Demand, E_I, and Cross-Price Elasticity of Demand, E_{CP}

Although price elasticity of demand is the one calculated most often, other types of elasticities exit, one of which is **income elasticity.** Another is called cross-price elasticity of demand, E_{CP}.

Income elasticities are calculated the same way as price elasticities:

$$E_I = \frac{\%\Delta quantity\ demanded}{\%\Delta income} = \frac{(Q_2 - Q_1)}{\frac{(Q_2+Q_1)}{2}} \div \frac{(I_2 - I_1)}{\frac{(I_2+I_1)}{2}}$$

For a normal good, **E_I is positive (>0):**

- If E_I is between 0 and 1, the good or service is income inelastic.
- If E_I is greater than 1, the good or service is income elastic, and the good is referred to as a **luxury good.**

For an inferior good, E_I **is negative (<0):**

- The more necessary the good or service is in the consumption pattern of a consumer, the lower its income elasticity.
  - Vegetables, bread, and cereals have $0 < E_I < 1$ (necessities).
  - Top meat cuts, wine, and jewelry have $E_I > 1$ (luxuries).

Cross-price elasticities, E_{CP}, are also calculated the same way as price elasticities but require the percentage change in price of one good (say, good Y) and the percentage change in quantity demanded of ***another*** good (say, good X):

$$E_{CP} = \frac{\%\Delta quantity\ demanded\ of\ good\ X}{\%\Delta price\ of\ good\ Y} = \frac{(Q_{x2} - Q_{x1})}{\frac{(Q_{x2}+Q_{x1})}{2}} \div \frac{(P_{y2} - P_{y1})}{\frac{(P_{y2}+P_{y1})}{2}}$$

For complements, E_{CP} **is negative (<0).**

For substitutes, E_{CP} **is positive (>0).**

Cross-price estimates are important measures because

1. they allow firms to understand how changes in prices of other goods (which they do not sell) affect the demand for goods they do sell, and
2. they allow policy makers (government) to predict or understand how the taxation of one good affects the demand of another good.

For example, one study[14] that examined cross-price elasticities for milk with varying fat content found that for a 1% increase in the price of whole milk, purchases of low-fat milk increased by up to 0.5% and for skim milk by up to 0.029%. Thus, it seems that consumers prefer to substitute with low-fat milk rather than skim milk when the price of whole milk increases.

Economic Policy Applications Using Price Elasticity

APPLICATION EXAMPLE 1: HOW FOOD ELASTICITIES CAN DICTATE TAX RATES

For those who are interested in how price changes alter diets, it is important to understand price elasticities of various foods. Research[14] conducting a systematic review of the price elasticity of demand for food in the United States finds the following:

- Price elasticities for foods and nonalcoholic beverages ranged from 0.27 to 0.81.
- Food away from home, soft drinks, juice, and meats are most responsive to price changes (0.7–0.8).

What would a 10% increase in soft drink price suggest?

Assuming no substitution of soft drinks with other caloric beverages and no change in other factors affecting purchasing behavior, **the price elasticity of soft drinks suggests that a 10% tax on soft drinks could lead to a 7% to 8% reduction in purchases of these beverages.**

These relatively small changes can make a big difference. Another study[15] that estimated potential weight loss from various tax rates on salty snacks under a range of price elasticities predicted that a 10% price increase from a national sales tax could reduce body weight between 0.2 and 0.99 pounds (0.1–0.5 kg) per year. The tax would generate approximately $1 billion in tax revenue. State governments already target sales taxes for soft drinks and selected snack foods. As of January 2009, 33 states taxed the sale of soft drinks at an average rate of 5.2%. Of importance to policy makers, recent surveys show that the public is willing to pay increased taxes if the funds generated are used to address childhood obesity.

APPLICATION EXAMPLE 2: IMPORTANT ELASTICITY DECISIONS BY FIRMS THAT AFFECT OUR LIVES

Many firms take advantage of the fact that some goods or services have price elasticities of demand virtually equal to zero. One example is the drug Daraprim, which is used to combat parasites, especially for patients with immune system deficiencies like HIV. Martin Shkreli, a former CEO of Turing Pharmaceuticals, raised HIV drug prices by 5,000%. That is, the price per pill increased from $13.50 to $750. (He also increased the price of medication taken by children with incurable kidney disease.)[16]

APPLICATION EXAMPLE 3: IMPORTANT ELASTICITY DECISIONS BY FIRMS THAT AFFECT OUR LIVES

Mylan, the maker of EpiPen, has steadily increased its prices. A set of two devices reached $609 in 2016, an increase of more than 500% from 2008.

How, then, does a society reasonably regulate prices without removing the incentive to innovate? Should governments threaten to invalidate a drug's patent if the drugmaker charges a price that government officials deem "too high"? These are questions to which a society must provide an answer.

Elasticities and the Economics of Taxation

Consumers commonly react to the imposition of consumption taxes as if they will bear the entire burden of the tax. For example, if the government imposes a $1 sales tax on say, cigarettes, does this mean that the price of cigarettes will increase by exactly $1 and the consumer will pay the entirety of the $1 tax? Not necessarily—the answer to who will bear the burden of a tax depends on the price elasticity of demand for the particular good or service that is being tax. The analysis of who bears the burden of a tax is referred to as **tax incidence.**

We will analyze the tax incidence of an excise tax imposed on marijuana, which we calculated to have an $E_p = 1.65$. Given that $E_p = 1.65$, the price elasticity of demand for marijuana is elastic. Thus, in figure 4.7, the demand curve is relatively flat. To carry out a tax incidence analysis, we also include the marijuana market supply curve before the imposition of the excise tax, $S_{NO\ TAX}$. When the market has no tax imposed on it, the equilibrium price for marijuana is $300 per ounce. At this price, the quantity demanded is 9 ounces of marijuana per week.

Now, the government imposes a 10% sales tax (per ounce) on the sale of marijuana. Assume that this translates to a $30 tax on every ounce of marijuana. In order to show the effect of a tax on the diagram, one can shift either the demand or the supply curve. The results will be equivalent in both cases. So, given that sellers are legally required to pay the tax to the government, we will shift the supply curve to the left by the exact magnitude of the tax—by $30. The new, after-tax supply curve is S_{TAX}.

The new after-tax equilibrium price occurs at point 2. Consumers end up paying $312, which is substantially less than $330, the price consumers would pay if all of the tax were to be shifted to them. However, because of a relatively elastic demand curve, suppliers end up paying $18 out of the $30 tax, thus receiving only $282 for one ounce of marijuana. We determine the price suppliers receive by moving down vertically from point 2 to the original supply curve, which continues to correspond to the new, after-tax equilibrium quantity demanded. The point at which the new after-tax

FIGURE 4.7 The Tax Burden on the Marijuana Market

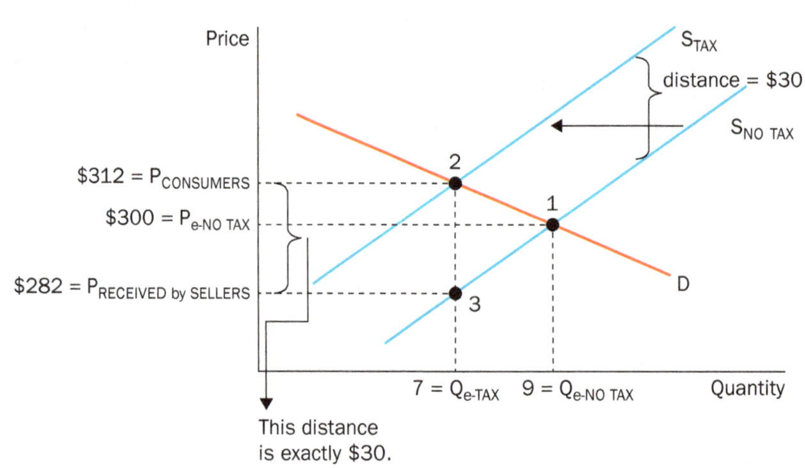

equilibrium quantity intersects with the original supply curve (i.e., point 3) is the point of reference for the new equilibrium price sellers will receive. The government, however, always receives the full amount of the tax—the $12 that is borne by the consumer plus the $18 that is borne by the supplier or seller.

In summary:

- When the demand curve for a good or service is relatively flat (elastic), more of a tax is shifted to the seller.
- When the demand curve for a good or service is relatively steep (inelastic), more of a tax is shifted to the consumer or buyer.
- When the demand curve for a good or service is vertical (perfectly inelastic), all of a tax is paid by the buyer.

Chapter Summary

In this chapter, we developed a metric that measures the extent of quantity demanded of a good or service response to a change in its own price. This metric is called the price elasticity of demand. The price elasticity of demand varies from 0 to positive infinity and it is calculated by dividing the percentage change in quantity demanded by the percentage change in price. If the price elasticity of demand is less than 1, then demand is deemed to be inelastic. When the price elasticity of demand is greater than 1, then demand is deemed to be elastic.

This chapter also illustrated that elasticity and total revenue of firms are interrelated. That is, if price elasticity of demand is less than 1, then a fall in price lowers total revenue for a firm. However, if the price elasticity of demand is greater than 1, then a fall in price raises total revenue for a firm.

There are other elasticities beside that of price elasticity of demand. This chapter considered income elasticity of demand and cross-price elasticity of demand. The importance of these types of price elasticity in economic policy applications are such that one can determine, quantitatively, how quantity demanded will respond when there are changes in consumer income and prices of substitutes or complements, respectively. Furthermore, price elasticity of demand will dictate whether consumers or firms will bear the greater burden of a tax. For instance, if the demand curve for a commodity is inelastic, then the imposition of a tax on that commodity will be paid mostly by the consumer.

SECTION 1: Testing Your Comprehensive Knowledge

Instructions

- After a thorough study of section 1, proceed with test 1.
- A well-prepared student should be able to complete this test within 75 minutes.
- Solutions to the questions follow the test.

Part 1: Multiple Choice (Please select the best answer.)

1. Which of the following is NOT a scarce resource?
   a. Fish
   b. Water
   c. Pollution
   d. Bicycles
2. Which of the following is an example of a positive economic statement?
   a. Inflation is more harmful than unemployment.
   b. Unemployment is more harmful than inflation.
   c. Lower taxes will encourage more spending.
   d. Climate change is the most serious economic problem.
3. Which of the following is an analytical statement?
   a. A rise in consumer incomes will lead to a rise in the demand for new cars.
   b. The level of duty on gas is too unfair and unfairly penalizes motorists.
   c. Labor unions help mitigate abuse and install important rights for workers.
   d. The government should increase the national minimum wage to $12 per hour in order to reduce relative poverty.
4. Which of the following is a feature of a good theory?
   a. It relies on a set of strongly held beliefs.
   b. It does not require data for testing.
   c. There are no assumptions used in constructing the theory.
   d. It is good at predicting actual behavior/outcomes.

The following figure shows the production possibilities curve of a government that has to divide its available time between producing foreign policy and domestic policy.

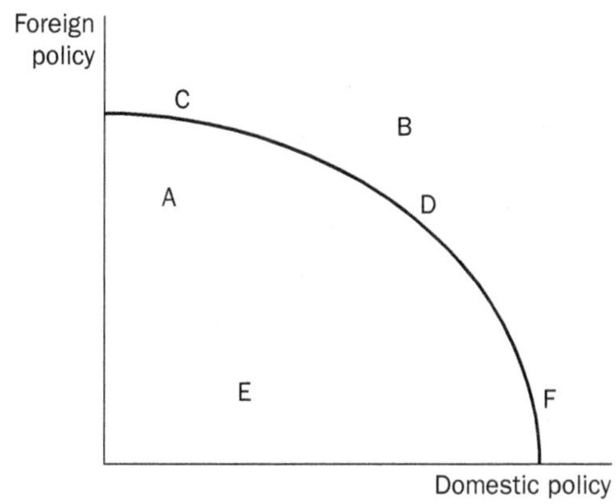

5. Refer to the figure above. Which of the following combinations is attainable but inefficient?
   a. A and E
   b. B
   c. C and E
   d. D and F
6. Refer to the figure above. Which of the following combinations is attainable as well as efficient?
   a. B
   b. C, D, and F
   c. D and E
   d. E and F
7. Refer to the figure above. Which of the following combinations is unattainable?
   a. A
   b. B
   c. D
   d. E
8. Refer to the figure above. Which of the following combinations has the same characteristics as combination C?
   a. A
   b. B
   c. D
   d. E

9. Which of the following statements is true of incentives?
   a. Incentives can be financial or moral, but not coercive.
   b. Incentives can be financial or coercive, but not moral.
   c. Incentives are designed to change behavior.
   d. Incentives are always in the form of rewards.
10. Which of the following statements is true?
    a. Economics is concerned with money, not choices.
    b. Economics can be used to predict people's actions.
    c. Economics does not provide insights into human behavior.
    d. Economic reasoning tends to reduce the quality of decision making.

The following figure shows the demand and supply curves for gas. D1 is the initial demand curve, and S is the supply curve.

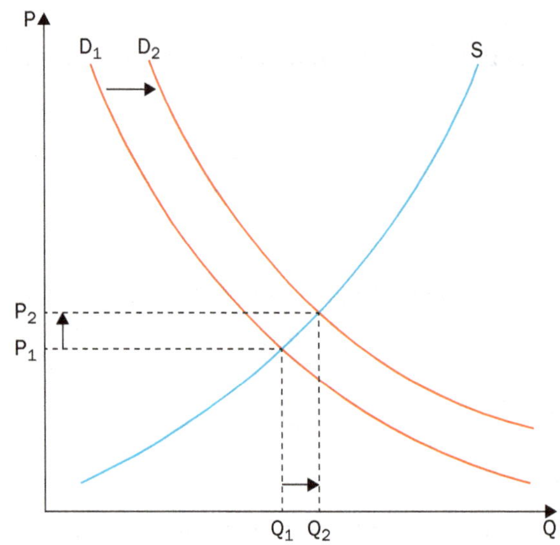

11. Refer to the figure above. When the demand curve for gas is D1 and the supply curve for gas is S, the equilibrium price is $10. Therefore, the equilibrium price for gas when D2 and S intersect must be
    a. $5.
    b. $10.
    c. $15.
    d. $8.

12. Refer to the figure above. When the demand curve for gas is D2 and the supply curve for gas is S, the government imposes a fixed price that is below P2. This will cause
    a. prices to revert to P1.
    b. a surplus.
    c. a shortage.
    d. an ambiguous effect.
13. Refer to the figure above. When the demand curve for gas is D2 and the supply curve of gas is S, the equilibrium quantity is:
    a. Q1.
    b. Q2.
    c. P1.
    d. P2.
14. Which of the following goods is likely to have the lowest price elasticity of demand?
    a. Life-saving drugs
    b. Gasoline
    c. Fruit
    d. Smart TVs
15. When the price of orange juice is $3 per bottle, you purchase 20 cartons. When the price increases to $6, you decide to purchase only 15 cartons. Your elasticity of demand for orange juice is:
    a. 0.22.
    b. 0.43.
    c. 0.55.
    d. 0.60.
16. Assume that a USB key is a normal good. Last year, when the price of USB keys was $25, 60 units were bought. However, this year, the equilibrium price of USB keys decreased to $15, but the equilibrium quantity increased to 70 units. Other things remaining the same, which of the following could explain this change?
    a. Shift of the supply curve of USB keys to the right
    b. Shift of the supply curve of USB keys to the left
    c. Shift of the demand curve for USB keys to the left
    d. None of the above

17. You consume two goods, shampoo and lipstick. Your demand for shampoo is inelastic, while your demand for lipstick is elastic. If there is an increase in the price of both shampoo and lipstick, then
    a. your expenditure on both shampoo and lipstick is likely to increase.
    b. your revenue on both shampoo and lipstick is likely to decrease.
    c. your expenditure on shampoo will increase and your expenditure on lipstick will decrease.
    d. your expenditure on both shampoo and lipstick is likely to decrease.
18. Your best friend consumes coffee, and his elasticity of demand is 2. If the price of coffee increases by 10%, the quantity demanded would fall by ________%. If the price of coffee increases by 40%, the quantity demanded would fall by ________%.
    a. 10; 40
    b. 2; 80
    c. 0.5; 5
    d. 20; 80

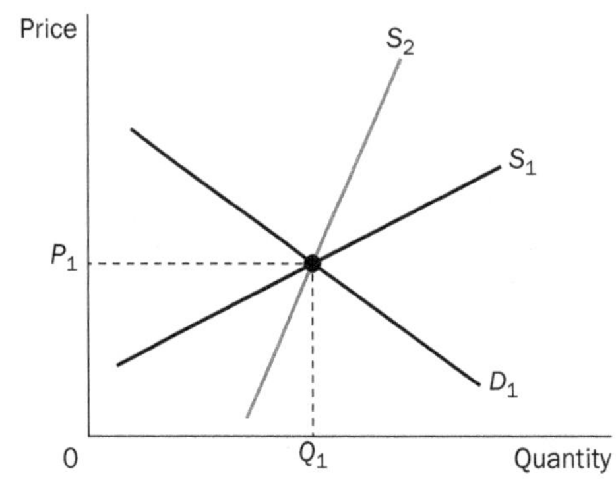

19. Examine the supply and demand graph above. Assume that the equilibrium price before a tax is $125 and the equilibrium quantity is 50,000. Which one of the following statements is true concerning the imposition of the tax?
    a. The producer bears a greater share of the tax burden if the supply curve is S_2.
    b. The new equilibrium price increases by $10.00 to $135.00 per unit.
    c. The entire tax burden falls on the seller.
    d. The entire tax burden falls on the buyer.
20. Examine the supply and demand graph above. Assume that the equilibrium price before a tax is $125 and the equilibrium quantity is 50,000. Which one of the following statements is true if the demand curve were to suddenly become perfectly horizontal (flat)?
    a. The entire tax burden falls on the seller only if supply is S_1.
    b. The entire tax burden falls on the seller only if supply is S_2.
    c. The entire tax burden falls on the seller regardless if the supply is S_1 or S_2.
    d. The entire tax burden falls on the buyer.

Part 2: Short Answer

1. Economists note that, generally, countries with the lowest female literacy rates have the highest birthrates. However, this does not necessarily mean that education causes smaller family sizes. Consider this: Poor countries that, in cooperation with world development agencies, invested most in literacy programs did not always experience a marked improvement in their rates of economic growth. In terms of incentives, how does one explain this observation?
2. Provide an example either from your own life or a world event/situation where a lack of incentives prevented a desired outcome from occurring.

Part 3: Analytical Reasoning

1. Use the table below to match the goods with their respective price elasticity of demand.

   Here are four price elasticities of demand: 2.17; 1.44; 0.88; 0.09.

Good	Price Elasticity of Demand
1. Cookies (all brands)	
2. Gasoline	
3. Mr. Christie's chocolate chip cookies	
4. Mr. Christie's (all cookies)	

2. Refer to the table that follows. An island nation produces only olives and garlic. The table below shows the maximum possible output combinations of olives and garlic when all island resources and currently available technology are employed.

Possible Output Combinations	Olives (thousands of kilograms)	Garlic (thousands of kilograms)
A	100	0
B	90	40
C	80	75
D	70	105
E	60	125
F	50	140
G	40	150
H	30	155
I	20	158
J	10	160
K	0	161

a. Graph the island nation's production possibilities frontier. Put olives on the horizontal axis and garlic on the vertical axis. Be sure to identify the output combination points on your diagram.

b. Suppose the island nation is currently producing at point D. What is the opportunity cost of producing an additional 10,000 kilograms of olives?

c. Suppose the island nation is currently producing at point D. What happens to the opportunity cost of producing more and more olives? Does it increase, decrease, or remain constant? Explain your answer.

Solutions to Test 1

Part 1: Multiple Choice

1C	11C
2C	12C
3C	13B
4D	14A
5A	15B
6B	16A
7B	17C
8C	18D
9C	19A
10B	20C

Part 2: Short Answer

1. When incentives are lacking, compelling people to go to school does not lead them to acquire an education. People will want to learn and will desire an education when they see future income from the acquisition of knowledge and skills (i.e., good jobs). Choice of family size (fewer children) is also freely made when economic opportunities are opened to them in a booming market economy.
2. Student answers may vary.

Part 3: Analytical Reasoning

1.

Good	Price Elasticity of Demand
1. Cookies (all brands)	0.88
2. Gasoline	0.09
3. Mr. Christie's chocolate chip cookies	2.17
4. Mr. Christie's (all cookies)	1.44

2a.

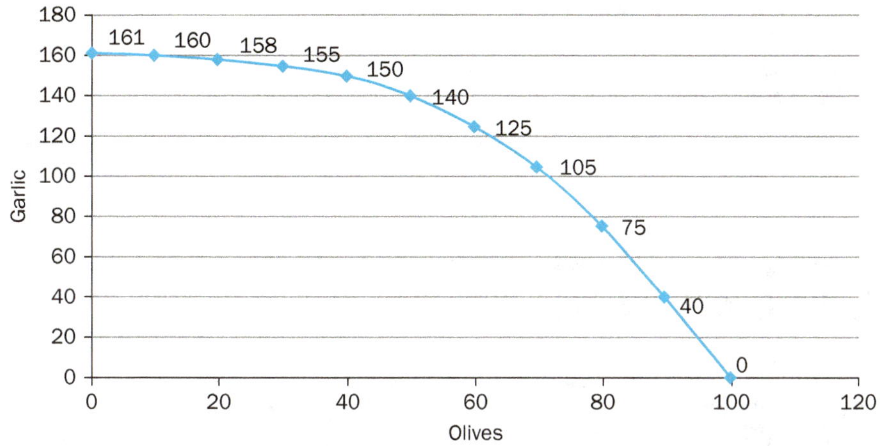

2b. 30,000 kilograms of garlic (to be given up)

2c. The opportunity cost increases. As more olives are produced, the nation must give up increasing amounts of garlic production.

SECTION 2

CHAPTERS 5–7

The Micro Side: Human Behavior and Firm Production

THE DANGERS OF MONOPOLIES: Political cartoon from Puck magazine from 1881 by Joseph Keppler illustrating the dangers of monopoly. A snake representing Monopoly has the U.S. Capitol in the coils of its tail. The body has stripes with the names of prominent businessmen of the era. The snake's head has risen as if prepared to strike, threatening Columbia. At left Puck draws Uncle Sam's attention to the threatening snake, asking "What are you going to do about it?"

Source: *https://commons.wikimedia.org/wiki/File:Puck_monopoly.jpg.*

CHAPTER 5

For Consumers' Sakes, Stop the Merger! Firm Costs and Firm Production

LEARNING EXPECTATIONS

- To understand how the theoretical production function is constructed
- To apply the concept of marginal analysis
- To differentiate and calculate the various firm costs

OMEN PREPARING SILK: 12th century China

urce: *https://commons.wikimedia.org/wiki/File:Court_ladies_pounding_silk_from_a_ inting_(%E6%8D%A3%E7%BB%83%E5%9B%BE)_by_Emperor_Huizong.jpg.*

There are approximately 28 million firms in the United States. A total of 99.7% of US firms are classified as small businesses; that is, firms that employ less than 500 employees. Small businesses are an important part of the US economy. They make up the following:

64 percent of net new private-sector jobs,
49.2 percent of private-sector employment,
42.9 percent of private-sector payroll,
46 percent of private-sector output,
43 percent of high-tech employment,
98 percent of firms exporting goods, and
33 percent of exporting value.[17]

The role and effect of firms on the economy is profound. Once it is determined what a society wants to produce, firms then play a pivotal role in deciding how to produce it, how to market it, and at what price to sell it based on the cost of making it. Additionally, some hold the view that the role of the firm, especially the role of the corporation, should not be based solely on competitiveness and profitability but should include corporate social responsibility, where the firm is accountable to a wide range of stakeholders, besides shareholders and investors. Corporate responsibility includes concerns about environmental protection, the well-being of employees, and civil society in general. The concept of corporate social responsibility is buttressed by the notion that corporations can no longer separate themselves from the broader society and act as siloed economic entities.

CORPORATE SOCIAL RESPONSIBILITY (OR LACK OF): AN EXAMPLE

Walmart made news when it eliminated health care insurance for 30,000 of its temporary employees. Thousands of full-time employees also faced insurance plans with very high deductibles and out-of-pocket expenses, where a single serious illness or hospitalization would have cost them as much as a year's earnings. The lack of an affordable health plan means that many full- and part-time employees forgo their health care needs completely or resort to public assistance for health care. Given that there are no free lunches in economics, the burden of the health care costs is shifted to taxpayers. Taxpayers, in essence, then subsidize what would have been a firm-provided health care plan. According to a University of California study, in 2003 Californian taxpayers subsidized Walmart by $20.5 million in medical care. Furthermore, families of Walmart employees in California utilized approximate 40% more in taxpayer-funded health care than the average for families of all large retail employees.[18]

A Firm's Production Function

The principal activity of firms is to turn **inputs** into **outputs.** Inputs are the resources that go into production, which include, for example:

- raw material, M, such as cotton, oil, energy;
- capital, K , such as sewing machines; and
- labor, L, usually measured in labor hours.

A production function presents the quantitative (or mathematical) relationship between inputs and outputs. A production function may take the form of a schedule, a graph, an algebraic equation, or a mathematical model. Many times, a production function represents the technology use of a firm. Mathematically, we can represent a production as follows:

$$\mathbf{Q = f(M, K, L, \ldots)} \tag{5.1}$$

where

Q = quantity of output
f(•) = "function of"
M = raw material
K = capital inputs such as machinery
L = labor inputs

Quantity output, Q = f(M, K, L, …), is the firm's production function for a particular good, q. For each different combination of inputs, the production function tells us the maximum quantity of output a firm can produce over some period of time. In addition to producing desired outputs such as cars or baseball caps, every time a firm engages in production, it generates **undesirable joint outputs.** Undesirable joint production outputs include generated wastes such as pollution, wasted heat, and wasted material, which are not part of the production function. If these waste outputs affect a third party in any detrimental way, they are termed **negative externalities.** Thus, firms do not always **internalize** (i.e., take into account by explicit costing) negative externalities such as pollution or acid rain.

Production Example: Wheat

For the sake of convenience of convenience, we reduce the number of variables used in a production function to only two: capital (K) and labor (L). Therefore, in the analysis of input-output relations, the production function is expressed as:

$$\mathbf{Q = f(K, L)} \tag{5.2}$$

Limiting the discussion to two inputs, such as L and K, allows us to describe the inputs in two-dimensional graphs.

We will begin our analysis of firm production by exploring the production costs of farming wheat. Before examining the production process and costs of producing goods, it is important to understand that there are different phases of production and that each phase is associated with different costs. In economics, we tend to classify phases of processes that change with time. This classification is not limited to firm behavior. Any economic agent—household, firm, government—will behave differently depending on the length of time it has to react to certain affecting factors called shocks. There are two classifications of time—the **short run** and the **long run.** The actually length of time—one week, one month, or one year—is not important. What is important is that when a phase is labeled "short run," it refers to the length of time in which an economic agent faces some or many factors that it cannot change or adapt to. In contrast, the "long run" is a period of time in which an economic agent can change any influencing factor or adapt to shocks. The following paragraph applies this idea to firm production.

In order to produce wheat, a variety of inputs are needed. Therefore, our production function will include inputs such as natural capital, manufactured capital such as tractors, human capital, and so forth. To some extent, production of wheat can use a varying amount of one or more inputs. For example, the amount of fertilizer applied to the land can be varied by the farmer in order to verify its effect on output or wheat yield. Any input that cannot be varied in the short term is referred to as a **fixed input.** A fixed input would be land (or its lease) because one cannot avoid/alter paying for it in the short term. A fixed input is a **limiting factor** that creates a **constraint** to increasing production.

Our production function is as follows:

- Q = f(natural capital, manufactured, human capital, social capital, financial capital)
- Q = f(seeds, land, fertilizer, pesticides, labor, ...)

To allow the analysis to be more tractable, we will consider only one input, fertilizer. Thus, our simplified production function is: Q = f(fertilizer). We will assume that the firm varies the amount of fertilizer to determine its effect on output (i.e., wheat yield). Figure 5.1 provides the amount of output for varying amounts of fertilizer, the input.

FIGURE 5.1 Production Output per Amount of Input

Input (fertilizer in kilograms)	Output (Wheat yield in bushels per acre)
0	50
10	100
20	135
30	155
40	165
50	174
60	182
70	190
80	196
90	199
100	202
110	202
120	202
130	202
140	202
150	200

When the data are tabulated as they are in figure 5.1, we can convert it to a graph, as shown in figure 5.2. As can be seen in the graph, increasing amounts of input or fertilizer increases the output yield. However, the increasing output yield increases at a decreasing rate when more fertilizer is added. Eventually, output yields level off at about 202 bushels per acre and 100 kilograms of fertilizer. Any additional fertilizer between 110 and 140 kilograms has no effect on the output. However, further increasing input levels to 150 kilograms of fertilizer actually causes a decrease in output from 202 wheat bushels per acre to 200 wheat bushels per acre. Now note that for this production function, we are only measuring the effect of one input variable, holding all other inputs constant. As discussed in the previous chapters, in order to determine the effect of one variable on another variable, we need to hold all other input variables at a constant level; otherwise, we could not isolate the effect of the variable of interest on our output variable.

FIGURE 5.2 Graphical Depiction of Wheat Output as a Function of its Fertilizer Input

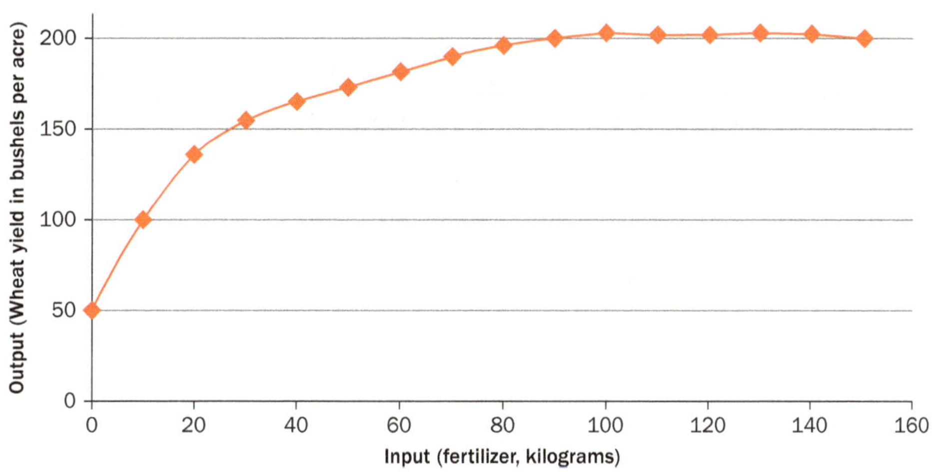

Note the following from figure 5.2:

1. The curve is the **total product curve:** It gives the maximum amount of output that can be produced at different levels of one input, assuming that the other inputs are fixed at a particular level. For example, the total product is 190 bushels per acre when the amount of fertilizer is 70 kilograms.
2. Yields per acre increase as more fertilizer is applied, but at **a decreasing rate.**

This is known as the **law of diminishing marginal returns.** This law is based on the fact that the slope of the production curve at any one point, called the **marginal product (MP),** becomes less positive when more input is added. Eventually, the MP becomes negative (at 150 kilograms of input).

The marginal product is calculated as follows:

$$MP = \frac{\Delta TP}{\Delta Q} \tag{5.3}$$

The law of diminishing marginal returns applies to any input. We can examine this law in action by changing the input from fertilizer to labor, holding all other inputs constant. We will graph wheat output and labor input in figure 5.3.

As figure 5.3 illustrates, a production process can exhibit three types of marginal returns when we consider the whole range of different production levels (as we increase inputs). Very small amounts of input lead to large changes in the quantity of output (delta Q). The increases in output grow larger as we increase the amount of inputs. This characterizes the portion of the figure from 0 to 2 workers and 0 to 90 bushels of wheat output. This range from 0 to 2 workers is called **increasing marginal returns.** Additional numbers of workers continue to increase wheat output, but at decreasing levels. We note in figure 5.3 that moving from 2 to 3 workers increases output from 90 to 130 bushels of wheat per acre, but increasing the number of workers by one extra unit from 3 workers to 4 workers increases output only from 130 bushels per acre to 161 bushels per acre. Thus, we are in a range of **decreasing marginal returns.**

FIGURE 5.3 Graphical Depiction of Wheat Output as a Function of its Labor Input

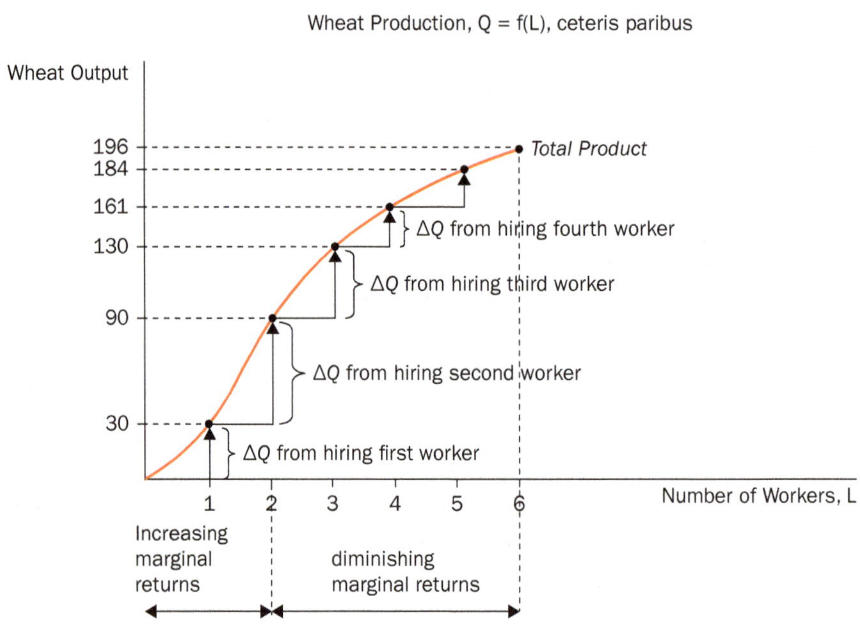

If output were to change by the same amount for every equivalent change in input, then we would be in the range of **constant marginal returns.** Figure 5.4 illustrates the three phases that a firm may go through in its production process. Firms need not have production functions that exhibit all three phases.

FIGURE 5.4 The Three Stages of Production: A Total Product Curve with Increasing, Constant, and Decreasing Marginal Returns

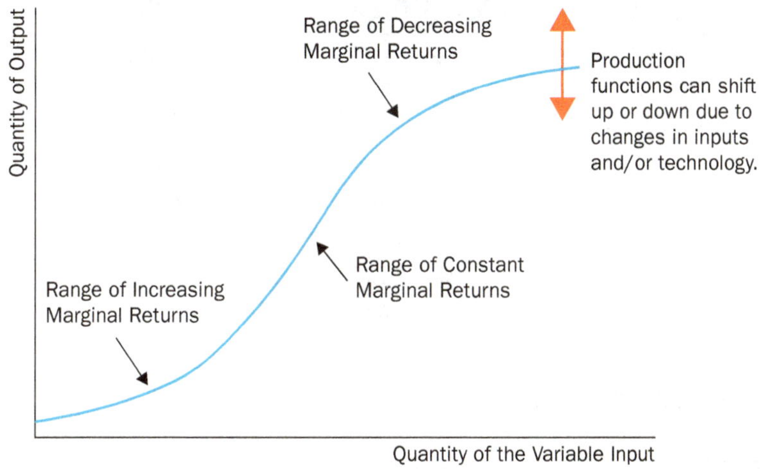

Marginal Analysis

Now that we are familiar with the concept of a changing marginal product along the total product curve, we can proceed in calculating marginal product. We will use the data in figure 5.3 to calculate MP using formula 5.3. The table below (figure 5.5) uses the MP formula to calculate the changes for each change in amount of fertilizer.

FIGURE 5.5 Calculating Marginal Product

Input (fertilizer in kilograms)	Output (Wheat yield in bushels per acre)	Marginal Product (MP)
0	50	—
10	100	$= \frac{(100-50)}{(10-0)} = 5$
20	135	$= \frac{(135-100)}{(20-10)} = 3.5$
30	155	$= \frac{(155-135)}{(30-20)} = 2$
40	165	1
50	174	0.9
60	182	0.8
70	190	0.8
80	196	0.6

FIGURE 5.5 Calculating Marginal Product (*continued*)

Input (fertilizer in kilograms)	Output (Wheat yield in bushels per acre)	Marginal Product (MP)
90	199	0.3
100	202	0.3
110	202	0
120	202	0
130	202	0
140	202	0
150	200	–0.2

Types of Production Costs

As firms engage in production, they incur a variety of costs. There are two types of costs we will consider: fixed and variable.

Fixed costs (also called sunk costs or overhead costs) are costs that cannot be changed in the short or medium term. Fixed costs do not generally vary with production volume. In the short run, a number of costs will be fixed. In other words, fixed costs are those that are spent and cannot be changed in the period of time under consideration.

Examples:

- Monthly payments on machinery
- Rent
- Mortgage costs

Variable costs are costs that can be relatively easily adjusted in the short term to market conditions or production targets. In the long run, there are no fixed costs. All costs are variable in the long run.

Examples:

- Wages
- Utilities

A firm's underlying expenses determine the profitable price level for its products or services, including aspects of its overall business strategy. Thus, a firm needs to calculate its total costs. Total costs are simply the sum of total fixed costs and total variable costs:

$$\text{Total Costs (TC)} = \text{Total Fixed Costs (TFC)} + \text{Total Variable Costs (TVC)} \quad (5.4)$$

or simply

$$\mathbf{TC = TFC + TVC} \quad (5.5)$$

A business owner will use her familiarity of her firm's fixed and variable costs to establish the firm's break-even point (the number of units or dollars at which total revenues equal total costs, TR = TC, so the company breaks even) and for rendering decisions related to the pricing of her goods and services. Recall that total revenue is the product of quantity sold and the price at which the units were sold.

Marginal Cost

Another type of cost that is of importance to firms is called the marginal cost (MC). ***Marginal cost is important in economic theory because firms, which seek to maximize profit, will produce up to the point where marginal cost equals marginal revenue (MR).*** Marginal revenue, which is the increase in revenue that results from the sale of one additional unit of output, will be discussed further in the next chapter. MR can remain constant over a certain level of output, but it eventually follows the law of diminishing returns as the output level increases.

Marginal cost is the additional cost incurred in the production of one more unit of output. MC is calculated from the variable cost of production, but not fixed costs because fixed costs do not change as output changes. There is no additional fixed cost that is incurred in producing another unit of an output (once production has been initiated).

We can write marginal cost as the change in total cost (delta TC) divided by the change in output (delta Q):

$$MC = \frac{\Delta TC}{\Delta Q} \tag{5.6}$$

MC tells us how much cost rises per unit increase in output. We will see in the following chapter that for competitive firms, the MC curve derives the supply curve.

What do MC curves look like? The typical MC curve is illustrated in figure 5.6, along with the typical TC curve.

FIGURE 5.6 The Typical MC and TC Curves

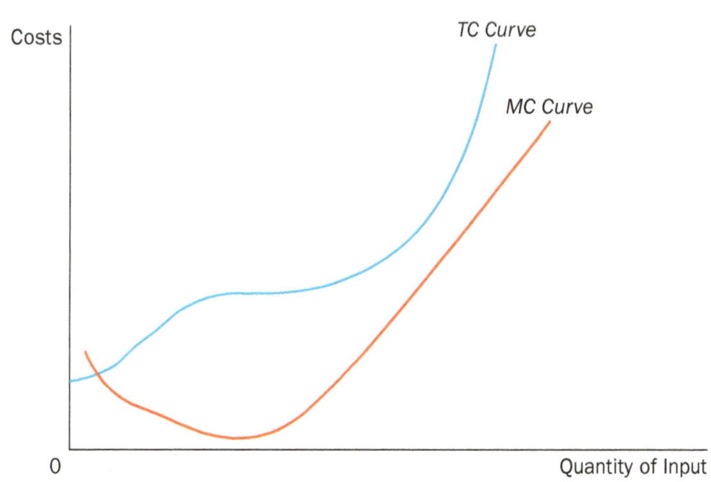

Average Costs

There are other costs that change when output changes. These are the **average variable costs (AVCs).** AVCs are easily obtained from the total fixed and total variable costs. There are three such costs:

1. **Average fixed cost:** Total fixed cost divided by the quantity of output produced:

$$AFC = \frac{TFC}{Q} \tag{5.7}$$

2. **Average variable cost (AVC):** Total variable cost divided by the quantity of output produced:

$$AVC = \frac{TVC}{Q} \tag{5.8}$$

3. **Average total cost (ATC):** Total cost divided by the quantity of output produced:

$$ATC = \frac{TC}{Q} \tag{5.9}$$

What do average cost (AC) curves look like? The typical AC curves are illustrated in figure 5.7.

FIGURE 5.7 The Typical AC Curves with the MC Curve

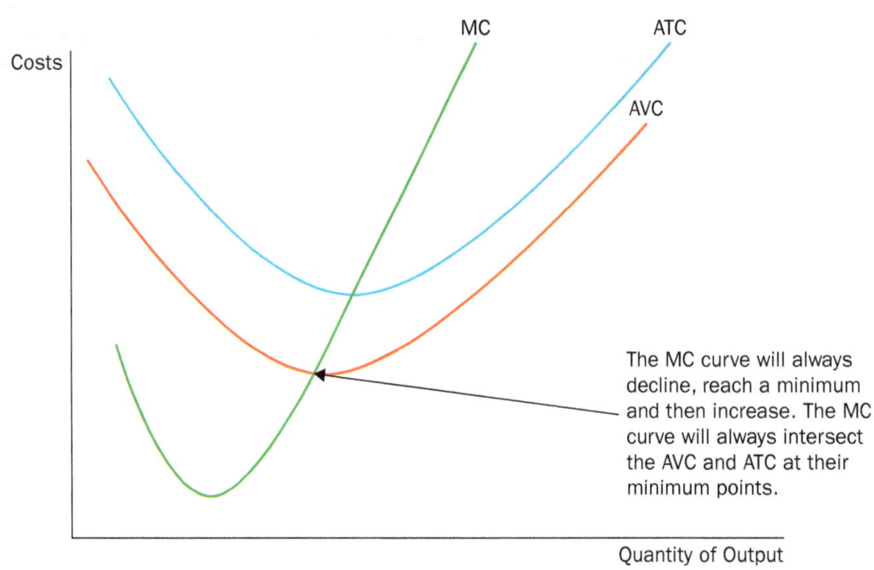

Achieving Minimum Costs Through Mergers: An Example of Real-World Cost Curve Application

One way a firm can maximize its profits is to minimize its costs. That is, it wants to operate where the AVC is at its minimum. All the curves illustrated thus far have been short-run curves. A firm can adjust its level of production in the long run to lower its average costs. How? By getting bigger. Sometimes, but not always (bigger is not always better), the bigger the firm's size, the lower its costs of production. This phenomenon is called **economies of scale.**

Economies of scale mean that average costs tend to decrease as the level of production increases, perhaps as a result of labor specialization or acquisition of more efficient capital or better design and development, and so on. Of course, there can also be situations of constant returns to scale and diseconomies of scale. For many production processes, there exists a **minimum efficient scale**—a point at which the long-run average cost curve begins to bottom out. Increasing output further is likely to eventually lead to the maximum efficient scale, beyond which long-run average costs will begin to increase again.

An example of a firm trying to achieve lower long-run average total costs is Bayer, the pharmaceutical/chemical giant. In 2016, Bayer announced that it intended to buy Monsanto, the world's largest seed producer. This announcement shocked farmers and consumers alike. The deal could have deep, largely negative effects for consumers and suppliers. The $62 billion deal would allocate considerable market power to one firm in an already highly consolidated global seed and chemical industry. Seed prices could rise for farmers, and consumers could see higher prices as well. Besides, it helps no one to have the global agricultural system dependent on a few companies to meet the world's agricultural needs. Even before this merger was announced, the seed and chemical industry had only six firms—Syngenta, Bayer, BASF, Dow, Monsanto, and DuPont—that control 60% of commercial seed and more than 75% of agrochemical markets.[19]

Market structure in general—and mergers and acquisitions in particular—raise important public policy issues:

- Low-cost production can benefit consumers—if it results in lower prices.
- Or it can hurt consumers with higher prices and by jeopardizing (e.g., food) security if competition is reduced such that only a few firms control the supply of one good or service.

Now, from Bayer's perspective, this merger will likely use newly acquired capital to create new amounts of output so as to also create new short-run average cost curves that will be enveloped by a **long-run average total cost curve (LRATC).** Assume figure 5.8 represents Bayer's cost curves. Bayer's LRATC curve is derived from its short-run average cost (SRAC) curves. In the short run, Bayer cannot make large changes to its plant size. In the long run, however, it can vary its plant size, say, via the merger with Monsanto.

For each short-run fixed plant size, Bayer takes the lowest average total costs for that size plant. For example, if Bayer has one plant in the short run, it faces ATC_0, which has its minimum at an output of 190 units. If Bayer has three plants in the short run, it faces

ATC_2, which has its minimum at an output of 1,960 units. For each of the four different numbers of plants, Bayer can operate at different short-run minimums. These lower portions (i.e., minimums) of the different short-run cost curves constitute the long-run average cost curve, with new minimums at points A and E on the LRATC. Note that points A and E are at the same output levels as points B, C, and D, respectively, but the latter points were not necessarily minimums on the short-run ATC curves. Thus, Bayer's LRATC curve (i.e., after the merger) is the "envelope" of the bottom points of the firm's SRAC curves.

FIGURE 5.8 Bayer—From Short-Run ATCs to LRATC

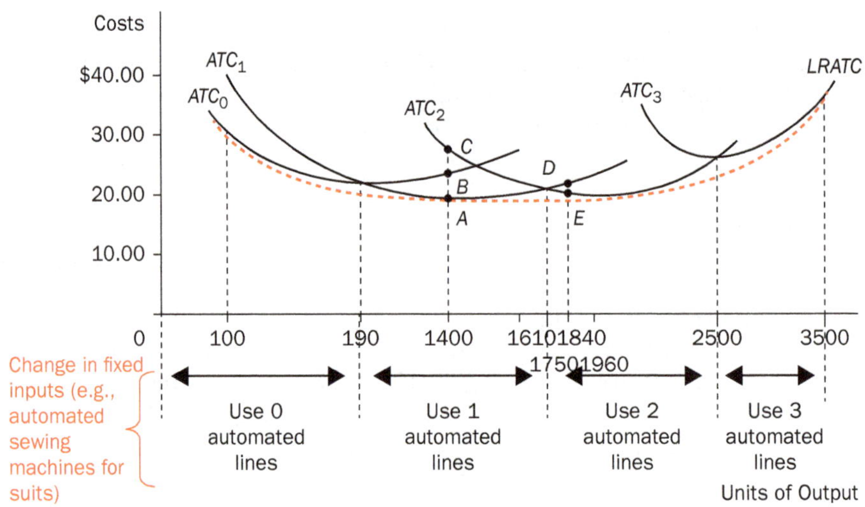

Application Questions

COST CALCULATIONS AND GRAPHING

Assume the table that follows represents the production costs for Monsanto. Its production process involves both fixed and variable costs. The fixed cost of producing seeds is $100,000. The following table describes some of these costs. Note that all entries are in thousands of dollars. Find solutions to the following:

1. Complete the table. Then graph the total variable cost and total cost curves.
2. On a separate chart, graph the average total cost, average variable cost, and marginal cost curves.
3. What are the output levels at which the average total cost and average variable cost curves intersect the marginal cost curve? Indicate whether these costs are short- or long-run costs. Explain your answer.

COST TABLE FOR MONSANTO

Output (seeds in billions)	Total Variable Cost (TVC) ($, 000)	Total Cost (TC) ($, 000)	Average Variable (AVC) ($, 000)	Average Total Cost (ATC) ($, 000)	Marginal Cost (MC) ($, 000)
0	0	100	—	—	—
10	100				
20				13.00	
30		290			
40					6
50	330		6.60		
60					10
70	560				

SOLUTIONS

Output (seeds in billions)	Total Variable Cost (TVC) ($, 000)	Total Cost (TC) ($, 000)	Average Variable (AVC) ($, 000)	Average Total Cost (ATC) ($, 000)	Marginal Cost (MC) ($, 000)
0	0	100	—	—	—
10	100	200	10.00	20.00	10
20	160	260	8.00	13.00	6
30	190	290	6.33	9.67	3
40	250	350	6.25	8.75	6
50	330	430	6.60	8.60	8
60	430	530	7.17	8.83	10
70	560	660	8.00	9.43	13

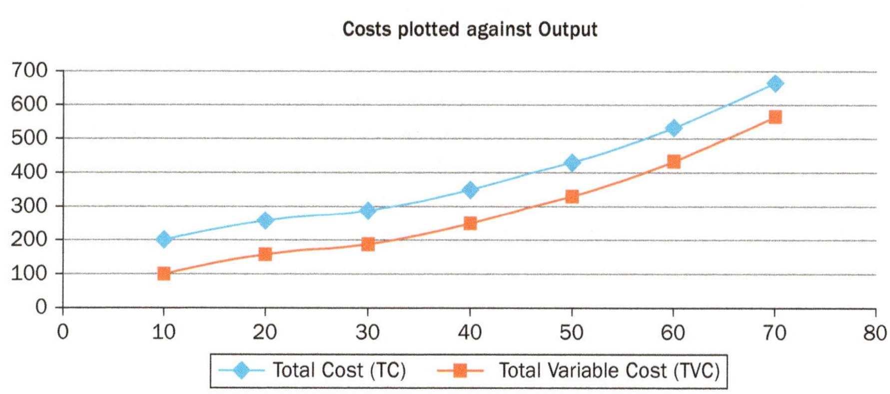

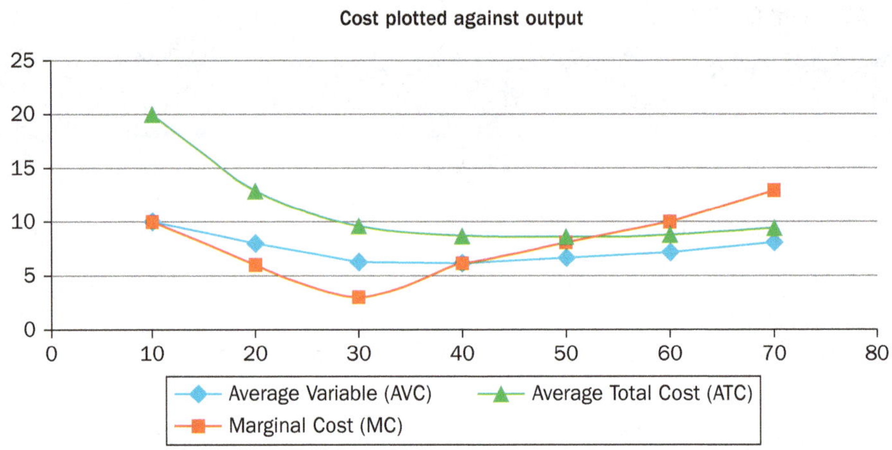

The marginal cost curve intersects the average variable cost at an output level of 40 billion seeds. The marginal cost curve intersects the average total cost at an output level of 50 billion seeds.

These costs are short-run costs because at least one input, the number of plants (i.e., capital equipment), remains fixed in this production process.

Chapter Summary

In this chapter, we introduced the theoretical production function for firms. The inputs used in the production function have several important properties that one should note:

1. Economists find that the supply of capital (K) is inelastic (usually perfectly) in the short run and elastic in the long run. Thus, in the short run, firms can increase production only by increasing labor.
2. In the long run, firms can employ more of both capital and labor.
3. As long as marginal benefits (MB), which is the gained value for every additional unit of output, exceed marginal costs (MC), which is the cost value of every additional unit of output, firms should expand production.

The chapter also made a distinction between short-run and long-run costs. SRAC curves are U-shaped because the average productivity of firms is expected to increase for small amounts of output, but it eventually declines as output increases. In the long run, there are no fixed inputs, and the long-run cost curve is one in which it envelopes all the firm's SRACs over a range of output amounts.

CHAPTER 6

Market Structure and Games

LEARNING EXPECTATIONS

- To understand and recognize the different types of market structures
- To understand how game theory works and to engage in game strategies using the payoff matrix
- To determine Nash equilibria

JOHN FORBES NASH, Game Theorist.

Source: *Copyright © European School of Economics (CC BY-SA 4.0) at https://commons.wikimedia.org/wiki/Category:John_Forbes_Nash#/media/File:John_Forbes_Nash_(2).jpg.*

In this chapter, we briefly introduce **market structures. While an industry is a group of firms that produce similar goods or services, a market structure** is the environment in which firms make pricing and output decisions and that is characterized by the number of sellers, the ability to control price, and the freedom with which firms can enter or exit.

There are four market structures. Figure 6.1 lists these four structures and their defining characteristics. Note that only firms that operate in a purely competitive market structure have no real influence over the setting of prices. Hence, they have a *perfectly horizontal demand curve* and are called **price takers.**

FIGURE 6.1 The Four Market Structures

	Characteristics	
Market Structure	Price Taker or Price Searcher?	Demand Curve Facing the Firm
Pure Competition	Price Taker—the firm chooses quantity but takes price from the market	Perfectly elastic
Monopolistic Competition	Price Searcher	Very elastic, but not perfectly elastic because close substitutes exist
Oligopoly	Price Searcher	Inelastic, to be an effective oligopoly
Pure Monopoly	Price Searcher	Inelastic, to be an effective monopoly

Market structures can also be characterized by the number of firms that participate in the market and the type of product that they sell. Figure 6.2 lists these defining characteristics for each of the four market structures. Once again, firms in a purely competitive market stand out as the only ones selling **homogeneous** goods or services; that is, goods or services that are nearly identical to each other and can be easily substituted.

FIGURE 6.2 Market Structure and their Product Characteristics

Market Structure	Number of Sellers	Number of Buyers	Homogeneous or Differentiated Product?	Example
Pure Competition	Many	Many	Homogenous (all goods are perfect substitutes)	Most agricultural products, items (e.g. books) sold on the Internet
Monopolistic Competition	Many firms with *non-interdependent* pricing and quantity decisions	Many	Differentiated products, but close substitutes for consumers so their demand curves are elastic	Spas Hairdressers Restaurants

FIGURE 6.2 *(continued)*

Market Structure	Number of Sellers	Number of Buyers	Homogeneous or Differentiated Product?	Example
Oligopoly	Few firms with *interdependent* pricing and quantity decision	Few or Many	Can be either homogenous or differentiated	Oil industry Airlines Pharmacies Beer
Monopoly	One	Few or Many	Single, homogenous product with no close substitutes	Telephone, cable companies (historically) Utilities

The Perfectly Competitive Market

An *individual firm* (as opposed to an industry) in a perfectly competitive market faces a perfectly elastic demand curve. Therefore, the demand curve, D, is completely horizontal. Given that the individual firm is a price taker, the demand curve that an individual firm faces is equal to the market price, P_e. If the firm were to set its price above the market price, it would sell nothing, because its product is perfectly substitutable with another of lower price. The individual firm's demand curve is also equal to the firm's marginal revenue, MR. This is illustrated in figure 6.3.

FIGURE 6.3 The Demand and Cost Curves for a Firm in a Perfectly Competitive Market

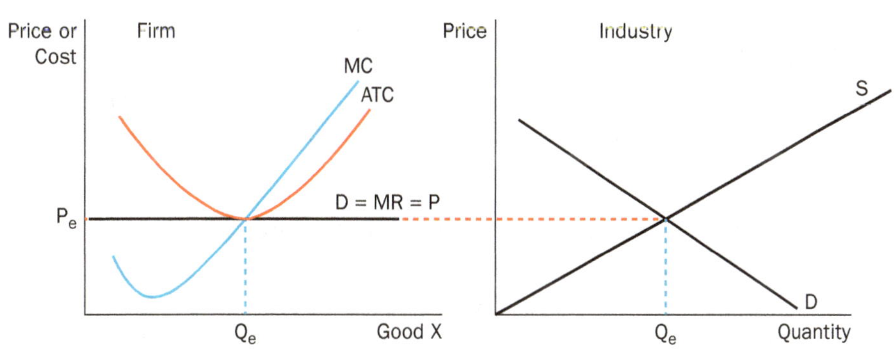

From Marginal Cost to the Supply Curve: Perfectly Competitive Firms

In order to decide how many units to produce in a perfectly competitive market structure, one needs a firm's marginal cost, MC, and the market price. If the MC is less than the price, firms will produce. Firms continue to produce as long as the cost of the next unit of output (i.e., its MC) is less than the market price. As figure 6.4 illustrates, the portion of the MC that is above the AVC curve is the supply curve for a firm operating in a perfectly competitive market. The portion of the MC curve below its intersection with the AVC curve is not part of the supply curve, because a firm would not operate at a price below which it cannot even cover its variable costs. The point at which a firm cannot receive a market price that is sufficient to cover its (average) variable costs is called the firm's **shutdown point.** The optimal decision is to produce no output if the price is less than the minimum of the firm's AVC (if P < AVC, then for every unit the firm sells, it makes a loss).

FIGURE 6.4 A Firm's Output Decisions in a Perfectly Competitive Market

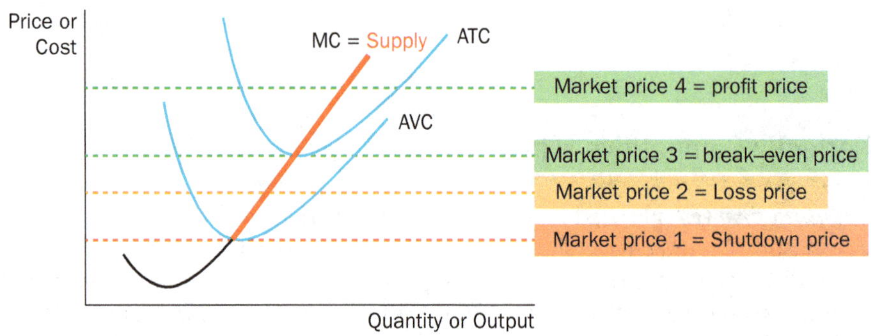

The Monopoly

This market structure is characterized by a **single supplier** of goods and services. Competition is severely restricted by **barriers to entry.** There are two types of entry barriers: legal and natural.

1. LEGAL MARKET POWER

Although barriers can be created by government, such as is the case with permits for New York taxi cabs, legal barriers that prevent other firms from entering the market are a result of either patents or copyrights.

- **Patents** ® are government-granted permission to be the sole producer and seller of a good.
- **Copyrights** © are government-granted rights to the creator of literary or artistic work.

Note that, in the United States, a patent gives a firm the exclusive right to a new product for 20 years from the date the product is invented. A copyright, on the other hand, grants the exclusive right to use the creation of literary or artistic work to the creator during the creator's lifetime and to his or her heirs for 70 years after the creator's death.

2. NATURAL MARKET POWER

Natural market power is gained when a single firm obtains market power through barriers to entry created by the firm itself. The firm controls key resources. Examples of natural monopolies that control key resources, which are essential for the production of a good or service, are:

- the National Hockey League (NHL), which controls all the labor resources; and
- the De Beers diamond company, which controls the vast majority if the world's diamond mines.

CHARACTERISTICS OF A NATURAL MONOPOLY

1. A natural monopoly occurs when the most efficient number of firms in the industry is **one**. In other words, **a natural monopoly occurs when a firm can supply the entire market at a lower price than can be achieved by two or more firms.**
2. A natural monopoly will typically have **very high fixed costs.** This implies the impractically of having more than one firm producing a good or service.

Let us examine telephone networks and the provision of municipal tap water as two examples of production with very high fixed costs.

- It is far better to have just one firm providing a network of telephone poles and cables or water pipes and sewers because of extremely high capital costs required in the initial setup of a regional or national network of poles and cables or pipes and sewage systems.
- What if there were more than one company supplying tap water or telephone services (some regions have or have had only one telephone service providers)? The average costs would be so high that having two firms would not make either firm viable. These firms would duplicate the work and cost of installing telephone poles and water pipes.

NATURAL MARKET POWER: POSITIVE NETWORK EXTERNALITIES

3. Natural monopolies are also characterized by positive **network externalities.** Network externalities occur when a product's value increases as more consumers use it. As markets get larger, as is the case for companies like eBay and Facebook, **positive network effects** raise the value received by consumers. This is similar to conventional firm-level economies of scale.

If we assume, *ceteris paribus*, that firms produce similar but incompatible products (called networks), and network effects operate only within the class of compatible products, then networks or competitors with larger market shares will have the advantage over smaller networks or competitors.

THE MONOPOLIST'S CURVES

Like firms in the competitive market, monopolies still choose to sell a quantity where MC = MR. However, the monopoly picks the combination of output and price that maximizes its profits, given its cost curves. The steeper the demand curve it faces, the higher the price at which a monopoly sells its quantity.

There is no unique relationship between a monopoly's profit-maximizing quantity and price. Therefore, there is no supply curve for monopolies. As figure 6.5 illustrates, the ATC is no longer U-shaped for a natural monopoly but strictly convex (slope is always negative). This is true of firms such as electric companies, telephone companies, cable companies, and the De Beers diamond company. If any of these monopolies would be broken up into two or more firms, each new firm would have a higher ATC because each firm would have to duplicate the initial fixed costs (e.g., a new, second set of electric, cable, or telephone wiring).

FIGURE 6.5 The Monopolist's ATC and MC Curves

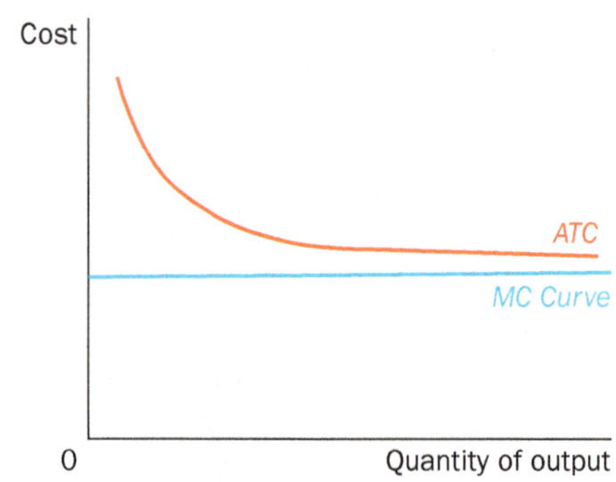

Creation of Monopolies and Antitrust Laws

Monopolies are sometimes very desirable. Monopolies generate much higher profits than perfectly competitive firms and thus can afford to invest those profits in research and development, which can generate new technologies that benefit all of society. However, monopolies can also be undesirable. Although monopolies are desirable because they avoid duplication in fixed resources and cost, monopolies can exploit consumers via much higher prices than would otherwise be the case in a perfectly competitive market. A lack of competition can lead to goods and services that command a high price but are of low quality.

REGULATION OF NATURAL MONOPOLIES

Natural monopolies are firms with no real competition. Without government intervention (regulations), they could abuse their market power and set higher prices and/or deliver poorer quality. Therefore, natural monopolies often need government regulation. For example, the Water Services Regulation Authority, or Ofwat, regulates the water sector in England and Wales, and the US Environmental Protection Agency enforces US federal clean water and safe drinking water laws. Without these government regulators, there is little consumers can do to force a monopoly to provide the highest-quality goods or services.

The Federal Trade Commission (FTC) is the governmental body that regulates the actions of monopolies through **antitrust laws.** Congress passed the first antitrust law, the **Sherman Act,** in 1890. Antitrust laws disallow unlawful mergers and business practices but do so in broad terms. As a result, antitrust laws let the courts decide which mergers and business practices are unlawful on a case-by-case basis, each based on its particular circumstances. Furthermore, the FTC and the Antitrust Division of the US Department of Justice jointly provide guidance to the business community on antitrust laws, outlining the parameters of permissible conduct.

Antitrust cases occur quite frequently, and courts have applied the antitrust laws to changing markets since the introduction of the Sherman Act and other antitrust acts that followed it. The entire premise of antitrust laws is the protection of consumers from anticompetitive behavior by firms. Such anticompetitive behavior reduces the incentives for firms to operate efficiently, keeping prices low and quality high.

THREE EXAMPLES OF ANTITRUST CASES

1. AMERICAN AIRLINES GROUP VERSUS BOOKING SERVICE SABRE

In 2016, American Airlines accused Sabre of conspiring with its competitors in the airline booking market to not compete with each other for airline flight and fare information. It was claimed that this resulted in airlines paying unfair fees and signing unfair contracts that suppressed competition and innovation. Although the courts rejected the claim that Sabre conspired with its competitors to not compete with each other, a federal jury awarded American Airlines approximately $5.1 million because it was convinced that Sabre had violated federal antitrust laws in 2011 after signing a contract with US Airways.

2. THE US GOVERNMENT VERSUS STANDARD OIL COMPANY OF NEW JERSEY

By the end of 19th century, the Standard Oil Company of New Jersey had acquired an overwhelming market share of the US oil-refining market. Under the direction of its founder and chair, John D. Rockefeller, the Standard Oil Company then began using its large market share of refining capacity to create a vertical integration of the entire oil sector, from oil exploration to refining to crude and retail distribution. It was alleged that the Standard Oil Company of New Jersey used its size to bully and undercut its competitors through anticompetitive behavior, which included underpricing its services and products and threatening its suppliers and distributors to engage in exclusive business with Standard Oil. This behavior so unnerved the US government that it filed court proceedings against Standard Oil for alleged antitrust violations under the Sherman Act. The US Supreme Court applied the Sherman Act and upheld it, resulting in a realignment of the US oil industry. The Standard Oil Company of New Jersey was divided into 34 separate companies, each of which would then compete with each other. Later, on November 30, 1999, the merger of Exxon (formerly the Standard Oil Company of New Jersey) and Mobil (formerly the Standard Oil Company of New York) created ExxonMobil, which became the largest oil company in the world.

3. THE US GOVERNMENT VERSUS THE MICROSOFT CORPORATION

In 1998, the United States government and 20 states accused Microsoft of becoming a monopoly and engaging in anticompetitive behavior. The issue was Microsoft's bundling of the web browser Internet Explorer with its Microsoft Windows operating system. It was alleged that the bundling restricted the market for competing web browsers. Although Microsoft argued that the bundling was the result of innovation and competition, and that consumers were benefiting by receiving essentially one product, not two separate products (i.e., a web browser and an operating system), the presiding judge found that Microsoft was a monopoly and that it was engaged in anticompetitive behavior. Microsoft appealed the decision and then settled with the US Department of Justice by making a deal to share its application programming interfaces with third-party companies.

Thought Question: When are Monopolies Desirable?

Hint: The economies of ideas/innovation suggest that it is critical that firms be allowed to price above their marginal costs. It is this difference that provides the profits that are the incentive for firms to innovate. (Think about the necessary incentives of high profits for a pharmaceutical company to take large risks in drug development.)

Oligopolies

The last market structure that we consider is that of the **oligopoly.** An oligopoly is a market type in which a small number of producers compete with each other. If there are only two firms in an industry, it is called a **duopoly.** Examples include firms in the following industries:

- Oil and gas production
- Breakfast cereals
- Beer brewing
- Airlines

This market structure is characterized by difficulty of entry by other firms not already in the market—similar to that of the monopoly. Products produced in the oligopolist's market may be identical (homogeneous) or differentiated. A defining feature of an oligopolistic market, however, is that each firm needs to be aware of its competitor's or competitors' actions. In particular,

- firms must act in a way that takes into account the expected behavior of others, and
- firms must recognize the interdependence of each firm's actions.

When firms in an oligopolistic market act in a way that

1. takes into account the expected behavior of others and
2. recognizes the interdependence of each firm's actions,

we call this **strategic behavior.**

Strategic behavior is analyzed by the method of **game theory.** In game theory, we have

1. rules,
2. strategies, and
3. payoffs.

In an oligopoly or duopoly game, we have

1. laws (rules) and
2. strategies.

Examples of strategies include

- increase price, decrease price, or leave price unchanged;
- increase quantity, decrease quantity, or leave quantity unchanged; and
- increase/decrease advertising price or change product feature.

Examples of payoffs include

- profits and
- losses.

How Game Theory Works: An Example of Nonidentical (Not Perfect Substitutes) Goods Duopoly Market: Beer Brewing

Assume that there are two market leaders that compete with each other for market share:

A. Molson Breweries, which has 60% market share
B. Labatt Breweries, which has 35% market share

The remaining shares are held by microbreweries.

The two main firms can pursue the following strategies:

1. spend on technology/research and development (R&D) to increase production rate from 5,000 bottles/hour to 7,000 bottles/hour so that the ATC for the firm decreases, or
2. do not spend on R&D.

Their payoff when pursuing either strategy is illustrated in the **payoff matrix** (figure 6.6), which is a table that shows the payoffs that each firm earns from every combination of strategies by the firms involved in the strategic game.

FIGURE 6.6 The Payoff Matrix for the Two Beer Companies

Labatt's Strategies	Molson's Strategies: *Engage in R & D*	Molson's Strategies: *No R & D*
Engage in R & D	Molson: +$5 million; Labatt: +$5 million	Molson: -$1 million; Labatt: +$50 million
No R & D	Molson: +$100 million; Labatt: -$5 million	Molson: +$7.5 million; Labatt: +$25 million

How will Molson proceed in this game? It will consider its best strategy based on its competitor's strategy. That is:

- If Labatt decides to engage in R&D, then Molson will generate revenue of $5 million if it also engages in R&D. However, Molson will incur a loss of $1 million if it decides not to engage in R&D. Thus, it prefers to engage in R&D.
- If Labatt does not engage in R&D, then Molson will generate revenue of $100 million if it engages in R&D, but only $7.5 million in revenues if it does not engage in R&D. Thus, Molson again prefers to engage in R&D.

We can examine the strategic behavior from Labatt's perspective as well in the same manner. As with Molson, Labatt will also prefer to engage in R&D whether or not Molson engages.

The payoff matrix in the beer industry illustrates that R&D is the **dominant strategy** for both players. A strategy is dominant if, regardless of what any other players do, the strategy earns a player a larger payoff than any other. A better outcome (i.e., larger profits or revenues) can be had if the two beer firms enter into a **collusive agreement,** which is an agreement to restrict output in order to raise prices and profits. A group of firms that enter into a collusive agreement is called a **cartel.** The Organization of the Petroleum Exporting Countries (OPEC) is a good example of an international producers' cartel, involving 14 member countries.

Member firms (or countries) in a cartel face two strategies:

1. comply with the collusive agreement, or
2. cheat on the collusive agreement, which may trigger a price war.

The Prisoner's Dilemma

The type of game we played with the beer companies is a particular type of game referred to as the **prisoner's dilemma.** The prisoner's dilemma is a game in which pursuing dominant strategies results in noncooperation that leaves everyone worse off. You can see from figure 6.6 that although the two beer companies prefer to engage in R&D, they would be better off colluding and not engage in R&D. If they were to both not engage in R&D, then they both would command bigger revenues of $7.5 million and $25 million, respectfully.

The prisoner's dilemma gets its name from a problem faced by two suspects the police arrest for a crime. Each suspect is offered a suspended prison sentence in exchange for confessing to the crime and testifying against his accomplice. The dominant strategy for each suspect is to confess. However, if both suspects confess, then they both go to prison for a longer sentence. If they risk not confessing and they BOTH remain silent, then they will go to prison with a shorter sentence. The payoffs for each prisoner are illustrated in figure 6.7. Let us examine the prisoner's dilemma in detail.

THE PRISONERS' SITUATION

- Prisoners A and B have been caught stealing a car.
- A and B will each receive 2 years for his crime.
- Each prisoner, A and B, are placed in separate rooms and cannot communicate with each other.
- Each prisoner is told that he is also suspected of having committed a bank robbery.
- If both prisoners confess to the crime of bank robbery, then each will receive a sentence, for both crimes, of 3 years.
- If only one prisoner confesses, but the accomplice does not, then the one who confesses receives a shorter sentence of 1 year for both crimes, and his accomplice will receive a 10-year sentence.
- If neither prisoner confesses, they will each only receive 2 years for the car theft.

There are 2 players, each with 2 strategies. Therefore, there are 4 possible outcomes:

1. Neither player (prisoner) confesses.
2. Both players confess.
3. A confesses, but B does not.
4. B confesses, but A does not.

FIGURE 6.7 The Payoff Matrix for the Prisoner's Dilemma

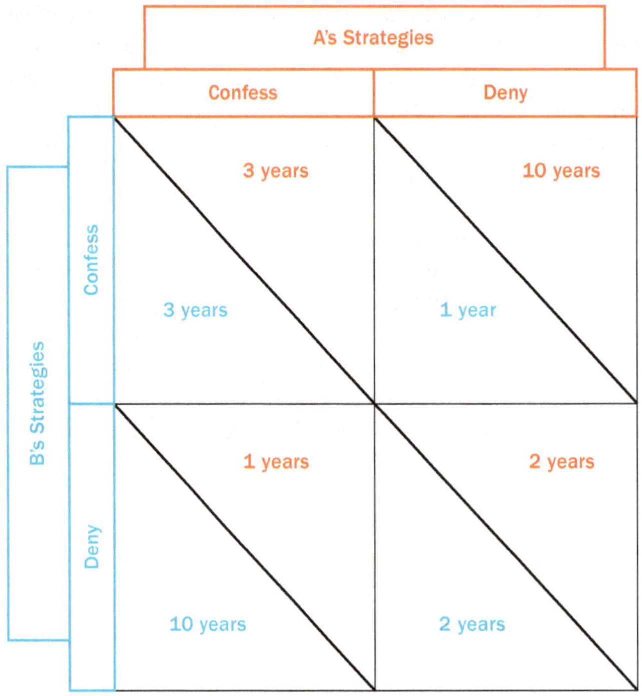

The prisoners pursue a dominant strategy in an environment of noncooperation. A game with a **noncooperative equilibrium** in which players do not cooperate but pursue their own self-interest is called a **Nash equilibrium.** Many game theorists concentrate on noncooperative equilibriums because of antitrust laws that limit cooperation among firms. If players coordinated their actions by forming pacts, then one could have a **cooperative equilibrium,** which is an equilibrium in a game in which players cooperate to increase their mutual payoff.

Application Question

LET'S PLAY

Assume that there are only two firms selling vitamin-fortified water: PepsiCo and Coca-Cola.

PepsiCo and Coca-Cola must each choose their respective strategy in pursuance of the goal of increasing revenues. We assume that for their new beverage line for vitamin-fortified water, they can charge either \$1.99 or \$2.99 per bottle.

The payoff matrix in figure 6.8 illustrates the combination of strategies that can be chosen, which will determine their revenues.

FIGURE 6.8 Pricing strategies for Coca-Cola and PepsiCo

		Coca-Cola's Strategies	
		Charge $2.99	*Charge $1.99*
Pespi's Strategies	*Charge $2.99*	+$40 million / +$50 million	+$55 million / +$10 million
	Charge $1.99	+$10 million / +$55 million	+$15 million / +$15 million

How will PepsiCo proceed in this game? It will consider its best strategy based on its competitor's strategy. That is:

- If Coca-Cola sets a price of $2.99, PepsiCo will generate revenues of $50 million if it also sets its price at $2.99. However, PepsiCo will generate $55 million in revenue if it charges $1.99. Thus, it prefers to charge $1.99.
- If Coca-Cola sets a price of $1.99, PepsiCo will generate revenues of $10 million if it sets its price at $2.99. However, PepsiCo will generate $15 million in revenue if it charges $1.99. Thus, it again prefers to charge $1.99.

Since PepsiCo prefers to set its price at $1.99 in both cases, then it must be that charging $1.99 is a **dominant strategy** for PepsiCo. It is a dominant strategy because it is the strategy that is best for PepsiCo, regardless of the strategies used by its competitor.

Now let us play the game from Coca-Cola's perspective.

How will Coca-Cola proceed in this game? It will consider its best strategy based on its competitor's strategy. That is:

- If PepsiCo sets a price of $2.99, Coca-Cola will generate revenues of $40 million if it also sets its price at $2.99. However, Coca-Cola will generate $55 million in revenue if it charges $1.99. Thus, it prefers to charge $1.99.
- If PepsiCo sets a price of $1.99, Coca-Cola will generate revenues of $10 million if it sets its price at $2.99. However, Coca-Cola will generate $15 million in revenue if it charges $1.99. Thus, it again prefers to charge $1.99.

Since Coca-Cola prefers to set its price at $1.99 in both cases, then it must be that charging $1.99 is a **dominant strategy** for Coca-Cola. It is a dominant strategy because it is the strategy that is best for a Coca-Cola, regardless of the strategies used by its competitor.

In this game, we arrive at a Nash equilibrium when both firms charge $1.99. It is a Nash equilibrium because it is an outcome in which each firm chooses the best strategy, given the strategies chosen by the other firms, but their choices are **not necessarily** their dominant strategies. If fact, both Coca-Cola and PepsiCo could have better revenue outcomes if they engaged in collusion; that is, agreed to charge the same price and not compete with each other. If they were to collude, they would agree to both charge $2.99. This is tempting to do, and if undertaken, it undermines the efficiency of the competitive market. Consumers will forgo the benefit of lower prices, best quality, and/or choice. For such reasons, collusion is illegal in many countries, including the United States.

Requirements for Nash Equilibria and Game Theory

Game theory only works if the players are rational. Furthermore, all players engaged in strategic games are assumed to understand the game and the payoffs of each strategy, and all players recognize that the other players understand the game and payoffs. Note that the prisoner's dilemma is a simultaneous move game, with a dominant strategy. It is a simultaneous move game because each player makes his or her decision at the same time as the other player—there is no communication or negotiation of any kind. The players will arrive at a **Nash equilibrium** if each player chooses a strategy that is best, given the strategies of others. In other words, changing strategies does not make anyone better off. Finally, note that the dominant strategy equilibria are always Nash equilibria.

Application Question

LET'S PLAY AGAIN—BUT AT THE INTERNATIONAL LEVEL

Earlier, we briefly made reference to the international oil cartel, OPEC. Although OPEC members would be able to command higher oil prices if they colluded to reduce the supply of oil, many members cannot agree among themselves on the level of supply, and some end up cheating on their agreements. Let us exam a game that can be played among two of the organization's members who are also bitter regional (geopolitical) rivals: Iran and Saudi Arabia. Note that Saudi Arabia's decision on the amount of oil that it will supply will have a larger effect on oil price because it can produce many more (millions of) barrels of oil than Iran.

In the fall of 2016, OPEC members, including Iran and Saudi Arabia, agreed to cut output, limiting the production range to 32.5 million and 33 million barrels per day. This cut in supply benefits Saudi Arabia because higher oil prices will help curb its growing debt, but the cut in supply is not as welcomed in Iran, because it would benefit most by actually producing more oil. Iran has wanted to increase its production capabilities for many years to regain a bigger share of the world oil market that it lost under nuclear sanctions that were imposed by the United States (and other countries). Let us consider the payoff matrix for these two countries (see figure 6.9).

From figure 6.9, we see that Saudi Arabia's profits would be highest ($50 million) if both countries agreed to reduce the supply of oil. **What are Iran's strategies?**

If Saudi Arabia reduced its supply of oil, then it is to Iran's benefit to increase the supply of oil, because Iran would make $25 million in profit rather than $20 million in profit. Iran's strategy would be to increase supply. If Saudi Arabia decided to increase its supply of oil, then once again, Iran's strategy would be to increase its supply of oil because it would make $20 million in profits rather than only $10 million in profit. In

FIGURE 6.9 Oil Production Strategies and Resulting Profits for Iran and Saudi Arabia

Saudi Arabia's Strategies \ Iran's Strategies	*Reduce Supply*	*Increase Supply*
Reduce Supply	+$20 million (Iran) +$50 million (Saudi Arabia)	+$25 million (Iran) +$15 million (Saudi Arabia)
Increase Supply	+$10 million (Iran) +$25 million (Saudi Arabia)	+$20 million (Iran) +$10 million (Saudi Arabia)

both cases, the strategy for Iran is to increase the supply of oil. This is Iran's dominant strategy. Therefore, Iran has a strong incentive not to cooperate in the reduction of the supply of oil. It is possible, as it sometimes happens in reality, for Saudi Arabia to punish a cheating OPEC member. To do so, Saudi Arabia, knowing Iran's dominant strategy, may decide to increase its supply of oil so that Iran's profits are reduced from $25 million to $20 million. However, by punishing Iran, Saudi Arabia will also hurt itself because its profits would decline from $15 million to $10 million.

Simultaneous Move Games with No or With Multiple Nash Equilibria

Notice that with the Iran-Saudi Arabia oil-production game, Saudi Arabia's dominant strategy is to always reduce supply regardless of what Iran decides to do. Iran's dominant strategy is to always increase supply regardless of what Saudi Arabia decides to do. Thus, this game does not have a Nash equilibrium. There are some games, however, that do not have dominant strategies but do have a Nash equilibrium. We will use the concept of the **tragedy of the commons** to illustrate this concept.

A **commons** is a natural resource shared by many individuals. No agent has exclusive ownership to any part of the resource but rather can use of a portion of it for his own benefit. Examples include groundwater, a city park, shared grazing land, a shared lake, the atmosphere, and so forth. The tragedy is that each agent will have an incentive to exploit the commons to his own advantage, typically without limit. The commons will be depleted and eventually ruined. The cause of the tragedy is the unrestrained self-interest of agents. Even if they agree not to engage in unsustainable practices like overfishing or polluting, there is an incentive, like OPEC members, to cheat on that agreement. Unless there are enforcements, like governmental or international regulations to prevent cheating, it is unlikely that individuals, firms, or even governments will honor the agreement. Figure 6.10 illustrates a tragedy of the commons (a case of overfishing) that destroyed the Grand Banks, which is a group of underwater plateaus southeast of Newfoundland that were once one of the richest fishing grounds in the world. The extensive use of advanced fishing technology such as sonar contributed to the destruction of the Grand Banks.

For this example, illustrated in figure 6.10, we will assume that there are only two countries that are competing for fish in the Grand Banks: Canada and Portugal. Both countries can decide to employ the use of sonar to improve their catches.

FIGURE 6.10 The Tragedy of the Commons: The Grand Banks and Overfishing

Canada's Strategies	Portugal's Strategies: *Employ Sonar*	Portugal's Strategies: *Do Not Employ Sonar*
Employ Sonar	+$2 million +$2 million	+$0.5 million +$5 million
Do Not Employ Sonar	+$5 million +$0.5 million	+$3 million +$3 million

We see from figure 6.9 that if Portugal employs sonar to capture more fish stock, then Canada should as well. If Portugal does not employ sonar, then Canada should continue employing sonar for a bigger profit. Likewise, if Canada employs sonar to capture more fish stock, then Portugal should as well. If Canada does not employ sonar, then Portugal should continue employing sonar for a bigger profit. No matter the choice by either country, the dominant strategy equilibrium (and Nash equilibrium) is always to employ sonar. This dominant strategy equilibrium, however, is not the best outcome for either country.

If, however, there were some joint-governmental regulation that rewards (but not very well) those that do not use sonar, we could have a different payoff matrix, as illustrated in figure 6.11. Notice that if Canada decides to employ sonar, then Portugal should too. If Canada does not, then Portugal should not as well. Similarly, if Portugal decides to employ sonar, then Canada should too. If Portugal does not, then Canada should not as well.

FIGURE 6.11 The Tragedy of the Commons with Partially Effective Regulation

Canada's Strategies	Portugal's Strategies: *Employ Sonar*	Portugal's Strategies: *Do Not Employ Sonar*
Employ Sonar	+$2 million +$2 million	+$1.5 million +$2.5 million
Do Not Employ Sonar	+$2.5 million +$1.5 million	+$3 million +$3 million

There are two Nash equilibria for this game, but no dominant strategy:

1. Both should employ sonar.
2. Both should not employ sonar.

Chapter Summary

In this chapter, we introduced the four different types of market structures. It was noted that only in pure competition are firms price takers and that the firms face perfectly elastic demand curves. Individual monopolies and oligopolies, however, face inelastic demand curves. With the former, competition is severely restricted by barriers to entry: legal and natural. Furthermore, because monopolies avoid duplication in fixed resources and cost, they can exploit consumers via much higher prices than would otherwise be the case in a perfectly competitive market. Therefore, monopolies in most countries are regulated by the government through some form of antitrust laws.

Oligopolies, on the other hand, do face competition, albeit limited competition. This creates an interesting dynamic between firms. Production, marketing, and investment decisions must consider the competitor's response in an oligopoly situation; hence, the application of game theory. In game theory, actors are assumed to be rational and strategic in their behavior. In some games, like the prisoner's dilemma, there exists a dominant strategy. In other games, a Nash equilibrium exists if each player chooses a strategy that is best, given the strategies of others. The chapter discussion also noted that the dominant strategy equilibria are always Nash equilibria.

CHAPTER 7

Rational and Irrational Consumer Behavior

LEARNING EXPECTATIONS

- To define utility and rationality
- To learn and play common behavioral games
- To appreciate how behavior leads to decision making

OLD LADY BUYING FLOWERS

Source: *https://commons.wikimedia.org/wiki/File:Old_lady_buying_flowers.JPG.*

Utility and Rationality

Economists refer to the enjoyment or satisfaction people receive from consuming goods and services as **utility.** Utility is a subjective notion. Utility is difficult to measure and has no units, but none of the important conclusions of the economic model of consumer behavior depend on utility being directly measurable. We assume that individuals are able to rank in order all possible situations (or choices) from least desirable to the most desirable.

- Thus, if a person prefers situation A to situation B, we would say that the *utility* assigned to option A, U(A), exceeds the utility assigned to option B, U(B).
- If an individual maximizes her utility (or self-interest), she is acting *rationally*.

NEOCLASSICAL AXIOMS OF RATIONAL CHOICE

Individuals are assumed able to rank in order all possible situations from least desirable to the most desirable because of the following axioms:

1. **Completeness:** If A and B are any two situations, the individual can always specify exactly one of three possibilities:
    - A is preferred to B,
    - B is preferred to A, or
    - A and B are equally attractive.
2. **Transitivity:** If "A is preferred to B" and "B is preferred to C," then an individual must also report that "A is preferred to C." That is, choices must be consistent.
3. **Continuity:** If "A is preferred to B," then situations close to A must also be preferred to B.

Utility is an *ordinal concept*—all one can say is that utility is higher or lower from the viewpoint of an individual. Consumers experience diminishing additional satisfaction (i.e., marginal utility = change in utility/change in consumption) as they consume more of anything during a given period of time. This is referred to as the **law of diminishing marginal utility.** The law of diminishing marginal utility is so important in economics that it is *axiomatic* in nature; that is, it is *irrefutably true*.

Behavioral Economics and Rational Decisions

We assume individuals act rationally, thus maximizing their utility. Is this always true? Behavioral economics avoids overarching neoclassical assumptions and relies on statistical experiments on firm and consumer decisions in different contexts to determine why people make certain decisions.

So, what is rational choice, really?

- In the standard economic view, rational choice is defined to mean the process of determining what options are available and then choosing the most preferred one according to some consistent criterion.[20]
- Thinkers following Adam Smith put forth refined ideas of an economic system based on the economic agent's self-interest.
- Utilitarian philosophers used the concept of rationality for policy where the objective criterion would be the "greatest good for the greatest number" (but they would need to find a utility index that could measure how beneficial different policies were to different people).[20]
- In contrast, according to Levin and Milgrom (2004), "psychological theories (with strong support from laboratory experiments) predict that many choices depend systematically on a much wider array of factors, such as the way information is presented to the subjects, the noise level in the laboratory and other variables that might influence the subject's psychological state."[20]
- Although the rational choice approach is quite attractive, experiments in behavioral economics and psychology have generated interest in new behavior modeling. Alternative models have been proposed.

According to Levin and Milgrom (2004), two such models are:

1. **Learning models,** in which individuals make choices like those that have worked well for them in the past, have attracted particular attention from economic theorists and experimenters; and
2. **Bounded rationality models** in which decision makers adopt rules that evolve slowly have had some empirical successes.

   Recent research tries to identify parts of the brain involved in decision-making and model how brain processes affect decisions.[20]

Although these various alternatives appear to have advantages for some purposes, economics continues to use, in most cases, the still useful and still dominant model of rational choice.[20]

Application Questions

LET'S PLAY SOME BEHAVIORAL GAMES

While it may be difficult to get a perfect understanding of the following games when reading in isolation, assume that you are involved in a classroom setting, where appropriate, and think how you would react to each scenario. Then decide whether *you* would have made a rational decision.

GAME 1: THE ULTIMATUM GAME

There are 2 players, A and B, and they CANNOT communicate with each other

Players A and B are told that they will be given $100 to share.
Player A will decide how to split the money, if at all, in any way he or she would like.
Player B will either accept or reject the offer.
If Player B rejects the offer, both players get nothing.
If the offer is accepted by Player B, the money will be split as proposed by Player A.
What would you do if you were Player A?
What would you do if you were Player B?

Before reading the results that follow, try game 2 first.

GAME 2: THE DICTATOR GAME

There are two groups.
Group 1, the dictators, each receive $20.
The dictators can allocate their $20 in only two ways:

1. $18 for themselves and $2 for the recipient (group 2) or
2. $10 for themselves and $10 for the recipient.

The recipient is NOT ALLOWED to reject either offer.

What would you do if you were the dictator?
What would you do if you were the recipient?

RESULTS OF GAMES 1 AND 2:

- For the ultimatum game, the rational decision is to offer as little as possible, but not $0.
- The rational decision is to accept any offer above $0, since the recipient started off with $0.

Studies find that during the ultimatum game, both allocators and recipients act as if fairness is important: Allocators usually offer recipients at least a 40% share, and recipients almost always reject offers of less than 10%.

- For the dictator game, the allocator should allocate only $2 if he is acting to maximize utility, but studies show that most dictators allocate an even split.

These two games are about fairness, and there is a business implication concerning fairness: Firms do not always raise their prices to equate quantity supplied to quantity demanded, if the price increase is viewed as unfair by consumers. Thus, firms will give up some profit in the short run to keep their customers happy and increase their profits in the long run. Adam Smith would have been astonished to know that people often interpret his concept of the invisible hand to mean that people should always behave with self-interest, since he wrote an early book entitled *The Theory of Moral Sentiments*, which presented a more nuanced view of human motivations.

If economic agents take emotion, fairness, and other variables into consideration when making decisions, does that mean the standard economic model of rational agents maximizing their utility is wrong? Traditional economists often answer no, for the following reasons:

1. Unrealistic assumptions are necessary to simplify complex decision-making problems, in order to focus on the most important factors.
2. Models are best judged by the success of their predictions, rather than the accuracy of their assumptions.

Indeed, models based on a standard economic model of rationality are quite successful in predicting many types of consumer behavior, but there are ways to manipulate decision making. We explore this theme in the next section.

INFLUENCING DECISIONS

Behavioral economists say that it *does* matter that consumers do not usually make "optimal" consumption choices. They believe modeling how people *actually* make decisions is important. Some important "irrational" consumption behaviors include:

- *Anchoring*: The use of "irrelevant" information can often influence behavior.
- *Example: Posting "limit 10 items per customer" will often induce people to buy 10 items, even if they would have bought fewer without the sign.*

Application Question

ANCHORING

Another example of anchoring used by this author in class was to present half of the students with the following "fun facts about the number 10":

- The Korean alphabet has 10 vowels.
- Virginia was the 10th state to enter the Union.
- The metric system is based on the number 10.
- In England, a person can be convicted of a criminal offense at the age of 10 and can receive a life sentence if found guilty of murder.
- The atomic number of neon is 10.
- The Ten Commandments are ethical and religious principles in both Christianity and Judaism.

The other half of the students were presented with "fun facts about the number 85":

- The Royal Canadian Air Cadets 85th Tornado Squadron parades from September until June.
- The atomic number of astatine is 85.

- The ISBN Group Identifier for books published in Brazil is 85.
- Arabigere 85 is a village in India.
- E85 fuel is 85% ethanol.
- Rick Hall, the "Father of Muscle Shoals Music," died at age 85.

After the "fun facts" were reviewed, a question that was completely unrelated to the fun facts was presented, and the students recorded their answers. The question read, "*Random Bonus Question for the Semester: What is your best guess of the percentage of African nations in the United Nations?*" The answer is 28%. If the students were rational, then their answers would have been random, or close to 28% for those who had a good idea of the number of countries in Africa. However, the group that reviewed the facts concerning the number 10 mostly replied with percentages in the range of 5% to 15%, while the group with the fun facts about the number 85 mostly replied in the range of 75% to 90%, which is obviously an unrealistic proportion.

Application Question

YOUR TURN AGAIN: TRY GAME 3—MAKE A DECISION

Imagine that the United States is preparing for the outbreak of an unusual Asian disease, which is expected to kill 600 people. One possible program to combat the disease has been proposed. Assume that the exact scientific estimate of the consequences of this program is as follows:

Options A and B:

- A: If this program is adopted, 200 people will be saved.
- B: If this program is adopted, there is a one-third probability that 600 people will be saved and a two-thirds probability that no people will be saved.

Choose A or B

Options C and D:

- C: If this program is adopted, 400 people will die.
- D: If this program is adopted, there is a one-third probability that nobody will die and a two-thirds probability that 600 people will die.

Choose C or D

WHAT ARE YOUR TWO CHOICES?

Game 3 is a game about the **effect of framing.** The robust experimental finding is that subjects tend to prefer the sure thing when given options A and B, but tend to prefer the gamble when given options C and D. Note, however, that options A and C are equivalent, as are options B and D. Subjects thus appear to be risk-averse for gains and risk-seeking for losses. In behavioral economics, these outcomes are described by **prospect theory.** In prospect theory, it is decision makers' private framing of the problem in terms of gains or losses that determines their evaluation of the options.

A "framing effect" is usually said to occur when equivalent descriptions of a decision problem lead to systematically different decisions. Framing has been a major topic of research in the psychology of judgment and decision making and is widely viewed as carrying significant implications for the "Rationality Debate."[21] Framing effects are commonly taken as evidence for incoherence in human decision making, and for the empirical inapplicability of the rational actor models used by economists and other social scientists.[21] The most common result is that subjects are more likely to engage in the activity when the disadvantages of not engaging, rather than the advantages of engaging, are emphasized.[22] (Example: Most students will be more inclined to study when failure is emphasized over passing.)

Application Question

ONE MORE TIME—GAME 4

You are given two choices for a subscription to your favorite magazine:

1. An online only subscription for $75
2. An online plus print subscription for $150

Which do you prefer?

Now you are given three choices for a subscription to your favorite magazine:

1. An online only subscription for $75
2. An online plus print subscription for $150
3. A print only subscription for $150

Which do you prefer?

What were your choices?

Game 4 is about the **dominated alternatives/phantom decoys effect.** That is, introducing a third decoy option makes you more likely to choose the option that someone secretly wants you to choose. A large majority of people chose the first option ($75), although the second option ($150) was preferable to, say, the publishers. The publishers then introduced a third decoy option that they knew nobody would prefer—$150 for print only. As expected, no one chose the third option, but then something interesting happened. An overwhelming majority now chose the second option ($150 for online + print)! The mere introduction of this third option made option #2 look very attractive—you were getting online version for free now! Sometimes consumers have a very poor understanding of worth. They had no idea what a print or online subscription of their favorite magazine is truly worth in monetary terms. With the first scenario with two options, consumers had nothing to which they could compare worth. But with the introduction of the third option, option #2 and #3 are comparable, and #2 wins. Option #1 has nothing comparable, so it gets left out.

This principle has been demonstrated successfully in different scenarios. For example, participants of a study were shown pictures of three individuals of the opposite sex and asked which one they would prefer to date. They were tricked because there were only two different individuals in the pictures. The third individual was a digitally altered, slightly inferior version of one of the two other individuals. So, the participants were present with individual 1, individual 2, and less-good individual 2. An overwhelming majority chose individual 2 in this scenario. The idea is the same as above. There is nothing comparable for individual 1, so 1 gets left out; individual 2 and less-good individual 2 look similar, with 2 being more attractive. Therefore, individual 2 wins.

Chapter Summary

In this chapter, we learned that for an economist, rational behavior implies that an agent maximizes his or her utility. However, research into human behavior shows that maximizing one's self-interest is not always the predictable outcome. In fact, many agents do make irrational decisions and can be lead to do so. As a result, many behavioral games can be played, given the assumption of rational or irrational decision making. Irrational behavior does not discount the use of utility maximization in neoclassical economic models, but it does highlight that predictions of economic phenomena sometimes require subject input.

SECTION 2: Testing Your Comprehensive Knowledge

Instructions

- After a thorough study of section 2, proceed with test 2.
- A well-prepared student should be able to complete this test within 75 minutes.
- Solutions to the questions follow the test.

Part 1: Multiple Choice (Please select the best answer.)

1. Utility
   a. is easily measured in units called utils.
   b. exists, but is not a concept of great concern to economists.
   c. is subjective and difficult to measure.
   d. is the consumption of a good that brings about good health.
2. The principle of diminishing marginal utility illustrates the tendency for additional units of consumption to
   a. total satisfaction received from consuming a given number of units of a product.
   b. increase total utility at a decreasing rate.
   c. decrease total utility at an increasing rate.
   d. decrease total utility at a decreasing rate.
3. Imagine that John obtains a marginal utility of 100 after drinking the first cup of coffee, a marginal utility of 80 after drinking the second cup of coffee, and a marginal utility of 50 after drinking the third cup of coffee. What is John's total utility when he drinks two cups of coffee?
   a. 100
   b. 150
   c. 230
   d. 180
4. In the ultimatum game, allocators usually offer recipients at least a 40% share of the money, and recipients almost always reject offers that are between 0% to 15% of the share. Which of the following is not a reason allocators offer recipients a large proportion of the money and why recipients reject small offers?
   a. Allocators worry about the recipients' disgust and anger.
   b. Recipients, like the general public, will take a loss in the face of perceived unfairness.
   c. Allocators know that recipients only care about monetary gain.
   d. Allocators simply do not want to offend the recipient.
5. Assume that in an experiment that employed the dictator game, allocators were given the option of dividing $100 in only two ways: (1) $190 for themselves and $10 to a recipient, or (2) $50 for themselves and $50 to

another recipient. Which of the following would be a likely outcome from this experiment?

a. Most of the allocators would chose to give themselves $190 and $10 to the recipients.

b. Male allocators would choose option (1).

c. Female allocators would choose option (1).

d. Most of the allocators would act fairly and choose option (2).

6. A firm that could not sell a kitchen stove for $1,000 started offering a "deluxe" model for $1,500. After it started offering the deluxe model, the firm significantly increased the sales of the $1,000 model. This is because of framing.

a. True

b. False

7. In a competitive market, there are a ________ number of buyers and a ________ number of sellers.

a. large; small

b. small; large

c. small; small

d. large; large

8. Sellers in a perfectly competitive market

a. are price takers.

b. sell differentiated goods and services.

c. are equal to the number of buyers.

d. are small in number.

9. A production function establishes the relationship between

a. the market price of a good and the elasticity of demand.

b. the quantity of output produced, the revenues, and the firm's profit.

c. the quantity of inputs used and the quantity of output produced.

d. the market price of a good and the quantity of output supplied.

10. Which of the following inputs can be changed in the short run?

a. Machinery

b. Real Estate (Land owned)

c. Technology

d. Labor employed

11. It is beneficial for firms in an oligopoly to collude, but they do not do so very often. Why?

a. Because collusion is illegal in most countries.

b. Because collusion lowers sales and profits.

c. Because collusion stifles innovation.

d. Because collusion decreases the cost of production but increases competition.

The following table shows the total output, number of workers employed, variable costs, and fixed costs of a firm. Use this table to answer questions 12 through 14.

Number of workers	Total output (units)	Variable costs ($)	Fixed costs ($)
0	0	0	210
1	25	10	210
2	60	20	210
3	100	30	210
4	115	40	210
5	130	50	210

12. Refer to the table above. When the ________ is employed, diminishing marginal returns sets in.
    a. second worker
    b. third worker
    c. fourth worker
    d. fifth worker
13. Refer to the table above. What is the total cost of producing 100 units of the good?
    a. $210
    b. $30
    c. $80
    d. $240
14. Refer to the table above. What is the average variable cost of producing 100 units of the good?
    a. $33.33
    b. $0.33
    c. $30.00
    d. $210
15. Software Inc. has the exclusive right to produce and sell its new voice recognition software for 21 years. The right granted to Software Inc. is called a
    a. trademark.
    b. patent.
    c. success.
    d. copyright.
16. Which of the following is an example of a good produced under monopoly?
    a. cars
    b. toothpaste
    c. water
    d. patented specialty drug

17. Which of the following is an example of differentiated goods?
    a. McDonald's restaurants located inside Walmart stores
    b. Gasoline and fruit juices
    c. Milk produced by different dairy farms
    d. Chewing gum and bricks
18. Which of the following is an example of a variable cost?
    a. The mortgage on a building
    b. The cost of electricity used in a manufacturing firm
    c. The land transfer tax paid for acquiring new land for manufacturing purposes
    d. The annual rent paid for an office space

Assume that you and your best friend have been caught cheating on an examination. You are both taken by your professor to separate rooms for questioning. Your payoff matrix is given below. The first (or top) payoff listed in each box is your payoff, while the second (or bottom) payoff listed in each box is your best friend's payoff.

		Your Best Friend	
		Confess	Do not Confess
You	Confess	25% penalty 25% penalty	No penalty Suspended
	Do not confess	Suspended No penalty	10% penalty 10% penalty

19. Refer to the scenario above. Which of the following is true?
    a. Your best friend's best response is to hold out if you confess.
    b. Your best response is to hold out if you expect your best friend not to confess.
    c. Your best response is not to confess irrespective of what your best friend does.
    d. Your best friend's best response is to confess irrespective of what you do.
20. What best characterizes the game played in question 19?
    a. It has no dominant strategy.
    b. It has one dominant strategy.
    c. It has two Nash equilibria.
    d. It is a sequential game.

Part 2: Short Answer

1. Answer both questions below.
   a. Describe in about three to four sentences what it would mean for two sellers to act noncooperatively, in a prisoner's dilemma manner.
   b. What, instead, would it mean for two sellers to collude?
2. Posting "Limit of 5 items per customer" will often induce people to buy 5 items, even if they would have bought fewer without the sign. Why?

Part 3: Analytical Reasoning

1. Assume that a firm that manufactures computer tablets can produce 4 tablets at a total cost of $3,100. In producing its tablets, the firm has fixed costs of $1,000.

   If the firm produces 5 tablets, the total cost of production is $3,800. What is the variable cost of producing 4 tablets?

2. Suppose that a seller in a duopoly needs to decide whether to invest a lot or a little on new technology. If a firm spends a lot on new technology, it will succeed in drawing customers away from its rival, thus generating higher profits. Draw a payoff matrix illustrating this case with options "spend a lot" or "spend a little" and outcomes of low, moderate, or high profits. Describe the noncooperative solution.

Solutions to Test 2

Part 1: Multiple Choice

1C	11A
2B	12C
3D	13D
4C	14A
5D	15B
6B	16D
7D	17A
8A	18C
9C	19D
10D	20B

Part 2: Short Answer

1a. In a prisoner's dilemma situation, each firm would benefit from having the lower price. However, with both firms taking a low-price strategy and no cooperation, neither firm will gain a price advantage. The result will likely be lower profits for both due to a price war.

1b. If the two firms collude to set price, then they can both maintain high profits. Note, however, that each firm also has an incentive to lower price and capture a larger market share and higher profits.

2. This is an example of anchoring, which results in behavioral change influenced by irrelevant information.

Part 3: Analytical Reasoning

1. Variable costs of producing 4 tablets total $2,100.
2. The noncooperative outcome is for both firms to spend a lot on new technology.

		Options for Firm 2	
		Spend a lot	Spend a little
Options for Firm 1	Spend a lot	Low profit Low profit	Loss (firm 2) High profit (firm 2)
	Spend a little	High profit (firm 2) Loss (firm 1)	Moderate profit Moderate profit

SECTION 3

CHAPTERS 8–11

The Macro Side: National Income, Prices, Money, and Engaging in Global Trade

THE GREAT DEPRESSION IN THE UNITED STATES: SOCIAL SECURITY: Public Health nursing made available through child welfare services.

Source: *https://commons.wikimedia.org/wiki/File:Public_Health_nursing.gif.*

CHAPTER 8

Rich, by What Measure?

AN INTRODUCTION TO GROSS DOMESTIC PRODUCT AND THE CONSUMER PRICE INDEX

LEARNING EXPECTATIONS

- To define and calculate real and nominal gross domestic product
- To define and calculate price indices, including the consumer price index
- To understand the limitations of gross domestic product as a measure of national income and wealth

A FEW OF THE BUILDINGS IN DUBAI MARINA IN DUBAI, UNITED ARAB EMIRATES AT NIGHT.

Source: *Copyright © Imre Solt (CC BY-SA 3.0) at https://commons.wikimedia.org/wiki/File:Dubai_Marina_at_Night_on_27_February_2007.jpg.*

Who Is Rich? Who Is Poor?

We now consider the behavior of the macroeconomy. Until now, we have focused our analyses on the behavior of the individual economic agent—households, firms, and even governments. This was the realm of **microeconomics.** When we incorporate and study the interaction of microeconomic behaviors on an economy-wide scale, we are in the realm of **macroeconomics.** We will begin our study of macroeconomics with a seemingly easy question. If you were asked to list the top 10 richest countries in the world for 2016, which countries would you list? Take a moment to draw up your list. Many students, when asked this question, tend to include the United States, China, Saudi Arabia, Switzerland, and Japan. Does your list include these as well? Now compare your list to figure 8.1, which lists the actual top 10 richest countries in the world for 2016.

FIGURE 8.1 Top 10 (projected) Richest Countries, 2016

Rank	Country	Income per Capita ($International)
1	Qatar	132,870
2	Luxembourg	99,506
3	Singapore	85,382
4	Brunei	79,508
5	Kuwait	70,542
6	Norway	68,591
7	United Arab Emirates	67,217
8	Ireland	65,806
9	San Marino	62,938
10	Switzerland	58,647

Source: International Monetary Fund, 2016 projections.

At this point, the astute reader should protest. We have not defined the word *rich*. Under what measure are we classifying a country as rich? This is an important question because our list will change based on the definition and thus the measure that we use for classification.

There are two ways of defining rich. One is to take into account the absolute size of an economy. The other is to calculate the size of the economy on a **per capita** basis—that is, the total income generated by the economy divided by the number of people in the country. We care about income on a per capita basis because it provides a good deal of information about the **standard of living** of the average citizen in a country. The standard of living is a measure of economic welfare, which refers to the availability and enjoyment (consumption) of goods and services by an individual. While a standard of living is not the same as a person's happiness or well-being, it is correlated with such measures. An acceptable measure for standard of living is **real gross domestic product (GDP) per capita,** which we will define and study in detail in the sections that follow. For now, think about real GDP per capita as the total amount of income generated by a country at fixed prices over the years.

The income values next to each country in figure 8.1 are expressed in GDP per capita in **international dollars.** The international dollar (also known as the Geary-Khamis dollar) is a currency unit used by economists and international organizations to compare the values of different currencies. Using this measure, the United States comes in at number 11, with 56,084 international dollars per capita.

If one were to measure rich as the absolute size of an economy, then a different list is generated. Figure 8.2 displays both a list and a chart of the top 10 rich countries for 2015. We note that the United States ranks first at $18,037 billion. More importantly, one should recognize that none of the top 10 richest countries listed in figure 8.1 are found in figure 8.2. This is not a result of using two different years, 2015 and 2016 projections. For the average citizen, holding all else constant, it is better, in terms of standard of living, to live in a country listed in figure 8.1 than in a country listed in figure 8.2. Per capita GDP is a better measure of the total income or output of a country because it takes GDP and divides it by the number of people in the country. A country can have a very big GDP value, but if it also has a very large population, then not much income is distributed among the average citizen. This would be the case with countries such as India. Although India generated US$2,095.40 billion in 2015, its per capita GDP is relatively small because the US$2,095.40 billion is divided by a population of approximately 1.3 billion. San Marino, a separate, landlocked country located in Italy, however, only generated about US$1.4 billion, but it is divided among barely 32,000 citizens Therefore, per capita GDP is far more useful when comparing one country to another, because it shows the relative performance of the countries. A rise in per capita GDP is an indication of economic growth and has a tendency to reflect increases in productivity.

GDP: Its History and Its Definition

The modern conception of GDP was a result of ignorance—the ignorance of not knowing exactly what a country was producing and the extent to which it produced goods. This ignorance came to full light and importance during the Great Depression because no one, especially the government, knew the full extent of the Great Depression.[23] As a result, in 1932 the US Congress asked the Russian-born economist Simon Kuznets to develop a measure that would estimate national income over the preceding four years.[23] It took Kuznets a little over a year to develop his estimate.

Kuznets's estimate was not the first time that someone tried to estimate national income. Colin Clark, a British civil servant, had been collecting statistics on national income since the 1920s.[23] However, it was not until 1940 that the prominent economist John Maynard Keynes argued for more statistical oversight on the British ability to produce weapons, such as guns, tanks, and airplanes.[23] From his insistence to include more statistics, Kuznets established the modern definition of GDP, to which we will now turn.

In order to measure national income, economists divide the economy into four aggregate sectors, from which they then sum the production of goods and services:

1. **Households/consumers and nonprofit institutions**
   We label this sector C, for consumption.

2. **Business sector (for-profit institutions)**
   We label this sector I, for investment.

FIGURE 8.2 Top 10 Richest Countries, 2015 (in US$ billions)

Country	Total Gross domestic Products, $US billions
United States	18,036.60
China	11,007.70
Japan	4,123.30
Germany	3,363.40
United Kingdom	2,858.00
France	2,418.80
India	2,095.40
Italy	1,821.50
Brazil	1,774.70
Canada	1,550.50

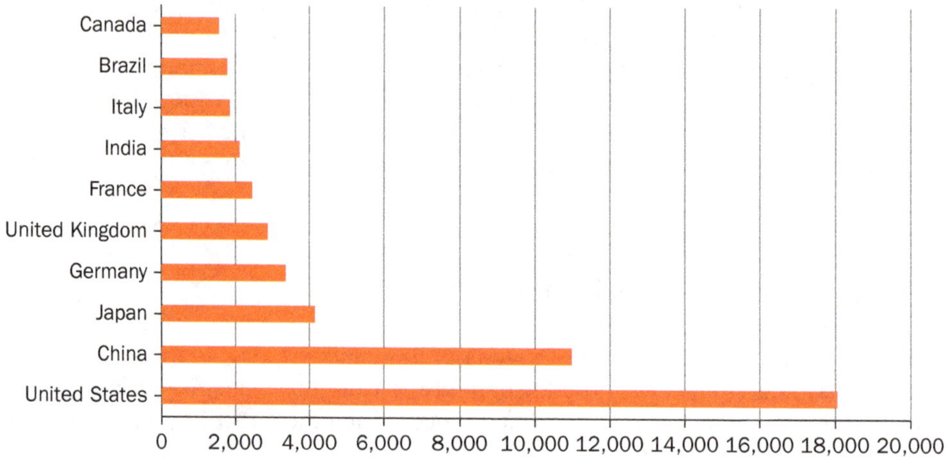

Source: World Bank, 2016.

3. **Government sector (municipal, state, federal)**
   We label this sector G, for government.

4. **Foreign: all entities and production located outside a country**
   We label this sector Ex, for exports; Im, for imports; and NX, for net exports; where NX = Ex – Im.

Finally, we arrive at our formal definition: ***GDP is a measure of the total value, in prices, of final goods and services produced in a country during a given year.*** Understanding the definition of GDP is very important, so we will partition it and explain each part of the definition separately.

(i) GDP is measured using market values, not quantities. GDP is the total value in market prices (i.e., dollars) of all goods and services produced.

(ii) GDP includes only the market values of *final goods* and services for *which payment is rendered*. A final good or service is one that is purchased by a final user—for example, a car—but not the individual tires. Only counting final goods and services avoids *double counting*. In contrast to final goods and services, an **intermediate good or service** is one that is used as an input to produce another good or service, such as apples in an apple pie.

(iii) GDP includes only current (new) production. GDP is a flow variable because it measures the amount of production during a time period, usually quarterly or yearly. For example, the value of buying a new home in 2017 is included in GDP statistics for 2017. However, buying an older home (e.g., one that was constructed in 1989), regardless of its price, in 2017 is not included in GDP statistics for 2017.

(iv) GDP measures production *within* a country regardless of who does the production. Imports of goods and services produced outside a country are not included. In fact, the value of imports is subtracted from a country's GDP calculations.

(v) GDP includes some inputed values. For example, police services and services provided by an owner-occupied home are estimated to provide a cost value.

(vi) In the United States, GDP data are collected by the **Bureau of Economic Analysis (BEA).** The BEA does not count some types of production. For example, goods and services produced by the underground, volunteer work, and home production are excluded from GDP. Note that reports on GDP and related statistics are released by the BEA every three months.

The Three Methods for Calculating GDP

Statistical agencies around the world, such as the BEA, have three accounting methods for the calculation of GDP:

- **The expenditure approach** sums the value of goods and services sold to final users.
- **The income approach** sums the income payments and other costs incurred in the production of goods and services. This measure is used to examine the purchasing power of households and the financial status of businesses.
- **The value added approach** is a measure of the sum of all the differences between an industry's gross output and its intermediate inputs.

We will use and only be concerned with the expenditure approach. We can write the expenditure approach as an accounting identity to facilitate its use:

- **Y = C + G + I + NX**

where

Y = national income or GDP
C = consumption by households and nonprofit institutions
G = government spending
I = investment spending by businesses (for-profit institutions)
NX = net exports (exports minus imports)

AN ECONOMIST'S NOTE ON THE TERM *INVESTMENT*

Economists use the term *investment* to mean acquisition of nonfinancial assets, as opposed to the common layperson's use of the term *investment* to refer to financial investments, such as the purchase of stocks and bonds.

EXAMPLE 1: SOFTWARE, EQUIPMENT AND STRUCTURES

Economists generally use the term *investment* to refer to investment in productive capacity. The BEA limits this to only investments in equipment, software, and structures. So buying a share is not "investment" in BEA terms. Buying a share in a company is a financial investment—it transfers ownership rights to the company, but does not in itself create new productive capacity.

EXAMPLE 2: EDUCATION (SPENDING ON)

Spending on education is considered consumption expenditure. It should be considered an investment in human capital but is not, since human capital is not recognized as a form of capital in the national accounts.

Using data from the BEA, we can see from figure 8.3 that household expenditures, at 69%, constitute the biggest share of GDP. The US government's expenditure share was 18% of GDP. In comparison, the world average for household expenditures' share of world GDP is 58.3%, and world governments' expenditure share of world GDP is 17.2%. We also note that for 2016, net export's share of GDP was negative 2%. This implies that imports exceeded exports. In fact, the United States imported \$0.46 trillion (or \$460 billion) more goods and services from other countries than it exported to other countries.

FIGURE 8.3 A Look at the Expenditure Approach, 2016, US GDP in \$ Trillions

Sector	GDP per Sector	Percent Share of Total GDP
Gross domestic product, Total	**18.68**	
Personal consumption expenditures, C	**12.83**	**69%**
Goods	4.11	22%
Durable goods	1.41	
Nondurable goods	2.70	
Services	8.72	47%

FIGURE 8.3 *(continued)*

Sector	GDP per Sector	Percent Share of Total GDP
Gross private domestic investment, I	**3.02**	**16%**
Fixed investment	3.01	
Nonresidential	2.31	
Structures	0.50	
Equipment	1.05	
Intellectual property products	0.76	
Residential	0.70	
Net exports of goods and services, NX	**−0.46**	**−2%**
Exports	2.28	12%
Goods	1.50	
Services	0.78	
Imports	2.74	15%
Goods	2.22	
Services	0.51	
Government consumption expenditures and gross investment, G	**3.29**	**18%**
Federal	1.25	7%
National defense	0.74	4%
Nondefense	0.52	3%
State and local	2.03	11%

Source: Author's modification from data obtained from www.bea.gov.

Figure 8.4 plots the size of each component of GDP for the United States from 1970 to 2014. It is clear that as total GDP for the United States (dashed line) has increased, so have its individual components. It is difficult to ascertain from the chart, however, whether each component's share of total GDP has changed over time. We note this information in figure 8.5. Household consumption expenditures as a share of total GDP have increased by 7 percentage points over the past 50 years, making it by far the biggest component of GDP. This implies that household spending is an even bigger player in today's economy than it was after the World War II. The importance of trade for the United States is also clear—import and export expenditures as shares of total GDP have increased at least threefold over the past 50 years. Government expenditures as a share of GDP is one component that has actually declined over the same period. So, the *relative* size of government has gone down, not up, as is commonly portrayed.

FIGURE 8.4 Growth in Each GDP Component for the United States, 1970–2014

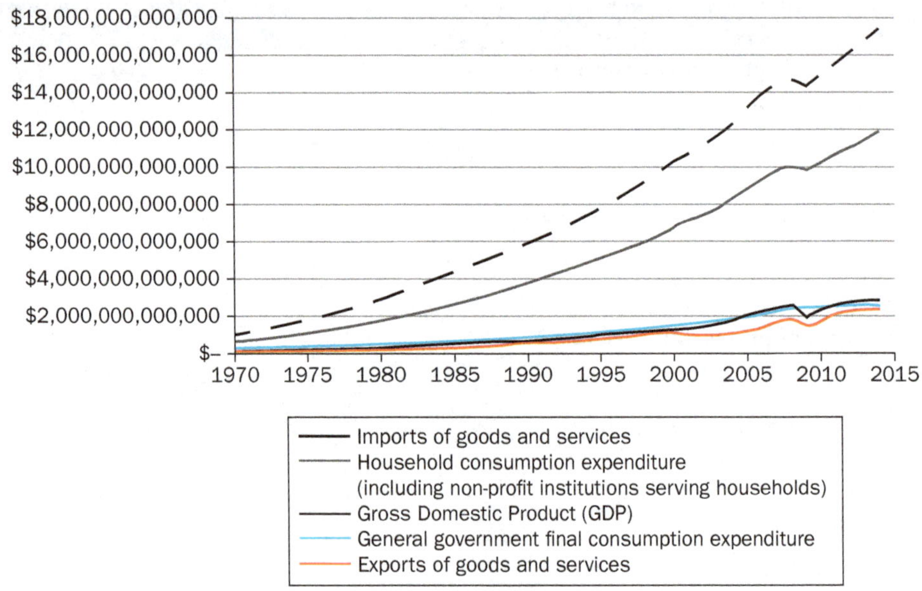

Source: Author's modification of data obtained from the United Nations, 2016.

FIGURE 8.5 Have US Expenditure Shares of GDP Fluctuated or Remained Constant over Time?

Expenditure	1960	1975	2015
Household consumption, C	61.05	61.15	68.10
Government consumption, G	15.56	17.67	14.44
Exports, Ex	4.97	8.20	12.60
Imports, Im	4.20	7.30	15.40

Source: World Bank, 2016.

We will now turn to learning how to calculate GDP using the expenditure approach. However, we will first pause for an exercise to test our understanding of the GDP.

Application Questions

WHICH OF THE FOLLOWING WOULD BE INCLUDED IN THIS YEAR'S GDP CALCULATION?

1. Someone has a tooth extracted by a dentist.
2. Sam rents an apartment in Plattsburgh.
3. You buy a new house in Vermont.

4. You buy an old home in New York.
5. John smuggles $100,000 worth of drugs into the United States from Mexico.
6. Lockheed Martin increases production of helicopters that are exported to India.
7. Americans consume Australian wines.
8. Ford opens a new factory in South Dakota, producing new cars.
9. Kate buys 100 shares from AT&T telecom.
10. A professor teaches a boring economics class.
11. You sell your car to your friend.
12. Your neighbor mows your lawn for you.
13. John receives cash payment of $1,000 (dividends) from AT&T.
14. Steve, a real estate agent, receives a $5,000 commission for the sale of a condo.
15. Joe works for Burger King.

SOLUTIONS

1. Someone has a tooth extracted by a dentist.

   Yes

2. Sam rents an apartment in Plattsburgh.

   Yes

3. You buy a new house in Vermont.

   Yes

4. You buy an old home in New York.

   No

5. John smuggles $100,000 worth of drugs into the United States from Mexico.

   No

6. Lockheed Martin increases production of helicopters that are exported to India.

   Yes

7. Americans consume Australian wines.

   No

8. Ford opens a new factory in South Dakota, producing new cars.

   Yes

9. Kate buys 100 shares from AT&T telecom.

   No

10. A professor teaches a boring economics class.

    Yes

11. You sell your car to your friend.

    No

12. Your neighbor mows your lawn for you.

    No

13. John receives cash payment of $1,000 (dividends) from AT&T.

    Yes

14. Steve, a real estate agent, receives a $5,000 commission for the sale of a condo.

    Yes

15. Joe works for Burger King.

    Yes

Calculating GDP Using the Expenditure Method

Calculating GDP via the expenditure method (also called the expenditure approach) requires one to sum up the value of each final good produced by an economy. The value is obtained by multiplying the price of a good or service by the quantity sold. We will carry out this exercise by considering a simple economy that produces only two final goods: peaches and wine. Figure 8.6 lists the production for the country of San Armando.

Notice that in figure 8.6, there are two years, 1989 and 1990. Thus, we will need to calculate GDP for each year using the prices from each respective year.

Thus, our calculations will be as follows.

For 1989, GDP_{1989}, contribution from peaches = $(P_{1989}) \times (Q_{1989})$ = (\$1/lbs) × (100 lbs) = \$100.

For 1989, GDP_{1989}, contribution from wine = $(P_{1989}) \times (Q_{1989})$ = (\$2/bottle) × (50 bottles) = \$100.

For 1989, total GDP_{1989} = GDP contribution from peaches + GDP contribution from wine = \$100 + \$100 = \$200.

We can simplify these calculations by writing out the steps mathematically, as below:

$$GDP_{1989} = P_{1989}^{Peaches} \times Q_{1989}^{Peaches} + P_{1989}^{Wine} \times Q_{1989}^{Wine}$$

Now, we calculate total GDP for 1990:

$$GDP_{1990} = P_{1990}^{Peaches} \times Q_{1990}^{Peaches} + P_{1990}^{Wine} \times Q_{1990}^{Wine}$$

Thus, for 1990, total GDP_{1990} = (\$1.50/lbs) × (100 lbs) + (\$2/bottle) × (75 bottles) = \$300.

FIGURE 8.6 Output by San Armando

(1) Description	(2) Price per Pound or Bottle (P)	(3) Quantity in Pounds or bottles (Q)	(4) Contribution to Nominal GDP [column (2) × column (3)]
Year 1–1989			
Peaches	\$1.00	100	\$100
Wine	\$2.00	50	\$100
			\$200
Year 2–1990			
Peaches	\$1.50	100	\$150
Wine	\$2.00	75	\$150
			\$300

We use prices in the year in which the goods were produced.

At this point, we have to make a distinction about the two types of GDPs that can be calculated using the expenditure approach. The calculations we have just used to determine total GDP values for 1989 and 1990 used the current market prices in each respective year. When one calculates total GDP using the given market price in each respective year, then one is calculating what is called **nominal GDP. Thus, the nominal GDP for San Armando for 1989 and 1990 is \$200 and \$300, respectively.**

Nominal and Real GDP

An increase in GDP will record both increases in actual production and increases in prices of those goods and services. Given that GDP is measured in value terms, we have to be careful about interpreting changes over time. If we are to track changes in an economy's ability to produce more, we want to see increases in GDP that reflect increases in output, not increases in prices. Thus, we need to calculate GDP without including the effect of increases (or decreases) in prices. GDP calculated in such a manner in which prices are maintained fixed at some constant level is called **real (or constant) GDP.** If one is to consider only increases in actual production, but not prices, one therefore needs to distinguish between nominal GDP and real GDP.

We will now recalculate GDP for San Armando using a constant price level. We do this by fixing prices using a specific **base-period year.** We will choose year 1 (1989) as the base year. This means that our GDP calculation for 1989 and 1990 will use ONLY 1989 prices for peaches and wine. Here are the real GDP values for San Armando:

$$Real\ GDP_{1989} = P_{1989}^{Peaches} \times Q_{1989}^{Peaches} + P_{1989}^{Wine} \times Q_{1989}^{Wine}$$

Thus, for 1990, total real GDP_{1990} = (\$1/lbs) × (100 lbs) + (\$2/bottle) × (50 bottles) = \$200.

Now, we calculate total real GDP for 1990:

$$GDP_{1990} = P_{1989}^{Peaches} \times Q_{1990}^{Peaches} + P_{1990}^{Wine} \times Q_{1990}^{Wine}$$

Thus, for 1990, total GDP_{1990} = (\$1/lbs) × (100 lbs) + (\$2/bottle) × (75 bottles) = \$250.

We see that although GDP increased from year 1 to year 2, the real increase was less than indicated by the nominal amount. The reason is that nominal GDP increased as a result of both increases in prices and increases in output, but real GDP increased only as a result of increases in output. Figure 8.7 compares and contrasts the results of using real and nominal GDP calculations.

FIGURE 8.7 Nominal and Constant-Dollar Real GDP for San Armando

(1) Description	(2) Price per Pound or Bottle	(3) Quantity in (Pounds or Bottles)	(4) Contribution to Nominal GDP [column (2) × column (3)]
Year 1, 1989			
Peaches	$1.00	100	$100
Wine	$2.00	50	$100
			$200
Year 2, 1990			
Peaches	$1.50	100	$150
Wine	$2.00	75	$150
			$300
(1) Description	**(2) Price per Pound or Bottle *in Base Year***	**(3) Quantity (Pounds or Bottles)**	**(4) Contribution to Real GDP [column (2) × column (3)]**
Year 1, 1989			
Peaches	$1.00	100	$100
Wine	$2.00	50	$100
			$200
Year 2, 1990			
Peaches	$1.00	100	$100
Wine	$2.00	75	$150
			$250

Real GDP and Nominal GDP Growth in the United States, and the GDP Deflator

As discussed in the previous section, changes in nominal GDP from one year to the next reflect changes in the output of goods and services and changes in their prices. *Real* GDP changes, however, are more meaningful because they indicate changes in output levels, independent of changes in prices. Changes in real GDP per capita provide a much better measure of changes in our material standard of living.

If we examine trends in nominal and real GDP for the United States using a time series from 1969 to 2015 (figure 8.8), then we note that both real and nominal GDP have grown steadily for the past 50 years, with real GDP outpacing nominal GDP for most of that time period. Only in 2009 did real GDP and nominal GDP equate to each other. After 2009, nominal GDP has been larger than real GDP. This indicates that post-2009 (i.e., after the Great Recession), increases in prices have outpaced increases in output.

FIGURE 8.8 Real versus Nominal GDP, Chained 1992 Dollars, 1969–2015 ($ billions)

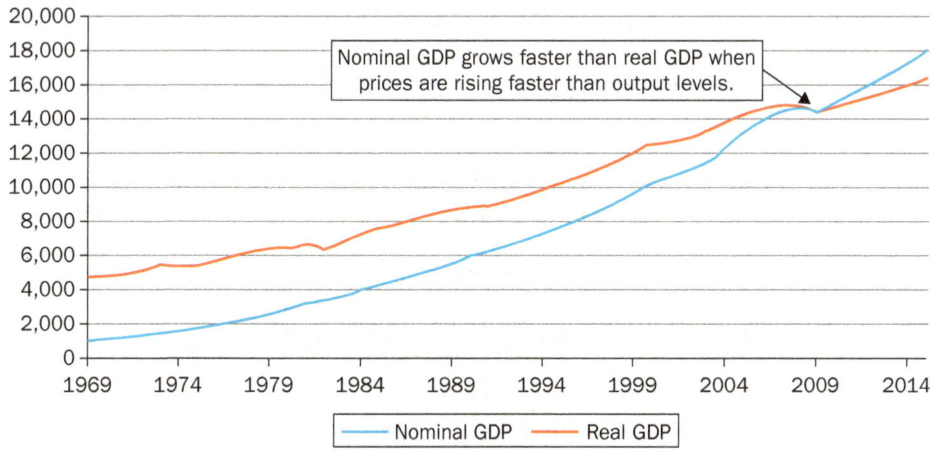

Source: Author's drawing using data from www.bea.gov.

In terms of growth rate of real and nominal GDP, which are measured by average annual changes in real and nominal GDP, respectively, we note from figure 8.8 that growth in real GDP slowed in 2001 when the United States entered a recession. A significant drop in real GDP (with negative growth rate) occurred during the Great Recession of 2008–2009. The rate of increase in real GDP was relatively high in the latter half of the 1990s when compared to the 1970s, 1980s, and early 1990s. Economic growth rates were 4.4% in the 1960s but decreased during the 1970s to 3.3%, then to 3.0%. Real GDP growth rates have been between 1.5% and 2.6% since the Great Recession.

How are growth rates in real or nominal GDP calculated? These growth rates are simply percentage changes from one year to the next or from one decade to the next, or any other combination of years. A growth rate is defined as a percentage change. The *percentage change* is the change in some economic variable, usually from one period to the next, expressed as a percentage. We calculate percentage changes using the following formula:

$$\text{Percentage change} = \left(\frac{\text{Value in the second period} - \text{Value in the first period}}{\text{Value in the first period}}\right) \times 100$$

Thus, if we were to calculate the growth rate of GDP from 2012 to 2013 using the percentage change formula, we would write it as follows:

$$\left(\frac{GDP_{2013} - GDP_{2012}}{GDP_{2012}}\right) \times 100$$

To calculate the percentage change in real GDP for San Armando, we have

$$\frac{Real\ GDP_{1990} - Real\ GDP_{1989}}{Real\ GDP_{1989}} \times 100 = \frac{250 - 200}{200} \times 100 = 25\%.$$

Thus, real GDP increased by 25% between 1989 and 1990. We can also apply the percentage formula to the growth rate in nominal GDP or changes in price. To calculate the percentage change in peach prices from 1989 to 1990 for San Armando, we have

$$\frac{P_{1990} - P_{1989}}{P_{1989}} \times 100 = \frac{1.50 - 1.00}{1.00} \times 100 = 50\%.$$

Thus, prices for peaches increased by 50% from 1989 to 1990. Give that there was no change in wine prices, the percentage change for the price of wine from 1989 to 1990 is 0%.

To calculate the percentage change in nominal GDP for San Armando, we have

$$\frac{nom\ GDP_{1990} - nom\ GDP_{1989}}{nom\ GDP_{1989}} \times 100 = \frac{300 - 200}{200} \times 100 = 50\%.$$

Thus, nominal GDP increased by 50% between 1989 and 1990.

We notice that the percentage increases in nominal GDP and peach prices were 50%. There was an increase in price for half of the goods produced by San Armando. We also notice that real GDP increased by half of nominal GDP.

There is a relationship between nominal GDP and real GDP that involves the percentage change in prices. If we look at the percentage difference in real GDP in 1990 and nominal GDP in 1990, we see a 20% difference in the two values that was brought about by price changes from the base year:

$$\frac{Real\ GDP_{1990} - nom\ GDP_{1990}}{nom\ GDP_{1990}} \times 100 = \frac{300 - 250}{250} \times 100 = 20\%.$$

We can determine the exact nature of the relationship between real and nominal GDP by defining a new variable called the **GDP deflator.** The GDP deflator shows how much a change in the base year's GDP relies on changes in the price level. It is also known as the **GDP implicit price deflator.** To compare GDP over time, we convert nominal GDP to real GDP for any year using the **GDP deflator:**

$$GDP\ deflator = \frac{Nominal\ GDP}{Real\ GDP} \times 100$$

Thus, the GDP deflator for San Armando for 1990 is:

$$GDP\ deflator_{1990} = \frac{Nominal\ GDP_{1990}}{Real\ GDP_{1990}} \times 100 = \frac{300}{250} \times 100 = 120$$

The GDP deflator tells us the percentage increase or decrease in prices from the base year.

If the GDP deflator value is 100, then there were no changes in the price level.

If the GDP deflator value is greater than 100, then there was an increase in the price level.

If the GDP deflator value is less than 100, then there was a decrease in the price level.

Thus, prices increased by 20% (i.e., 120 – 100) from the base year, 1989. This is the same result obtained when we calculated the percentage difference between real and nominal GDPs for the same year, 1990.

Application Questions

GDP CALCULATIONS

1. Assume that an economy's nominal GDP is $350 and its real GDP for the same year is $320. Find and interpret the value of the GDP deflator.

SOLUTION

$$GDP\ deflator = \frac{Nominal\ GDP}{Real\ GDP} \times 100 = \frac{\$350}{\$320} \times 100 = 109.35$$

Thus, prices increased by 9.35% (i.e., 109.35 – 100) from the base year.

2. Consider the economy of the Isle of Hildebrand. This island country produces only two goods: bottles of tomato sauce and pizza, as shown in the yearly production table.

Year	Sauce production (in bottles)	Price of a bottle of tomato sauce	Pizza production	Price of a pizza
2010	100	$2	50	$10
2011	105	$3	45	$12
2012	105	$4	45	$13

Using the information in the table, answer the following questions.

a. Calculate the nominal GDP for 2010, 2011, and 2012.

b. Given your answers to (a), can one conclude that the economy is more productive in 2011 and 2012 than it was in 2010?

c. Using the year 2010 as the base year, calculate the real GDP for each year. Can one now conclude that 2011 and 2012 were more productive years than 2010?

d. Calculate the GDP deflator for each year.

SOLUTION

a. nominal $GDP_{2010} = (100) \times (\$2) + (50) \times (\$10) = \$700$
nominal $GDP_{2011} = (105) \times (\$3) + (45) \times (\$12) = \$855$
nominal $GDP_{2012} = (105) \times (\$4) + (45) \times (\$13) = \$1005$

b. No, because we are considering nominal GDP, which includes changes in prices. One should never use nominal GDP as an indication of economic growth or productivity.

c. real $GDP_{2010} = (100) \times (\$\mathbf{2}) + (50) \times (\$\mathbf{10}) = \$700$

real $GDP_{2011} = (105) \times (\$\mathbf{2}) + (45) \times (\$\mathbf{10}) = \$660$
real $GDP_{2012} = (105) \times (\$\mathbf{2}) + (45) \times (\$\mathbf{10}) = \$660$

A comparison of real GDP over the three years shows that this economy is actually less productive than it was in 2010.

d. GDP $deflator_{2010} = (\text{Nom GDP/Real GDP}) \times 100 = (\$700)/(\$700) \times 100 = 100$
GDP $deflator_{2011} = (\$855)/(\$660) \times 100 = 129.5$
GDP $deflator_{2012} = (\$1005)/(\$660) \times 100 = 152.3$

3. Consider the economy of ancient Rome, as shown in the table, and answer the following questions.

	Year 1 = 209 B.C.	Year 2 = 208 B.C
Nominal GDP (in billions of dinari)	2,397	2,528
GDP deflator (base year is 215 B.C.)	110	112
Population (in millions)	81.77	81.6

a. Find the appropriate statistic that can be used to calculate the growth rate of the economy, and then calculate the rate of growth.

b. Has the standard of living increased or decreased for the citizens of ancient Rome during these two years? Find the growth rate for the measure of standard of living.

c. If nominal GDP increases by 7% next year (i.e., 207 B.C.), what will be the nominal GDP for next year (207 B.C.)?

SOLUTION

a. The appropriate statistic for the growth rate of the economy is the percentage change in real GDP. However, the table description of the economy does not provide the real GDP for the two years. We must first calculate it from the nominal GDP and the corresponding GDP deflator. Rearranging the GDP deflator formula, we now have

$$Real\ GDP_{209\ B.C.} = \frac{Nominal\ GDP}{GDP\ deflator} \times 100 = \frac{2397}{110} \times 100 = 2179$$

And

$$Real\ GDP_{208\ B.C.} = \frac{Nominal\ GDP}{GDP\ deflator} \times 100 = \frac{2528}{112} \times 100 = 2257$$

Now, we calculate the percentage change in real GDP from 209 B.C. to 208 B.C.:

$$\frac{Real\ GDP_{208\ B.C.} - Real\ GDP_{209\ B.C.}}{Real\ GDP_{209\ B.C.}} \times 100 = \frac{2257 - 2179}{2179} \times 100 = 3.58\%$$

The Roman economy grew by 3.58% from 209 B.C. to 208 B.C.

b. To determine standard of living, one needs to calculate real GDP per capita. Thus, real GDP per capita for 209 B.C. is 2,179,000,000,000/81,770,000 = 26,649 dinari per capita.

   Real GDP per capita for 209 B.C. is 2,257,000,000,000/81,770,000 = 27,661 dinari per capita.

   The standard of living has increased.

c. If nominal GDP increases by 7% next year, this means that it is 7% bigger than it was in 208 B.C. Therefore, nominal GDP for 207 B.C. is 2,528 + (0.07) × (2,528) = 2,705 dinari.

Price Indices and the Consumer Price Index

The GDP deflator is an **index number** that relays information on the price level of the overall economy. Any index number is a ratio that measures the value, in percentage terms, of an item (or group of items) at a point in time relative to the value of an item (or group of items) at another point in time. Index numbers can be constructed for any purpose and are frequently employed in every field, such as medicine, business, and economics, as indicators of change in an activity or variable of interest. The reason for this wide use is because an index is a handy way to express a change in any collection of objects of interest. This convenience of comparison was recognized long ago, and some credit the Italian economist Gian Rinaldo Carli with the compilation in 1764 of some of the earliest index numbers concerning historical price fluctuations in Europe.

There are many kinds of index numbers in economics, including price indices, quantity indices, value indices, and so forth. As mentioned, the GDP deflator is one type of price index. Any price index can be constructed in order to compare the price of a good or service (or group of goods) in a particular point in time to the price paid for that good at a particular point in time in the past. There are two types of price indices: a **simple price index,** which follows the price of a single good or service, and an **aggregate price index,** which follows the prices for a group of goods and services. The latter group of goods and services is called a **market basket.** All price indices have a **base period,** which is the point in time in the past against which all comparisons are made.

The formula for a simple price index, I_i is as follows: $\mathbf{I_i = (P_i)/(P_{base\ year}) \times 100}$, where

I_i = price index for year i
P_i = price for year i
$P_{base\ year}$ = price for the base year

For example, if we were to use the price of peaches in the country of San Armando and set the base year as 1989, we have the following information for which we can construct an index number for 1990:

P_{1990} = price of peaches for the year 1990 = \$1.50
P_{1989} = price for the base year 1989 = \$1.00
I_{1990} = price index for year 1990 = $(P_{1990})/(P_{1989}) \times 100$ = (\$1.50)/(\$1.00) × 100 = 150

The resulting index number, 150, indicates that prices rose by 50% (i.e., 150 – 100) from the base year (1989) to the year of interest (1990). This is the same result we obtained in the previous section when we used the percentage change formula.

Let us practice using the simple price index formula and the percentage change formula by completing the following chart. The chart provides the average price for cars for the years 2007 to 2009. We are to calculate the percentage change in average price from the base year, 2007, and construct an index number for each year using 2007 as the base year.

Year	Average Car Price ('000)	% Change	Index Number
2007	20	0%	
2008	22		
2009	19.5		

SOLUTION: The index number for the base year is always 100.

The index numbers for 2008 and 2009 are calculated as follows:

$I_{2008} = (P_{2008})/(P_{2007}) \times 100$ = (\$22)/(\$20) × 100 = 110, which indicated that prices in 2008 were 10% higher than the base year, 2007.

$I_{2009} = (P_{2009})/(P_{2007}) \times 100$ = (\$19.5)/(\$20) × 100 = 97.5, which indicated that prices in 2009 were 2.5% lower than the base year, 2007.

The percentage changes in prices are calculated as follows:

(i) for changes from 2007 to 2008

$$\frac{P_{2008} - P_{2007}}{P_{2007}} \times 100 = \frac{22 - 20}{20} \times 100 = 10\%$$

(ii) for changes from 2007 to 2009

$$\frac{P_{2009} - P_{2007}}{P_{2007}} \times 100 = \frac{19.5 - 20}{20} \times 100 = -2.5\%$$

The completed table is as follows:

Year	Average Car Price ('000)	% Change	Index Number
2007	20	0%	100
2008	22	+10%	110
2009	19.5	−2.5%	97.5

Another commonly used price index in economics that you will often hear about in the news is the **consumer price index (CPI).** The CPI is an imperfect cost-of-living index that was first introduced in 1913. It is a measure that tracks movements in the level of consumer prices over time. The CPI compares the retail prices of a representative "shopping basket" of goods and services at two different points in time:

$$\text{CPI} = \frac{\text{cost of consumer basket in current year}}{\text{cost of consumer basket in base year}}$$

Specifically, the CPI represents changes in prices of all goods and services purchased for consumption by urban households.

In the United States, the **Bureau of Labor Statistics (BLS)** is responsible for the CPI program that produces monthly data on changes in the prices paid by urban consumers for a representative basket of goods and services. The BLS constructs a variety of consumer price indices. One is called the **all urban consumers (CPI-U),** which covers approximately 89% of the US population. It includes goods and services that are typically bought by consumers. It also includes items such as water and sewer service user fees, and sales and excise taxes paid by the consumer, but it excludes income taxes and investment items (like stocks, bonds, and life insurance). Prices for the goods and services used to calculate the CPI are taken through a given month and collected in 87 urban areas throughout the country. Data come from approximately 23,000 retail and service establishments.

Another BLS consumer price index that is quoted often is called the **CPI-U for all items less food and energy.** This index is more commonly known or reported by news agencies as the "core" CPI. According to the BLS, this measure strips out eight of the most volatile CPI components (fruit, vegetables, gasoline, fuel oil, natural gas, mortgage interest, intercity transportation, and tobacco products), as well as the effect of changes in indirect taxes on the remaining components. It is an index monitored by many economic policy makers because it is assumed that food and energy prices are volatile and are subject to price shocks that cannot be well controlled by the will of the government (technically, central bank policy—more on this in chapter 10).

WHY DO WE NEED BOTH THE CPI AND THE GDP DEFLATOR AS MEASURES OF CHANGING PRICE LEVELS?

The GDP deflator is a measure of price level, but it is very broad because it includes the price of every final good and service. That is, it includes goods such as steel and helicopters that the typically household never buys. Therefore, for the typical household, the CPI provides for a better measure of how prices are changing and how this affects household purchasing power. In fact, the percentage change in the CPI defines the rate of the all-important concept of **inflation. Inflation is the persistent rise over time in the average price of goods and services.** Inflation is the "cost of living." The **inflation rate** is the percentage change in the price level from one time period (e.g., year) to the next.

Figure 8.9 tracks the value of the CPI for the United States from 1946 to 2013, using 1984 as the base year. We can use percentage changes from any two CPI values in order to calculate the rate of inflation from any two periods of time. For example, if we are interested in the rate of inflation between 1950 and 1951, we need the CPI values for 1950 and 1951, which are 23.51 and 25.38, respectively. Thus, the inflation rate between these two years is:

$$\frac{CPI_{1951} - CPI_{1950}}{CPI_{1950}} \times 100 = \frac{25.38 - 23.51}{23.51} \times 100 = 7.95\%$$

Of course, if we are interested in knowing the inflation of any year relative to the base year, 1984, then no calculations are required. As with any index number, we simply subtract 100 from the index value to determine the percentage change. Thus, the percentage change (and therefore, the rate of inflation) between 2016 and 1984 is 142% (i.e., 242 – 100); average prices were 142% higher in 2016 than they were in 1984. The percentage change (and therefore, the rate of inflation) between 1970 and 1984 is –60.2% (i.e., 39.8 – 100); average prices were 60.2% lower in 1970 than they were in 1984.

IS THE CPI THE BEST MEASURE OF INFLATION?

A number of indices have been constructed to measure different aspects of inflation, including the following:

- The CPI measures inflation as experienced by households in their daily consumption.
- The GDP deflator measures inflation experienced by all economic agents.
- The producer price index measures inflation at the earlier stages of the production process.
- The employment cost index measures inflation in the labor market.

Thus, the "best" measure of inflation depends on how the information is used and for whom it is used. The CPI would then be the best measure for consumers if it is used as a means to adjust payments to consumers, such as Social Security, alimony and child support, and for collective bargaining agreements, rental contracts, insurance policies with automatic inflation protection, and so on.

FIGURE 8.9 CPI for All Urban Consumers–All Items, Index 1946–2013 (1984 = 100), Monthly, Seasonally Adjusted

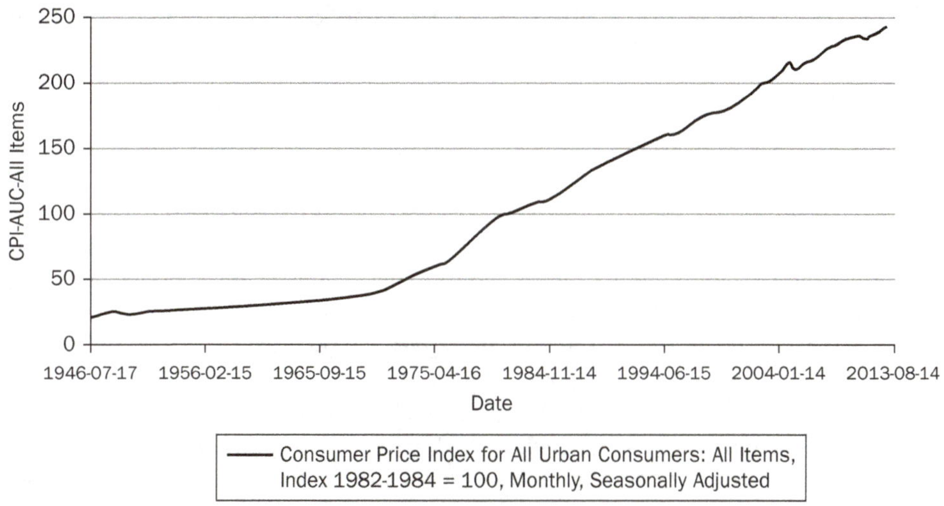

Source: Bureau of Labor Statistics, Consumer Price Index for All Urban Consumers: All Items [CPIAUCSL], retrieved from FRED, Federal Reserve Bank of St. Louis; https://fred.stlouisfed.org/series/CPIAUCSL.

What Are Some Limitations of the CPI?

The CPI-U is not perfect and has some limitations. Here is a list of some of the limitations:

1. The CPI may not be applicable to all population groups. The CPI-U is designed to measure inflation for the US urban population and thus may not be reflective of the price level experienced by those who live in rural areas.
2. The CPI may not be applicable to subgroups of the population. It may not accurately reflect the inflation experiences of the elder or poor, given that these groups may have different "shopping baskets" than the typical consumer.
3. The CPI cannot be used as a measure of total change in living costs, because not all factors that affect living costs are included in the CPI, such as social and environmental changes and changes in income taxes.

A Final Word on GDP and Its Shortcomings

As the previous sections highlight, GDP is a useful measure of total production in a country and can be used to form an understanding of how productivity and price levels change over time. When Keynes's idea of GDP found admirers, its use spread quickly. After World War II, the United States was ready to deliver its Marshall Plan, but countries that wanted to receive postwar aid had to produce an estimate of their GDP. Yet, GDP, as popular as it is as an economic measure, has shortcomings, some of which are quite serious. Even back in 1968, Robert Kennedy lamented in a speech about the use of GDP as the perfect indicator of a country's well-being by stating that GDP does not capture "the beauty of our poetry or the strength of our marriages."

To be sure, **GDP is not a measure of well-being,** and here are some of the shortcomings that explain why it is not such a measure:

1. If a society values **leisure time,** then increasing one's well-being by increasing one's leisure time (e.g., working fewer hours) can lead to a decline in GDP.
2. **GDP does not include household production** that can lead to a better quality of life. That is, goods and services produced for oneself are not counted, including homemaker services such as child care, meal preparation, building one's own cabinets, volunteer work, and so forth.
3. **GDP is not adjusted to subtract negative externalities,** which reduce one's well-being. Nondesirable outputs include generated wastes such as pollution, wasted heat, and waste materials are not subtracted from GDP. Negative externalities also include Walmart's minimization of worker hours so that they do not benefit from health insurance coverage, forcing them to use emergency rooms as the only venue for health care.
4. **GDP is not adjusted for changes in crime rates and other social ills.** Increases in crime lead to lower well-being but may increase GDP if more is spent on policing and on constructing more prisons. GDP does not account for changes in well-being from increasing divorce rates, drug addiction, and so on.
5. **GDP is a bad measure of income equality.** Income inequality reduces a country's well-being if it increases significantly. Certainly, GDP does not indicate how a nation's income is divided among its citizens (neither does GDP per capita). Rising income inequality can hinder economic growth and development even in developed countries like the United States. Recall our theme of incentives—wide income disparities can act as a powerful material and psychological disincentive to economic progress. Low income levels are manifested in poor health and education, which lead to lower economic productivity levels. A country may get richer, but it is how that richness gets distributed that matters. It is a fallacy to assume that if the richest segment of one's society gets relatively richer, they will spur economic activity by spending their money. The rich do not necessarily save and invest significantly larger portions of their incomes on productive domestic goods when they become richer.

Separate from well-being, it should also be noted that GDP does not measure the underground economy. It is estimated that the underground economy constitutes about 10% of GDP in the United States and as much as 50% of measured GDP in countries like Zimbabwe and Peru as a result of trade and trafficking of drugs, prostitution, and selling of goods to avoid taxes or to avoid government regulation.

To overcome some of these shortcomings, other measures of well-being or even happiness have been developed either to replace GDP altogether or to be used with GDP. Environmentally adjusted net domestic product is one measure that adjusts GDP by subtracting the costs of natural resource depletion and environmental degradation.

The genuine progress indicator (GPI), the better life index, and the human development index are three examples of measures that have been developed to replace GDP altogether. Let us consider the GPI.

The GPI uses the same personal consumption expenditure data that are included in GDP. It then adjusts personal consumption expenditures by adding factors such as the value of household and volunteer work, and subtracting factors such as the costs of crime and pollution. Both the GDP and the GPI are measured in monetary terms, so they can be compared to each other. Figure 8.10 provides a table with all the adjustments made to personal expenditures that are found in the GDP in order to arrive at the GPI. Figure 8.11 plots the values for GDP and the GPI on the same graph for the United States for the years 1950 to 2004.

From figure 8.11, we note that real GDP per capita increased about threefold, from $11,672 per capita in 1950 to $36,596 in 2004. The annual growth rate of GDP over this period was 3.81%. In contrast, real GPI per capita has remained fairly constant since 1978, at about $15,000. The GPI growth rate over the period 1950–2004 was only 1.33%. Thus, according to the GPI, residents of the United States are no better off today than they were in 1978.

FIGURE 8.10 Genuine Progress Indicator Components, United States, 2004

Component of GPI	Value (billions of dollars)
Personal consumption	7,589
Personal consumption after inequality adjustment	6,318
Value of household work and parenting	+ 2,542
Value of higher education	+ 828
Value of volunteer work	+ 131
Service value of consumer durables	+ 744
Service value of highways and streets	+ 112
Costs of crime	− 34
Loss of leisure time	− 402
Costs of underemployment	− 177
Costs of consumer durables	− 1,090
Costs of commuting and auto accidents	− 698
Costs of environmental defensive expenditures	− 21
Costs of pollution	− 178
Value of lost wetlands, farmland, and forests	− 368
Costs of nonrenewable energy depletion	− 1,761
Damages from carbon emissions and ozone depletion	− 1,662
Adjustment for capital investment and foreign borrowing	+ 135
Genuine Progress Indicator	**4,419**

Source: Talberth et al., The Genuine Progress Indicator 2006: A Tool for Sustainable Development. Redefining Progress, 2007. http://rprogress.org.

FIGURE 8.11 Comparison of Real GDP per Capita (black line) and Real GPI per Capita (blue line), in US$ (base year = 2000), United States, 1950-2004

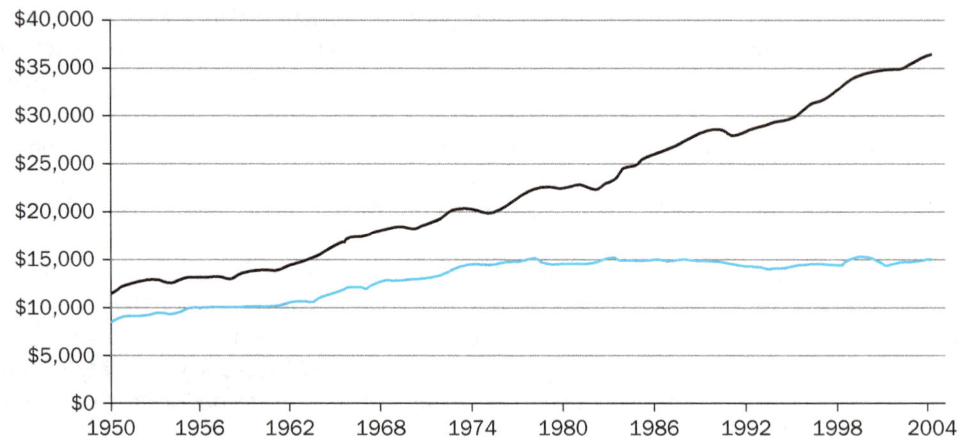

Source: Talberth et al., The Genuine Progress Indicator 2006: A Tool for Sustainable Development. Redefining Progress, 2007. http://rprogress.org.

Chapter Summary

In this chapter, we were introduced to the system of national income accounting. We saw that, in the world of macroeconomics, GDP is an invaluable metric. It is used as a measure of the value of all newly produced goods and services in an economy within a given year. This chapter noted that GDP on a per capita basis provides for a measure of standard of living of the average citizen in a country—albeit not a perfect measure.

This chapter used one of the three methods for calculating GDP in order to derive nominal and real amounts. The method that was used is the expenditure approach. Using the expenditure approach, we saw that GDP is the aggregation of all goods and services produced in an economy using market prices. However broad, GDP does not account for all economic and social activities in a country. GDP also does not account for negative externalities that damage the natural environment or human well-being.

Finally, the chapter noted that because nominal GDP may increase from year to year due to price increases irrespective of production changes, the GDP deflator is thus used to adjust nominal GDP to take price increases into account. The GDP deflator is an index number that allows us to calculate the level of inflation from one time period to another. Another price index that is of greater use to consumers is the consumer price index, or CPI. The CPI is calculated using a basket of consumer goods and services. It is also used as a measure of inflation.

CHAPTER 9

"We Are All Dead in the Long Run"

JOHN M. KEYNES—BUSINESS CYCLES, UNEMPLOYMENT, AND FISCAL POLICY

LEARNING EXPECTATIONS

- To understand and describe the phases and characteristics of a business cycle
- To define and calculate the rates of employment and unemployment
- To understand why unemployment always exists and how fiscal policy applies to the unemployed

ASSISTANT SECRETARY, U.S. TREASURY, HARRY DEXTER WHITE (LEFT) AND JOHN MAYNARD KEYNES, HONORARY ADVISOR TO THE U.K. TREASURY at the inaugural meeting of the International Monetary Fund's Board of Governors in Savannah, Georgia, U.S., March 8, 1946.

Source: *https://commons.wikimedia.org/wiki/File:WhiteandKeynes.jpg*

Business Cycles: A Short-Run Fluctuation

Spend more. It's good for the economy, right? Political leaders exhort people to spend more (which conversely means save less) so that the economy does not go into a recession. President George W. Bush encouraged Americans to keep spending after 9/11 so as not to affect the value of stocks. Are politicians right that spending is better for economic growth than saving? To answer this question, we will first need to define some terms and then analyze business cycles, unemployment, and fiscal policy.

First, we need to recognize that real GDP does not increase and has not increased every year since the beginning of the 20th century. There have been some years when GDP declined, sometimes drastically. Although real GDP per capita has risen about eightfold since the start of the 20th century, the US economy has experienced alternating periods of expanding and contracting economic activity. These alternating periods are called the **business cycle.** The US business cycles are similar to those in other countries with advanced economies. For at least 150 years, Western countries have experienced business cycles where periods of expanding production and employment are followed by periods of recession, during which production and employment decline. Although these cycles are recurring ones, they are not identical to each other. Periods of expansion are not all the same in every business cycle, and periods of contraction (or recession) are not all the same. However, it has been the case that every period of recession has been followed by a period of expansion. Figure 9.1 illustrates a typical idealized path for real GDP—rising, falling, then rising again. It is an *idealized* path because not all of the cycles are of the same length or size. The figure is simply a representation of stylized characteristics and phases of a cycle. Any stylized representation forms an important base for the manner in which one thinks (about the economy), but it is not always literally true. The phases of rising real GDP are known as *expansion phases*; the periods of falling real GDP are known as are *recessions*. We refer to the points at which the economy changes from one phase to the other as *peaks* or *troughs*, respectively.

FIGURE 9.1 A Stylized Business Cycle

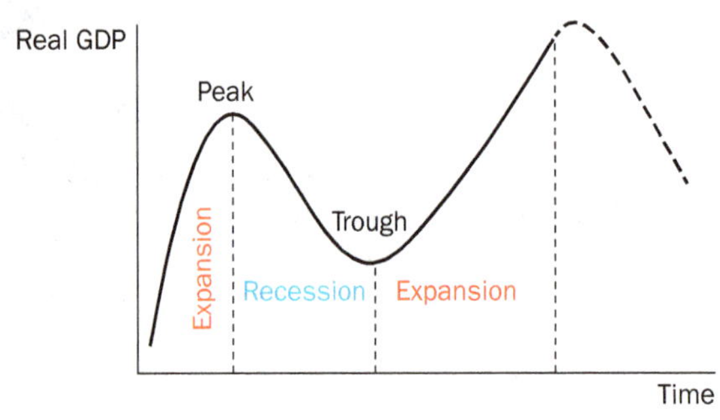

A NOTE ON THE DEFINITION OF A RECESSION

It is generally noted in the press or by the layperson that a recession occurs when two consecutive quarters of negative GDP growth take place. This is not entirely correct.

The designation of a recession is the conclusion by a committee of experts at the National Bureau of Economic Research (NBER), which is a private nonprofit research organization that focuses on analyzing the US economy.[24] A recession, as defined by the NBER, is a monthly concept. The committee of experts analyzes monthly indicators, including employment, personal income, industrial production, quarterly GDP growth, and others, to determine whether the US economy has entered or exited a recession.[24] Figure 9.2 lists all the business cycle peaks and troughs recorded by the NBER from 1890 to 2009. The period of recession starting in December 2007 and ending in June 2009 was the longest and most severe since the Great Depression of the 1930s. Consequentially, it was labelled the **Great Recession.** One should note that real GDP growth since the Great Recession has been slower than is typical at the start of a business cycle expansion.

FIGURE 9.2 Business Cycle Peaks and Troughs in the United States, 1890-2009

Peak	Trough	Peak	Trough
July 1890	May 1891	May 1937	June 1938
Jan. 1893	June 1894	Feb. 1945	Oct. 1945
Dec. 1895	June 1897	Nov. 1948	Oct. 1949
June 1899	Dec. 1900	July 1953	May 1954
Sep. 1902	Aug. 1904	Aug. 1957	Apr. 1958
May 1907	June 1908	Apr. 1960	Feb. 1961
Jan. 1910	Jan. 1912	Dec. 1969	Nov. 1970
Jan. 1913	Dec. 1914	Nov. 1973	Mar. 1975
Aug. 1918	Mar. 1919	Jan. 1980	July 1980
Jan. 1920	July 1921	July 1981	Nov. 1982
May 1923	July 1924	July 1990	Mar. 1991
Oct. 1926	Nov. 1927	Mar. 2001	Nov. 2001
Aug. 1929	Mar. 1933	Dec. 2007	June 2009

WHAT CAUSES BUSINESS CYCLES?

We have just noted that no two business cycles are alike. There is no prevailing reason why they should be alike. There is also no prevailing reason why business cycles should exist, either. Yet, they occur when there is some sort of shock (or disruption) to the economy. In the absence of shocks, the economy should, in theory, remain in a steady state. This steady state is one in which everyone who wants to be and can be employed is employed (called full-employment level) and in which there is a level of production in which all inputs, including labor, are being used efficiently. When the economy is at its steady state, inflation tends to remain constant, and in the absence of any external disturbance, the level of full employment grows at the same rate as population growth.

Finally, as long as new technologies are discovered, the economy will continue growing at its steady-state rate.

Unfortunately, shocks do occur, which give rise to business cycles. If there is a sudden increase in demand by consumers or firms as a result of optimism in the economy, then that optimism can lead to a rise in the inflation rate above that which maintains the steady state. Newly found optimism leads to increased spending by consumers and increased expenditures/investment by businesses. A demand shock can also occur as a result of increased government spending for, say, new military adventures. These collective actions can cause an economy to "overheat," pushing it toward a business cycle peak. Downturns toward troughs (i.e., recessions or depressions) can occur when these same factors work in reverse. Another possible cause of recessions or periods of expansion is the creation of too little or too much money by a country's central bank. Central banks are responsible for the amount of money that circulates in an economy. They conduct what is referred to as **monetary policy**, which is the subject of the next chapter. Monetary policy has played a crucial role in causing business cycles in the United States over the past 90 years (including the Great Depression of the 1930s). For this reason, we will devote an entire chapter to it.

If one were to examine the average length of business cycles since 1854 (see figure 9.3), one might conclude that business cycles have been less severe and less frequent in the post-World War period than in the prewar period. While many economists (but not all) would agree with this observation, which is called the **great moderation** (of the business cycle), the reader needs to be cautioned that the quality of the data is not consistent over the 155-year sample. This makes such comparisons problematic. Figure 9.4 uses the same data on real and nominal GDP as figure 8.8 in order to indicate some periods of recession in US history.

FIGURE 9.3 US Business Cycle Expansions and Contractions, Duration in Months

Period of Time	Contraction *Peak to Trough*	Expansion *Previous trough to this peak*	Cycle *Trough from Previous Trough*	Cycle *Peak from Previous Peak*
Average, all cycles:				
1854–2009 (33 cycles)	17.5	38.7	56.2	56.4
1854–1919 (16 cycles)	21.6	26.6	48.2	48.9
1919–1945 (6 cycles)	18.2	35.0	53.2	53.0
1945–2009 (11 cycles)	11.1	58.4	69.5	68.5

Source: NBER.

FACTORS THAT EXPLAIN THE GREAT MODERATION

There are four factors that can help explain why post–World War II business cycles occur less frequently and have become less severe.

FIGURE 9.4 Real versus Nominal GDP, Chained 1992 Dollars, 1969-2015 ($ billions)

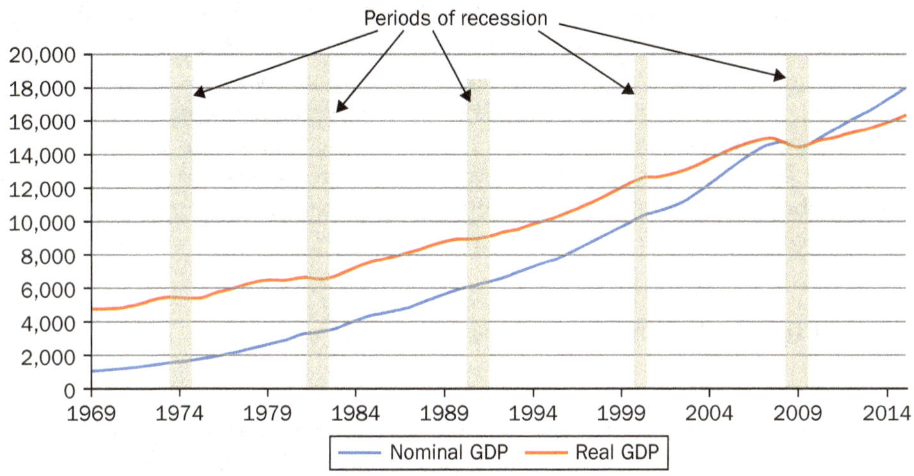

Sources: Author's drawing using data from www.bea.gov and NBER.

1. THE INCREASING IMPORTANCE OF SERVICES

The modern US economy is more dependent on the production of services. Manufacturing, especially the production of durable goods like furniture, appliances, and cars, is more strongly affected by recessions.

2. THE ESTABLISHMENT OF UNEMPLOYMENT INSURANCE

Before the 1930s, unemployment insurance and other government transfer programs like Social Security did not exist. These programs increase the ability of consumers to continue to purchase goods and services during recessions.

3. ACTIVE FEDERAL GOVERNMENT STABILIZATION POLICIES

Most economists view that active government policies (see the section on fiscal policy) have lengthened expansions and minimized the effects of recessions. A bigger government role in the economy since the Great Depression has been viewed as having had a positive effect on business cycles.

4. INCREASED STABILITY OF THE FINANCIAL SYSTEM

Although there are bank failures every year in the United States, bank failures prior to 1933 occurred in relatively larger numbers and were devastating to those whose accounts were affected. For example, over 9,000 US banks failed throughout the duration of the Great Depression, which represents the worst period of bank failures in the United States. Prior to 1933, any money in an account held at a failing bank was lost forever, regardless of the amount. In 1933, however, the **Glass-Steagall Act** created the **Federal Deposit Insurance Corporation (FDIC).** The purpose of the FDIC is to provide deposit insurance to the typical depositor so that the amount, up to a limit, is guaranteed by the government. The current guaranteed amount is $250,000 per depositor per insured bank. The existence of the FDIC and other financial regulations today have made the financial system, less (but not completely) unstable.

EFFECTS OF BUSINESS CYCLES ON FIRMS

When a recession hits, workers decrease their spending due to expectations about their current and future incomes decreasing. However, reduction in consumer spending does not affect all goods and services equally. There are two types of goods: **durable goods,** which by definition are expected to last three or more years; and **nondurable goods,** which are goods that are consumed immediately, like food and clothing, or are expected to last less than three years. The purchase of durable goods like furniture, appliances, and automobiles is more strongly affected by recessions. Thus, firms selling durable goods are more likely to be hit hard by a recession.

THE EFFECT OF THE BUSINESS CYCLE ON INFLATION

As discussed, the inflation rate measures the change in the price level (using the change in the CPI) from one year to the next. During periods of expansion, demand for goods and services by consumers and firms and even government is high relative to supply. This high level of demand results in price increases (i.e., high inflation). During recessions, demand for goods and services is low relative to supply, resulting in prices increasing more slowly or even decreasing, leading to low levels of inflation or even deflation. Inflation tends to rise toward the end of an expansion and fall over the course of a recession.

THE BUSINESS CYCLE IN SUMMARY

Typically, during contractions (i.e., recessions):

- Unemployment rises
- Inflation may fall (and may be negative)
- Output (GDP) falls

Typically, during expansions (i.e., booms):

- Unemployment declines
- Increase in the inflation rate (if recovery is strong)
- Output (GDP) rises

In the 1960s, economist Arthur Okun found that there is a quantitative relationship between changes in real GDP and the unemployment rate. This relationship is now referred to as **Okun's law.** It states that, for example, a 1% point drop in the unemployment rate, UR, is associated with a 0.5% point boost (increase) to real GDP.

Mathematically, Okun's law can be written as:

Percentage change in UR = 1.5% – 0.5 × (percentage change in real GDP)

We now turn the study of unemployment.

Employment and Unemployment

Statistics on unemployment are very important to the government and to a country's central bank. They provide vital information on the proportion of individuals that are actively producing goods and services in an economy. Furthermore, addressing the issue of unemployment requires information about the extent and nature of the problem. This information is used by government policy makers to make decisions on any government action that may need to be taken to correct the pain of unemployment.

In the United States, the BLS is responsible for analyzing information on the various aspects of employment. A monthly survey called the Current Population Survey (CPS) is used to measure the extent of unemployment in the country. The CPS has been conducted in the United States every month since 1940 and is the responsibility of the US Census Bureau. In particular, according to the US Census Bureau, the CPS provides a comprehensive body of data on the labor force, employment, unemployment, persons not in the labor force, hours of work, earnings, and other demographic and labor force characteristics. The CPS samples the civilian, noninstitutionalized population aged 16 years or older.

For the purposes of labor force statistics, the US population is divided into three groups:

- **Employed:** A person is considered employed if the majority of the previous week was spent working at a paid job.
- **Unemployed:** A person is considered unemployed if he or she is not working but

    (i) is looking for work and ready, willing, and able to work;
    (ii) is temporarily laid off; or
    (iii) is waiting to start a new job.

- **Not in the labor force:** Anyone who does not fit the definitions of *employed* or *unemployed* is deemed not to be part of the labor force. This includes children, the elderly, full-time students not working, members of the armed forced, and those who are institutionalized.

Important: The **labor force** is the sum of employed and unemployed individuals. Stated another way, the **total labor force = employed individuals + unemployed individuals**.

THE DETAILS

Individuals are considered employed if they engaged in any paid work, whether full-time or part-time, during the survey reference week. Individuals who have a job at which they did not work during the survey week because of reasons that include being on vacation, on maternity or paternity leave, taking time off for family or personal obligations, or being involved in a labor dispute are also considered employed.

Individuals are classified as unemployed if they did not have a job but were actively looking for work in the four weeks prior to the survey reference week and are currently available for work.

Individuals who were not holding paid jobs and those who are not looking for work are classified as "not in the labor force." A large number of those classified as not in the labor force are students and retirees.

Given these definitions, we can now calculate the following labor force statistics:

1. The **unemployment rate, UR:** the percentage of individuals who are part of the labor force but who are unemployed

$$UR = \frac{number\ of\ unemployed\ individuals}{labor\ force} \times 100$$

2. The **labor force participation rate:** the percentage of the adult population (greater than or equal to 16 years of age) that is in the labor force

$$UR = \frac{labor\ force}{adult\ population} \times 100$$

Application Questions

CALCULATING UNEMPLOYMENT RATES

Compute the (1) labor force, (2) unemployment rate, (3) adult population, and (4) labor force participation rate using these data from the country of San Marchello:

Number of unemployed individuals = 1,580,000
Number of employed individuals = 19,080,000
Number of individuals not in the labor force = 9,000,000

SOLUTIONS

$$\begin{aligned} Labor\ force &= employed + unemployed \\ &= 19{,}080{,}000 + 1{,}580{,}000 \\ &= 20{,}660{,}000 \end{aligned}$$

$$\begin{aligned} Unemployment\ rate &= 100 \times (unemployed)/(labor\ force) \\ &= 100 \times 1{,}580{,}000/20{,}660{,}000 \\ &= 7.65\% \end{aligned}$$

$$\begin{aligned} Population &= labor\ force + not\ in\ labor\ force \\ &= 20{,}660{,}000 + 9{,}000{,}000 \\ &= 29{,}660{,}000 \end{aligned}$$

$$\begin{aligned} LF\ partic.\ rate &= 100 \times (labor\ force)/(population) \\ &= 100 \times 20{,}660{,}000/29{,}660{,}000 \\ &= 69.7\% \end{aligned}$$

Unemployment Rates: The Demographics

The unemployment rate that is announced to the public is an average rate for all age, gender, and ethnic groups. Unemployment rates, however, are not uniform across all demographic groups, as illustrated in figure 9.5. Younger workers tend to have a higher unemployment rate, while middle-aged workers tend to have a much lower unemployment that is at or sometimes below the national average. When it comes to gender, men and women tend to have nearly identical average unemployment rates. Slightly different rates occur in both times of recession and boom, which is likely due to the types of jobs held by men versus those held by women. Since the late 1980s, recessions tend to hurt men more than women, such that men have a slightly higher unemployment rates than female. However, during the expansionary phase of a business cycle, men tend to have lower unemployment rates than women.

The unemployment rate for African Americans is higher than the rates for all other ethnic groups, which may be a result of both lower educational attainment than other groups and discrimination faced in the labor market. However, unemployment rates for African Americans reached their lowest level before rising again during the Great Recession of 2008–2009.

Thought Question

Although not depicted in figure 9.5, individuals with the least amount of formal education had the highest unemployment rates. What are some reasons for this observation?

FIGURE 9.5 Unemployment Rates for Different Groups

	Total		White		Black or African American		Asian		Hispanic or Latino	
Age and sex	3rd 2015	3rd 2016	3rd 2015	3rd 2016	3rd 2015	3rd 2016	3rd 2015	3rd 2016	3rd 2015	3rd 2016
Total, 16 years and over	5.2	5	4.5	4.4	9.5	8.5	3.7	4	6.5	5.8
16 to 19 years	16.6	15.9	14	14.2	31.7	28	14.7	12.4	20.2	17.8
25 years and over	4.2	4.1	3.7	3.6	7.5	6.8	3.1	3.5	5.4	4.7
Men, 16 years and over	4.9	4.8	4.3	4.3	9.7	8.9	3.5	3.6	5.7	5.2
16 to 19 years	17	16.4	14.2	13.9	34	33.3	17.7	15.5	20.2	19
25 years and over	3.9	3.8	3.4	3.4	7.6	6.6	2.9	3	4.5	4
Women, 16 years and over	5.5	5.2	4.8	4.5	9.4	8.2	4	4.5	7.6	6.6
16 to 19 years	16.2	15.3	13.6	14.6	29.9	23.1	11.2	8.9	20.3	16.3
25 years and over	4.6	4.4	4.1	3.8	7.5	7	3.4	4	6.6	5.7

Source: Bureau of Labor Statistics, "Labor Force Statistics from the Current Population Survey," January 19, 2018, https://www.bls.gov/cps/cpsaat24.htm.

Limitations of the Unemployment Rate

When presented with an unemployment rate, one would assume it is representative of the realities of the economy. That is, when the unemployment rate is low, we assume that the economy is functioning well. If it is high, then it indicates a poorly functioning economy. However, the unemployment rate can at times be misleading. Let us take three examples to illustrate this point.

Example 1

Assume a representative individual, John, loses his job and immediately starts searching for a new one. What happens to the unemployment rate? Does the unemployment rate give an accurate impression of what is occurring in the labor market? Certainly, in this case, the unemployment rate is on the rise, and it correctly indicates that the economy is not performing well.

Example 2

Assume in this example that Torsellini, a software engineer, has been laid off. He was earning $150,000 per year. Upon losing his job, he accepts another as a part-time Walmart greeter for $12 per hour. What happens to the unemployment rate? Does the unemployment rate give an accurate impression of what is occurring in the labor market? In this example, Torsellini remains employed through his transition from one job to the other. The unemployment rate would remain unchanged and would indicate no change in the economy or labor market. However, this is misleading. A well-paying full-time job was lost and a part-time, low-paying job was created. This is not a pattern one would like to see occur in the labor market.

Example 3

Now assume that Mario, a pulp and paper mill worker, lost his job last year when the mill ceased operations. He was looking for work, found none, and became discouraged. He has since given up looking for work. What happens to the unemployment rate in this case? Does the unemployment rate give an accurate impression of what is occurring in the labor market? There are two possible answers. One, the unemployment rate falls because Mario is discouraged (not looking for work) and thus no longer counted as unemployed. Two, given that Mario would not be counted as unemployed, he would also not be counted as part of the labor force. Thus, the unemployment rate can be approximately unchanged if we assume that the labor force (the denominator) is much greater than those unemployed (the numerator) such that one person will not significantly affect the overall rate. However, if we are talking about general effects of the average worker in these types of situations, we can simply conclude that the unemployment rate falls. A falling unemployment rate gives the impression that the economy and the labor market are improving. However, neither the economy nor the labor market are actually on the mend.

DISCOURAGED WORKERS

In the third example, we encountered Mario, a discouraged worker. This is an official BLS designation of individuals who would like to work but have given up looking for jobs. They are classified as "not in the labor force" rather than "unemployed." Individuals who give up looking for jobs and withdraw from the labor market altogether do so when there are few jobs available, and this is usually an indication of a poorly performing economy. Discouraged individuals may return to the labor market if they determine that the economy is doing better. When a discouraged worker begins to search for a job again, he or she will then be classified as "unemployed." Thus, the unemployment rate may rise even though economic prospects may be improving.

Why Are There Always Some People Unemployed? Three Types of Unemployment

Economists distinguish between three types of unemployment because each has a different effect on the economy. The three types of unemployment are the following:

1. **Cyclical unemployment**
   This type of unemployment, as the name suggests, is associated with business cycles and occurs when aggregate (total) demand is insufficient to create full employment. Cyclical unemployment is the deviation of unemployment from its "natural rate."

   Even when the economy is doing well, there is always some "natural" unemployment, which is the sum of the two following types of unemployment:

2. **Frictional unemployment**
   Frictional unemployment occurs when workers spend time searching for the jobs that best suit their skills and tastes. It is usually a short-term phenomenon for most workers.

3. **Structural unemployment**
   Structural unemployment occurs when there are fewer jobs than workers. There are several reasons that this type of unemployment exists:

   1. During economic downturns, it is difficult to adjust wages downward because of fixed contracts or unionization of workers. This makes some wages "sticky." Due to "sticky wages," employers are forced to lay off some workers. Sticky wages do not adjust quickly enough so that all workers with any given skill set would be employed.
   2. Structural unemployment may also arise due to a mismatch of skill and location (e.g., a skilled logger living in an area without rivers in which he can employ his logging skills).
   3. Structural unemployment can result when a new technology makes a worker's skill obsolete (e.g., cartoon drawers at Disney are replaced with digital cartoon creation software).

There is some evidence that unions (which restrict entry into specific occupations), license restrictions on professions, and minimum wage laws can increase structural unemployment. Government labor market policies influence how many jobs businesses wish to create, thereby affecting structural unemployment. This type of unemployment is usually longer-term unemployment.

Application Questions

Are the following cyclically, frictionally, or structurally unemployed?

a. A pulp mill worker is laid off because of excess inventory in British Columbia.
b. A fish plant worker is laid off because of lack of fish in the cod industry in the northeastern United States.
c. A typist is laid off because employees have been given their own computers.
d. A plumber quits her job in Boston and moves to Cleveland to find work.

SOLUTIONS

a. A pulp mill worker is laid off because of excess inventory in British Columbia.
   Cyclically
b. A fish plant worker is laid off because of lack of fish in the cod industry in the northeastern United States.
   Structurally
c. A typist is laid off because employees have been given their own computers.
   Structurally
d. A plumber quits her job in Boston and moves to Cleveland to find work.
   Frictionally

Help for the Unemployed and the Natural Rate of Unemployment

The US Department of Labor's **unemployment insurance** programs provide unemployment benefits to workers who become unemployed through no fault of their own as long as they meet certain eligibility requirements. These unemployment benefits are designed to help those who are cyclically unemployed during times of recession, but they are provided to those who are structurally unemployed as well during times of recession and boom. These benefits, along with other government labor policies, can have a long-term effect on the rate of structural unemployment. Any policy that affects structural unemployment will also affect the natural rate of unemployment. We will discuss such possible effects.

As we have discussed, the natural rate of unemployment = frictional + structural unemployment. It does not reflect cyclical unemployment. Rather, it is the unemployment rate that is estimated to prevail in the long-run macroeconomic equilibrium. Most economists consider the natural rate of unemployment to be about 5% for the United States. Although it is called "natural," the natural rate of unemployment actually differs for different countries. This is a result of differences in structural unemployment. As discussed in the previous section, some economists have suggested that structural unemployment may arise from two sources: government/labor market regulations that raise the costs of hiring new employees, and **hysteresis.** In labor economics, hysteresis refers to the delayed effects of unemployment. As unemployment increases, more workers adjust to a lower standard of living. This adjustment acclimatized workers to their new lower living standard, and consequently, they no longer desire to work as hard or at all to achieve the previously higher living standard.

Let us compare the unemployment rates of the United States with those of the four largest economies of continental western Europe; namely France, Germany, Italy, and Spain. The unemployment rate for the United States for the years 1998 to 2007 fluctuated between 4% and 6%. For the same time period, the unemployment rate in France never dropped below 7%, ranging between 7% and 11%. The unemployment rate of Italy ranged between 6% and 11%, while that of Spain ranged from 8% to 15% (as of December 2016, it stood at nearly 19%). Germany's unemployment rate fared a little better, ranging between 5% and 9% for the same period. These differences are not a result of recessions, but mostly due to differences in structural unemployment.

One difference between these European countries and the United States is that France, Germany, Italy, and Spain have not been able to fully recover from the unemployment disasters of the early 1980s—giving rise to hysteresis. The high unemployment levels from the 1980s reduced labor force participation and resulted in involuntary reductions in hours. This also happened in the United States, but to a lesser extent. Furthermore, wages in these four European countries are far more rigid or "sticky" than they are in the United States. The sticky wages do not adjust to clear the labor market so that adverse supply shocks (e.g., increase in taxes, unemployment insurance benefits or wages) that reduce the demand for labor create unemployment. Some economists have argued that these differences in unemployment rates are a result of union behavior and/or government policies. For example, in France, government policy requires employers to offer their workers long-term contracts. As a result, employers have less incentive to hire more workers because it becomes difficult for them to get rid of those who are unproductive. To address this structural unemployment issue, the French government provided subsidies to firms that hire younger worker as long as the firm promises not to replace older workers with those young workers.

On the supply side of the labor market, public policies to assist the unemployed can act as disincentives to look for work. For example, if a worker who loses a job is provided with numerous entitlements, such as unemployment insurance and government medical benefits, then the opportunity cost of being unemployed is lower than it would be otherwise. With a lower opportunity cost, the unemployed individual is less inclined to search for a new job. More importantly, it has been found that it is not just the amount of these benefits that reduces one's incentive to find a new job, but the length of time in which an unemployed individual can receive the benefits. A country like the United States that provides much less generous assistance for the unemployed may provide more of an incentive for finding employment than a country like France that provides far more generous help that can last for several years (depending on an individual's eligibility).

Fiscal Policy

Fiscal activity or policy refers to the federal government's taxation (revenue) and spending policies. The use of fiscal policy can have a positive or negative effect on the business cycle, depending on the timing and extent of the fiscal action taken by the government. Generally, the federal government uses fiscal policies to ensure adequate levels of employment. When the business cycle takes a downturn, the government has three fiscal tools to achieve full employment levels:

1. Direct spending
2. Taxation
3. Transfer payments

Increases in 1 and 3 and decreases in 2 result in **expansionary fiscal policy.**

Direct spending entails government spending on goods and services such as infrastructure repair and upgrading, spending on scientific and medical research, acquisition of military goods, and so on. An increase in direct spending increases overall or aggregate demand of goods and services in an economy and thus should result in increased employment levels and possibly in an increased rate of inflation.

Decreases in taxes allow households and firms to retain more of their income. This increased amount of income that is net of taxes, called **disposable income,** can either be saved or spent. Usually, there is some portion of the newly available disposable income (i.e., after the tax break) that is spent on goods and services. Thus, tax reductions increase overall demand for goods and services, which also leads to increased employment and inflation levels.

Transfer payments by the government entail payments such as grants and subsidies to firms and payments such as Social Security and unemployment benefits to households. An increase in these payments leads to higher incomes for firms and households. In turn, this additional income can be used for consumption and/or investment, which will result in increased demand and thus higher levels of employment and inflation.

In times of business cycle peaks, inflationary pressures may be of concern. Thus, the government may use fiscal policy to reduce overall demand of goods and services. Decreases in direct spending and transfer payments and increases in taxation levels result in **contractionary fiscal policy.** Contractionary fiscal policy can lead to a reduction in the rate of inflation, but it is usually not used when unemployment is high. An overly aggressive use of contractionary fiscal policy can lead to increased unemployment and cause recession (or make one worse).

Federal government spending is usually **countercyclical** (i.e., going against the business cycle) such that there is increased spending when the economy is depressed. State and local government spending is usually **procyclical** (i.e., going with the phases of the business cycle) such that spending increases when economy is doing well.

TO WHAT EXTENT DOES GOVERNMENT SPENDING HELP THE ECONOMY?

To summarize, an increase in government spending, which **has a similar effect to an increase in private investment,** increases an economy's aggregate demand for goods and services. The increase in demand for goods and services causes firms to employ more workers and expand production. As firms employ more workers, the unemployment rate decreases and households see an increase in their disposable incomes. Subsequently, aggregate demand increases again. The increase in aggregate demand causes firms to employ more workers, and the effect continues. This continued effect is called the **Keynesian multiplier effect.** The Keynesian multiplier effect differs based on the type of spending and basically magnifies the effect of government spending on the economy by some factor. For example, if the Keynesian multiplier is 2, then an increase in direct government spending, G, by $10 million will generate 2 times $10 million in GDP.

Mathematically, we can write it as follows: **change in GDP = multiplier × change in G.** Figure 9.6 lists the various Keynesian multipliers for different types of government fiscal initiatives. From the figure, we note, for example, that 2-year tax cuts for lower- and middle-income people result in a bigger change in GDP that a 1-year tax cut to higher-income people. If the federal government decides to cut taxes by $1 billion, then 2-year tax cuts for lower- and middle-income people increases GDP between $0.3 billion and $1.5 billion, while the same $1 billion in tax cuts for 1 year to higher-income people increases GDP between $0.1 billion and $0.6 billion. The ability of government to increase GDP beyond that of its own spending amount indicates that government budgeting is not equivalent to household budgeting, as is popularly expressed.

FIGURE 9.6 Ranges for US Fiscal Multipliers Based on Different Types of Government Spending

Spending Type	Fiscal Multiplier: Lower Bound Estimate	Fiscal Multiplier: Upper Bound Estimate
Purchases of goods and services by the federal government	0.5	2.5
Transfer payments to state and local governments for infrastructure	0.4	2.2
Transfer payments to state and local governments for other purposes	0.4	1.8
Transfer payments to individuals	0.4	2.1
Transfer payments to retirees	0.2	1.0
2-year tax cuts for lower- and middle-income people	0.3	1.5
1-year tax cut to higher-income people	0.1	0.6
Extension of first-time homebuyer credit	0.2	0.8

Source: US Congressional Budget Office, 2015.

MANDATORY VERSUS DISCRETIONARY SPENDING

Although the federal government uses fiscal policy to achieve certain ends, it cannot spend at will. There are two types of spending that the federal government undertakes: (1) mandatory spending and (2) discretionary spending.

Mandatory spending is not subject to Congress's annual appropriations process. It includes Social Security, Medicare, Medicaid, food stamps, federal employee pensions, and so on. Mandatory spending consituted 65% of federal government spending in 2015. **Discretionary spending,** however, is subject to Congress's annual appropriations process. It includes defense, highways, federal employee salaries, foreign aid, and so on. Discretionary spending constituted 29% of federal government spending. The remaining 6% of government spending was used to pay the interest on the national debt.

THE FEDERAL BUDGET

The federal government's revenues are generated from the collection of payroll taxes on wages and earnings, taxes on corporate profits, federal excise taxes, estate and gift taxes, customs duties, earnings from the federal reserve system, and other fees and charges. If government revenues are greater than government spending, called **outlays** (i.e., transfers plus direct spending), then we have a government **budget surplus.** If government revenues are less than government outlays, then we have a government **budget deficit.** Government deficits are sometimes expressed as a percentage of nominal GDP as a way to show effects of inflation and ability of the economy to "handle" the deficit. The federal deficit—as measured by government borrowing—reached 6% of GDP in 1983, a recession year. The deficit was reduced as a percentage of GDP from the early 1990s until 1998, when the budget went into surplus. When there is a surplus, some **debt,** which is the accumulation of deficits, is retired. From 1998 to 2001, the government retired some debt. After 2000, a recession that was coupled with tax cuts from the Bush administration tax cuts returned surplus budgets to deficit budgets. The Great Recession led to even larger deficits, reaching 10% of GDP. The deficit as a percentage of GDP began to decline shortly afterward. Automatic stabilizers were not present during the Great Depression. Figure 9.7 illustrates how total government spending in 2016 was divided among various activities.

FIGURE 9.7 Government Outlays, 2016, as a Percentage of Total Spending

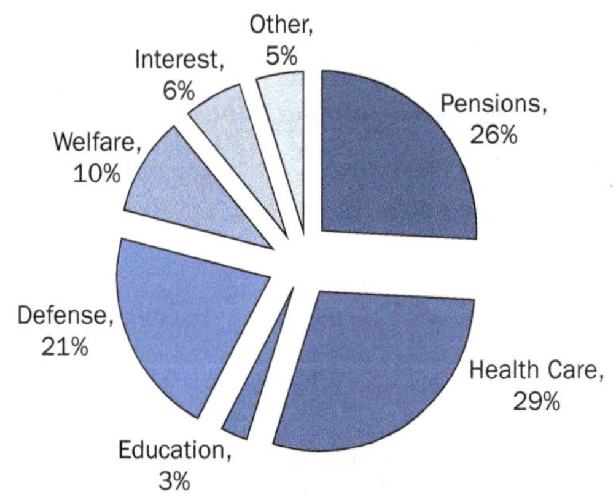

Source: US Government Publishing Office.

Chapter Summary

At the beginning of the chapter, we asked whether spending more is good for the economy. We now have an answer. Given that an economy uses investment goods and services to produce other goods and services, saving, to an extent, instead of consuming will promote rather than reduce economic growth.

This chapter also examined the different types of unemployment, noting that zero unemployment is not a realistic policy goal. The chapter noted that unemployment rates are not uniform if they are broken down by gender, ethnicity, or educational attainment. Helping the unemployed and discouraged workers can be achieved by fiscal policy—or fiscal policy can exasperate it. Lastly, it is important to note that business cycles have become a staple of the modern, advanced economy, and that government social safety nets have moderated the severity of business cycle troughs.

Roman coinage (Denarius, 46 B.C.) featuring Titus Carisius, who defeated the Astures in Hispania.

Source: *Copyright © Classical Numismatic Group, Inc. (CC BY-SA 2.5) at https://commons.wikimedia.org/wiki/File:Moneyer_issues_of_Imperatorial_Rome._T._Carisius._46_BC._AR_Denarius_%2817mm%2C_4.10_g%2C_7h%29.jpg.*

CHAPTER 10

Is Money Really Created With a Fountain Pen?

MONEY AND MONETARY POLICY IN A NUTSHELL

LEARNING EXPECTATIONS

- To differentiate between the concepts of money, money supply, and inflation
- To understand the complementary roles of commercial banks and central banks
- To describe monetary policy and apply its tools in different economic contexts

In this chapter, we will look at the basic nature and functions of money and the banking system. Although we all use money daily, we do not all consider exactly what money is, what it can do, where it comes from, and who controls the amount available in an economy. We will examine each of these inquiries, in turn.

What Is Money?

Money (or the "money supply") is anything that is generally accepted as payment for goods or services or in the repayment of debts. Thus, *money* has a very broad definition. Money is a stock concept (a variable measured at a specific point in time) and it is different from:

- **wealth,** which is the total collection of assets that serve to store value; and
- **income,** which is flow of earnings per unit of time (a flow, not a stock variable).

WHAT ARE THE FUNCTIONS OF MONEY?

We list three functions of money. Money can function as a medium of exchange, a unit of account, and a store of value. Money as a medium of exchange eliminates the trouble of finding a **double coincidence of wants,** as occurs in a barter system, and it reduces transaction costs. Without money, an individual who has extra chickens, for example, but wants salt for curing his meat would have to find someone who has salt to trade (i.e., barter) and also wants chicken in exchange for salt. This is difficult and time consuming for both parties. Thus, money allows a society to overcome the double coincidence of wants and thus use its time and resources more efficiently. The individuals who are no longer spending time looking for the appropriate person with whom to barter (called search costs) can devote their time to learning tasks and specializing in a trade.

1. As a **medium of exchange,** money must also have the following characteristics:
   - be easily standardized
   - be widely accepted
   - be divisible
   - be easy to carry
   - not deteriorate quickly
2. As a **unit of account,** money provides for a common way or unit by which the value of every good or service can be expressed. Rather than say that 4 socks buys 12 bananas or 1 haircut buys 7 bottles of water, every item or service is expressed in dollars, euros, or any other common currency unit. This also leads money to
   - be used to measure value in the economy, and
   - reduce transaction costs.

3. As a **store of value,** money is one way economic agents hold wealth. Of course, there are other forms of wealth that agents can hold, such as real estate, cars, stocks, bonds, precious metals, insurance policies, and so on. However, money is the only form of wealth that is the most readily convertible into other goods and service. Which is easier: to turn a car into groceries or money into groceries? This ready convertibility of money is referred to as liquidity. Thus, money is the most liquid of all forms of wealth and is used to save purchasing power over time, but it loses value during periods of inflation.

PAYMENT SYSTEMS (FORMS OF MONEY)

Physical goods, such as gold, silver pearls, feathers, cigarettes, and others, when used to accomplish trade, are called **commodity money.** Commodity money usually has *intrinsic value*; this is, it has value on its own such that it can be useful in some way other than as a medium of exchange.

Another form of money is called **commodity-backed money,** which is money whose value is backed by gold, silver, or any other commodity. Thus, if there is $1 million of paper money circulating in an economy, then it must be that a million dollars' worth of gold also exists to back up the amount of paper money. Historically, people used gold to help facilitate buying and selling. Individuals brought their gold to a goldsmith, who had secure storage facilities, and he would issue them a receipt (the rudiments of a banking system). The goldsmith-issued receipts were then used to buy goods, without the need to redeem the gold itself.

Our current use of money is **fiat money,** which is money authorized by a central bank or government and is the definitive money. Fiat money is neither convertible to nor backed by any gold, silver, or any other commodity. Furthermore, it has *no intrinsic value*. In the United States, Federal Reserve Notes are fiat money. What makes fiat money valuable is everyone's confidence or belief that it actually is valuable. A system in which the definitive money is money authorized by a governmental body is referred to as **legal tender.** If money is authorized as legal tender, then it must be accepted to discharge debts and to pay taxes.

COMMODITY MONEY: THE GIANT STONE MONEY OF YAP.

Surnce: *Copyright © Yanajin33 (CC BY-SA 2.5) at https://commons.wikimedia.org/wiki/File%3ALittle_world%2C_Aichi_prefecture_-_House_of_Yap_in_Micronesia_-_Stone_money_%28Replica%29.jpg.*

EXAMPLE OF COMMODITY MONEY: THE GIANT STONE MONEY OF YAP

Imagine large, circular stone disks carved out of limestone, where some stones weigh so much that scores of men are required to carry them. For hundreds of years, residents of the Pacific islands of Yap used these stone disks as money. The disks were quarried in the distant island Palau and returned some 500 kilometers (about 300 miles) to Yap in sailing canoes. The value of any particular stone depended on its size and the difficulty of transport, including the number of people who died quarrying it. There is still some limited use of these disks today.

Measuring the Money Supply

The gold trade led to modern banking. Understanding the modern system of banking is crucial to understanding how a country uses the system to stabilize inflation and unemployment rates. When goldsmiths provided depositors of gold with receipts, those receipts circulated widely and exchanged hands often enough that most people did not redeem their receipts for gold. As long as goldsmiths held some gold ***in reserve,*** there was enough left to cover redemptions of those receipts that were actually brought back to the goldsmith. Given this observation, the goldsmith actually issued more receipts than there was gold to back those receipts. Unless everyone came to the goldsmith at the same time to redeem the receipts, this system worked out fairly well. The result of this system where the amount loaned was greater than the gold held in reserve is an increase the **supply of money. The money supply** is thus broadly defined as the quantity of an object circulating in the economy at a point in time that can be used as money.

THE MONEY SUPPLY AND MONEY AGGREGATES: THE COMPONENTS OF M1 AND M2

How do we measure the money supply? Who measures it? Which particular "objects" or assets can be called "money"?

First, we must recognize that there are different measures of money supply. The **Federal Reserve System** (simply referred to as **the Fed**), which is the **central bank** or **monetary authority** in the United States, has developed definitions of money that include assets broader than currency, called monetary aggregates: ***M1, M2,*** *and* broader monetary aggregates. The measures or constructs of monetary aggregates all use the concept of **liquidity.** The more liquid an asset, the more readily available it is for spending.

The most liquid money aggregate is called M1. This measure of the money supply includes the following:

- Currency (cash and coins)
- Traveler's checks
- Demand deposits and other checkable deposits

The second measure of money is M2. M2 includes M1 plus a broader set of financial assets held principally by households. Thus, M2 = M1 + the following:

- Savings deposits
- Small-denomination time deposits (time deposits in amounts of less than $100,000)
- Balances in retail money market mutual funds

There are other, more inclusive money aggregates that central banks construct, such as M3. For the United States, however, the Federal Reserve System stopped publishing the M3 money supply aggregate as of March 23, 2006. M3 includes or included all of M2 (which also includes M1) plus large-denomination time deposits of $100,000 or more, balances in institutional money funds, repurchase liabilities issued by depository institutions, and Eurodollars, which are US dollar deposits by US residents held in Europe or elsewhere outside the United States, such as at foreign branches of US banks and at all banks in the United Kingdom and Canada.

The US M1 money supply totaled about $2.8 trillion in April 2014. Currency accounted for about 43% of M1, and checkable deposits accounted for 57%. Traveler's checks were a negligible fraction of the M1 money stock. By year end of 2016, the M1 money supply totaled $3.3 trillion, which is a 17.9% increase in less than two years. M2 increased to $13.3 trillion in 2016, up 18.8% from $11.2 trillion in April 2016. Figure 10.1 plots the time series trend of both M1 and M2 since 1982. Notice that the money supply has grown more rapidly since 2004 than any previous period. Changes in the monetary aggregates indicate the direction of monetary policy as well as the outlook for economic activity and inflationary pressures.

FIGURE 10.1 M2 Money Stock, Billions of Dollars, Weekly, Seasonally Adjusted, 1982-2016

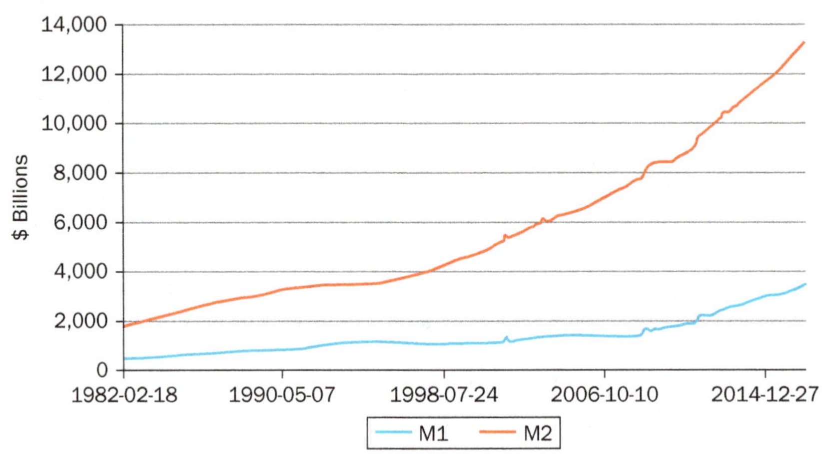

Sources: Board of Governors of the Federal Reserve System (US), M1 Money Stock [M1], retrieved from FRED, Federal Reserve Bank of St. Louis, December 15, 2016, https://fred.stlouisfed.org/series/M1.

Board of Governors of the Federal Reserve System (US), M2 Money Stock [M2], retrieved from FRED, Federal Reserve Bank of St. Louis, December 15, 2016, https://fred.stlouisfed.org/series/M2.

Thought Question

Does the M1 money supply emphasize money as a temporary store of value?

Central Banks

There are two different financial institutions that play a critical role in stabilizing the economy. The second type, commercial banks, serves you, the individual or household, and businesses. The first type is the central bank. Such banks do not accept deposits from households or from businesses. Rather, central banks serve commercial banks, and the majority of their deposits come from the federal government and from commercial banks. It is for this reason that central banks are sometimes referred to as the banker's bank. It is also the government's bank. Recall that in the United States, the central bank is called the **Federal Reserve System,** or the Fed for short.

A country's *monetary authority* is responsible for

- issuing currency and controlling the amount of money in circulation,
- serving as a bank to the government and as a bank to other banks, and
- influencing interest rates.

CONTROLLING THE MONEY SUPPLY

The Fed hopes that by controlling the money supply, it can influence important economic variables such as GDP, unemployment, and inflation. The Fed needs to find a measure of money that is strongly linked to those economic variables. The different measures of money—M1 and M2—are correlated with different objectives of the central bank, which is the reason why the Fed measures money in different ways.

The Fed really wants to keep its eye on GDP and its growth, the unemployment rate, and the rate at which prices grow. However, the Fed or any central bank cannot control any of these variables directly. It can only control the money supply. Fortunately, there is a strong correlation between the growth of money supply and the growth rates of GDP, unemployment, and inflation. Thus, by measuring and then controlling the money supply, central banks hope to influence the other economic variables indirectly.

Central banks influence the money supply by directly creating money. However, they are not the only ones that can create money. Commercial banks are also involved in money creation, but the process is quite different. In the next sections, we will examine how commercial banks create money and then examine how central banks, in a very different fashion, do so as well.

Money Creation by Commercial Banks

Commercial banks are financial institutions that accept deposits and makes loans directly from and to households and businesses. The assembly of all commercial banks is known as the **banking system.** *There are other* financial institutions that are part of the banking system, such as credit unions and savings and loan associations, but these are not in the strictest definition banks. The bank system is a powerful institution because it has massive power to potentially stabilize the economy in times of recessions or, alternatively, the power to potentially cause recessions if it acts irresponsibly (as it did in the years prior to the Great Recession of 2008–2009).

The two important functions of a commercial bank are to accept deposits and make loans. Commercial banks can provide personal loans to individuals and households, or they can extend commercial loans to firms. **Mortgage loans** are a type of loan made to those who wish to buy homes or other structures or lands. **Consumer** or **personal loans** are made to people who want to buy cars and personal fixtures such as furniture, appliances, renovations, and so forth. The process by which commercial banks provide loans is the process by which they concomitantly create money. It is true that commercial banks use deposits to make loans, but the amount of loans made far exceeds the amount of deposits any commercial bank has in reserves. Rather, commercial banks create money, in the form of bank deposits, by making new loans. For example, when a bank makes a mortgage loan of $500,000 to each of many clients, it typically does not have enough money on reserve for all the mortgage loans. Also, it does not typically provide clients with $500,000 in cash. Rather, the commercial bank will credit the borrower's bank account with a bank deposit equal to the amount of the mortgage. At the moment the deposit is made in the borrower's account, new money, which did not exist anywhere prior to the deposit, is created. For this reason, some economists have referred to bank deposits as "fountain pen money," which is money created at the stroke of bankers' pens when they approve loans.[25]

CONSTRAINTS ON HOW COMMERCIAL BANKS CREATE MONEY

Although commercial banks create money through lending, they cannot do so freely without limit.[25] However, there are limits on the amount of loans commercials banks can extend to borrowers. Regulations set forth by a country's central bank limit the activities of commercial banks so as to maintain the resilience of the financial system. If these regulations are too lax or are not followed, bad lending practices can cripple an economy. Commercial banks also operate in a competitive market with other commercial banks, so they must be able to extend profitable loans and to mitigate the risks associated with making risky loans.

BANK PANIC OF 1837.

Source: *https://commons.wikimedia.org/wiki/File:The_times_panic_1837.jpg*

Note that although commercial banks can create money with the stroke of a pen, household and firms "destroy" the same money when they repay their debts (referred to as outstanding loans). So, if money is created and then destroyed, then how does the money supply ultimately grow over time? The ultimate constraint or limit on money creation and growth is achieved by central banks through their monetary policy. By influencing the level of interest rates in the economy, monetary policy by central banks affects the desired borrowing levels by households and firms. We will now consider, in the next section, monetary policy.

Monetary Policy and the Central Bank

Monetary policy is the set of decisions a government makes, usually through its central bank, about the amount of money in circulation in the economy. In the United States, monetary policy is conducted by the Fed. The Fed adjusts very short-term interest rates to achieve a rate of monetary expansion consistent with maintaining a low and relatively stable rate of inflation (and low unemployment).

The Federal Reserve was created by Congress in 1913 to ensure that the United States had a more stable monetary and financial system. Why did Congress think it necessary to increase stability in the financial system? It was common for the United States in the 19th and early 20th centuries to suffer from financial panics and **bank runs,** albeit the bank failure rate was lower, on average, than that of nonbanking firms. A run on a bank occurs when a large number of depositors simultaneously attempt to withdraw all of their deposits because they fear that their particular bank will be unable to repay their deposits in full. As we indicated earlier, banks only hold a small amount of depositors' money in reserve, so if the majority of depositors seek to withdraw their money, the bank will not be able to meet their demands. When this occurs, banks will shut their doors, and the depositors who had not yet retrieved their money lose it forever. Thus, the Federal Reserve has been mandated by Congress to conduct monetary policy in such a way so as to tie it to the broader goal of **promoting** a productive and stable US economy. This then contributes to higher standards of living for US citizens.

In the United States, a committee within the Federal Reserve called the **Federal Open Market Committee (FOMC)** is responsible for implementing monetary policy. The FOMC is made up of the **Board of Governors** and five reserve-bank presidents. The FOMC meets eight times throughout the year to set key interest rates. Decisions on whether there should be any increase or decrease to the money supply are also made during these meetings. Seven members, nominated by the president and confirmed by the Senate, constitute the Board of Governors. Members begin their term on the Board of Governors on February 1 of even-numbered years. A full term is 14 years. No member can be reappointed after serving a full term.

FOMC policy makers monitor and analyze a variety of economic and business information in order to assess movements in the US economy, which informs monetary policy. The economic data and surveys from business and financial markets are used to develop forecasts on the direction of economic growth, inflation, and levels of employment. Once the Fed is satisfied with its analyses and has determined that some form of action needs to take place to correct the economy's trajectory, it has three monetary policy tools at its disposal:

1. The discount rate
2. Reserve requirements

3. Open market operations

The Board of Governors is responsible for the discount rate and reserve requirements. The FOMC is responsible for open market operations.[26] Using the three tools, the Federal Reserve influences the demand for, and supply of, balances that depository institutions, such as commercial banks, hold at Federal Reserve Banks.[26] By altering the demand and supply curves for deposits, the Federal Reserve influences the direction by which the **federal funds rate** moves. **The federal funds rate is the interest rate at which commercial banks (depository institutions) lend money to *each other*.** Changes in the federal funds rate ultimately lead to changes in other short-term interest rates, foreign exchange rates, long-term interest rates, and the amount of money and credit available to firms and households.[26] These changes will then affect economic variables, such as the price level, the unemployment rate, and the rate of GDP growth.

The Three Monetary Policy Tools in Some Detail

1. DISCOUNT RATE WINDOW LENDING—CHANGING THE INTEREST RATE

The Federal Reserve Bank's regional lending facility is called the discount window. The discount window is used by the Fed as an instrument of monetary policy. It carries out its monetary policy via the **discount rate,** which is the interest rate the Fed charges eligible institutions such as commercial banks and other depository institutions on loans they receive from the discount window. These discount window loans are usually on a short-term basis because some lending institutions may need to meet temporary liquidity shortages.

Through the discount window, the Federal Reserve can influence the volume of discount loans by setting the price of loans. That is, if the Fed increases the discount rate, commercial banks will find borrowing more expensive and will thus borrow fewer funds. This reaction reduces the **monetary base** (cash plus commercial bank reserves) and the money supply. A higher discount rate also leads to pressure on other short-term interest rates such as the federal funds rate. If the Fed decreases the discount rate, commercial banks will find it less expensive to borrow money and will likely do so. This reaction grows the monetary base and increases the money supply.

Not many economists advocate the use of the discount rate as a means of controlling the money supply, because it cannot force banks to accept discount loans. Thus, the Fed does not control this policy as completely as it would open market operations, which is discussed in the sections that follow. Historically, the federal funds rate has been both above and below the discount rate. However, since 2003, the practice of setting the discount rate 1 percentage point above the federal funds rate target helps discourage (a negative incentive) commercial banks from using this monetary tool in lieu of less expensive alternative monetary policies.

To summarize,

Decreasing the federal funds (interest) rate makes it easier for commercial banks and other depository institutions to borrow from the Federal Reserve and can lead to

- ***lower unemployment (job gains) and***

- ***inflation.***

Increasing the federal funds (interest) rate makes it more difficult to borrow and can lead to

- ***higher unemployment (job losses)and***
- ***deflation or a reduction in the rate of increase of inflation.***

2. RESERVE REQUIREMENTS

Commercial banks and other depository institutions must hold **reserves** in the form of vault cash or deposits with Federal Reserve Banks. **Reserve requirements** are the amount of funds that a depository institution must hold in reserve as a ratio of specified deposits. For example, in 2006, the reserve requirement on checkable deposits was 0% on the first $8.5 million, 3% on the next $45.8 million, and 10% on any amount greater than the $45.8 million. The Board of Governors has sole authority over changes in reserve requirements, but the Fed rarely uses a change in reserve requirements as a monetary policy tool. Changing the reserve requirement is expensive because banks would have to modify their policies.[27]

The Fed can use changes in reserve requirements to control liquidity in the market. A small reserve requirement is expansionary monetary policy since it allows more money in the banking system.[27] A high reserve requirement is contractionary. It allows less liquidity and slows down economic activity.[27]

The higher the reserve requirement, the less profit a bank makes with its deposits.[27] A high requirement is more burdensome on small banks since they do not have as much money as larger banks to loan. For this reason, small banks are exempt from the reserve requirements. A small bank is one with less than $12.4 million in deposits.[27]

3. OPEN-MARKET OPERATIONS

The Fed conducts **open-market operations** when it buys **government bonds** from or sells government bonds to commercial banks:

- When the Fed buys bonds, it increases the monetary base. Buying bonds causes the money supply to increase because commercial bank reserve accounts increase, which will be lent to borrowers.
- When the Fed sells bonds, it causes the money supply to decrease because commercial banks buy the bonds with their reserves. Commercial banks will then have less to lend out to consumers and businesses.

Government Bonds

- When the US government runs a deficit, the Treasury Department must *borrow* the funds by issuing new government bonds and selling them to the public.
- The Treasury is not legally entitled to create money; only the Federal Reserve can create money.

FIGURE 10.2 The Issuance and Purchase of Government Bonds

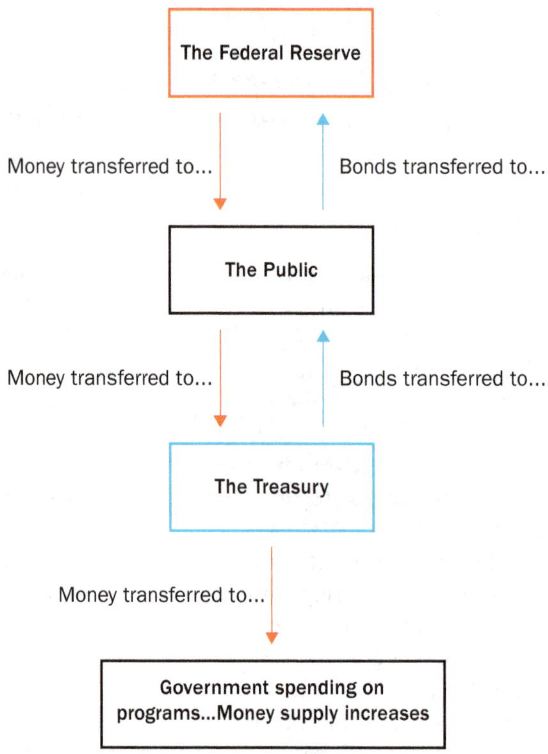

FIGURE 10.3 Summary of the Three Traditional Monetary Policy Instruments

Monetary Tool	How It Works	Who Sets the Policy/Uses the Tool
1. Discount window lending	The discount rate leads to changes on other short-term interest rates such as the federal funds rate. The federal funds rate, determines the interest rate at which banks lend money to each other.	The Board of Governors sets the rate.
2. Reserve requirements	Reserve requirements control liquidity in the market. A small reserve requirement is expansionary monetary policy since it allows more money in the banking system. A high reserve requirement is contractionary.	The Board of Governors sets the reserve requirement.
3. Open market transactions	The buying and selling of government bonds directly affects the volume of commercial bank reserves, which in turn affects the federal funds rate.	Open market transactions are directed by the Federal Open Market Committee (FOMC).

- When the public buys government bonds with money, there is a transfer of money from them to the Treasury. This action, while increasing the government debt, does not increase the money supply.
- When the Fed uses open market purchases—that is, the Fed buys government bonds from the public, which are the same bonds that the Treasury has issued/sold to finance the government's deficits—the money supply increases. This illustrates that running a government deficit and increasing the money supply are two separate decisions.
- We illustrate the buying and selling of government bonds in figure 10.2. Note that in the creation of money, the public plays the role of middleman.

While our analysis of deficit financing in the United States applies to most other countries, there are some countries that do not use the public as a middleman. In these countries, the central bank acts as if it were part of the government, issuing money by buying treasury bonds directly and usually at the will of government. This phenomenon of increasing the money supply so that the government can run a deficit is referred to as **monetizing the deficit.** This behavior can lead to uncontrolled increases in the money supply, which can lead to very large rates of inflation or hyperinflation.

The Costs of Inflation and Deflation

From an outsider's perspective, central banks seem to be obsessed with controlling price levels. Inflation, especially hyperinflation, and deflation can lead to serious socioeconomic problems and can destroy an economy very quickly. We will examine two recent cases that exhibit the deleterious effects of uncontrolled price changes on an economy: (1) hyperinflation in Zimbabwe and (2) deflation in Japan. Before we review the two cases, we will summarize the costs of inflation and deflation on an economy.

1. COSTS ASSOCIATED WITH INFLATION AND THE ZIMBABWEAN EXPERIENCE

It is important to realize that the presence of inflation is associated with nominal and real uncertainty in the movement of macroeconomic variables such as GDP, investment levels, and others. This uncertainty reduces incentive by firms to invest, which leads to lower economic growth. With inflation, market prices carry perceptions not related to scarcity. Thus, households and firms are unsure what to do—if they accelerate their purchases to avoid rising prices, then they end up stoking further rises in the price level. Inflation also leads to **tax distortions;** that is, inflation makes nominal income grow faster than real income. However, taxes like the income tax are based on nominal income and are not adjusted for inflation. So, inflation causes people to pay more taxes even when their real incomes do not increase.

Extreme levels of inflation, referred to as **hyperinflation,** destroy an economy and can lead to starvation as large parts of a society cannot afford to buy any food. Zimbabwe's severe and uncontainable inflation between 2000 and 2009 (2007–2009 were the most severe years) devastated its people. It is the only country so far in the 21st century to experience a hyperinflationary episode. By mid-2008, the International Monetary Fund put the annual inflation rate at 489 billion percent! The largest currency denomination in 2009 was the Zimbabwean 100 trillion dollar note (Z$100 trillion). Obviously, it was a worthless currency. Almost all transactions used the US dollar, South African rand, and Botswanan pula. The official exchange rate on December 31, 2008, was US$1 = Z$4 million.[28] Seven years of negative GDP growth per capita accompanied this period of inflation. The government attempted to control inflation by controlling the prices of basic goods and services, even trying to force merchants to adopt price ceilings using police force.[28]

Thought Question

What result do you think the Zimbabwean government achieved when it attempted to control inflation by controlling the prices of basic goods and services?

The result: As we learned in earlier chapters, this would lead to shortages. Indeed, in 2007 and 2008, price ceilings on food quickly resulted in food shortages because firms could not earn a profit selling at government-mandated prices.[28] Only when Zimbabwe, in 2009, abandoned its currency and adopted the US dollar did inflation decline to more manageable levels.

2. COSTS ASSOCIATED WITH DEFLATION

Deflation, meaning decreasing average prices over time, would increase the burden of household and business debts after adjusting for the decline in prices. Why? If deflation occurs, then holding cash is beneficial because $1 will buy increasingly more goods and services as prices continue to fall. However, the prospect of continuously falling prices discourages consumer spending. Consumers will put off spending indefinitely as they wait for lower prices. This decrease in demand will fulfill the prophecy of lower prices, which will in turn discourage spending. As demand falls unabated so will production of goods because inventories are kept full. As production falls, unemployment increases rapidly because wages do not adjust downward quickly enough and economic growth stagnates.

The above description of deflation describes the Japan experience since the late 1990s. The Japanese economy has been stagnant for more than 10 years. The average GDP growth rate for Japan from 1993 to 2003 was just above 1%. Given the lackluster performance in the past 15 years, including a record low of −4.80% GDP growth in the first quarter of 2009, the Japanese economy averaged only 0.51% GDP growth from 1980 until 2016.

Chapter Summary

In this chapter, we discussed the importance of money as a means to eliminate the inefficient double coincidence of wants. Money supply, in our modern economy, is tracked closely by centrals banks, which, along with commercial banks, can create new money. Although both central and commercial banks have the power to create new money, the manner in which they do so differs. Commercial banks create money, in the form of bank deposits, by making new loans. A central bank, specifically the US Federal Reserve System, creates money through open-market operations.

In addition to money creation, central banks' main role is to maintain a low and stable rate of inflation. A low and stable rate of inflation is conducive to economic growth. On the other hand, hyperinflation and deflation stifle economic growth. The control of inflation by the Federal Reserve can be carried out via three monetary policy tools—the discount rate, reserve requirements, and open-market operations.

CHAPTER 11

Will You Lose Your Job or Generate More Wealth?

MAYBE BOTH. MACROECONOMICS AND INTERNATIONAL TRADE

LEARNING EXPECTATIONS

- To define trade liberalization and describe its role in global economic growth along with arguments for and against free trade
- To describe the North American Free Trade Agreement and its effect on North American GDP
- To understand, describe, and calculate gains from trade

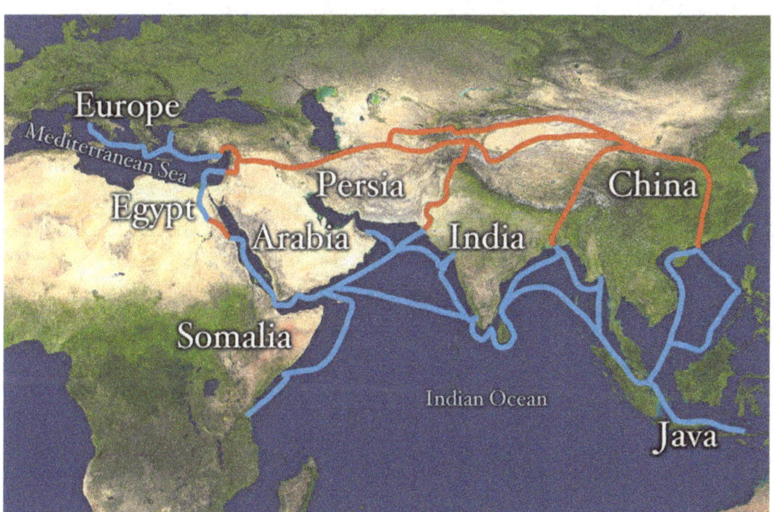

EXTENT OF SILK ROUTE/SILK ROAD: Red is land route and the blue is the sea/water route.

Source: *https://commons.wikimedia.org/wiki/File:Silk_route_copy.jpg*

The Growth of Global Trade

Trade is the exchange of goods and services between countries. Goods that are brought into a country are termed **imports,** and those sold to another country are termed **exports.** Since World War II, there has been an important shift in global trade patterns. As a share of total global output, international trade is now at about three times the level in the early 1950s, mostly as a result of the integration of rapidly growing emerging market economies.[29] Nevertheless, developed countries have a greater share of global trade than developing countries, and they usually export high-tech manufactured goods such as electronics and import low-tech primary products such as chocolate and coffee. Trading blocs such as the European Union dominate world exports.[29]

The expansion of global and regional trade (see figure 11.1) was driven by trade liberalization and subsequently by specialization in production and income convergence among the now developed nations. As a result, the greatest volume of trade occurs between the developed countries, especially between Japan, the United Kingdom, the United States, and Germany. The worldwide volume of trade, including both imports and exports, expressed as a percentage of global GDP, has been increasing over the past several decades.[30] The United States has also seen trade become an important part of its economy, although the foreign sector, as a percentage of GDP, is smaller than most other developed nations. An important development in trade occurred in 1994 when the **North American Free Trade Agreement (NAFTA)** came into effect. NAFTA created one of the world's largest free trade zones and helped foster strong economic growth and rising prosperity for Canada, the United States, and Mexico.

FIGURE 11.1 Trade Expressed as a Percentage of GDP, World and the United States, 1960-2015

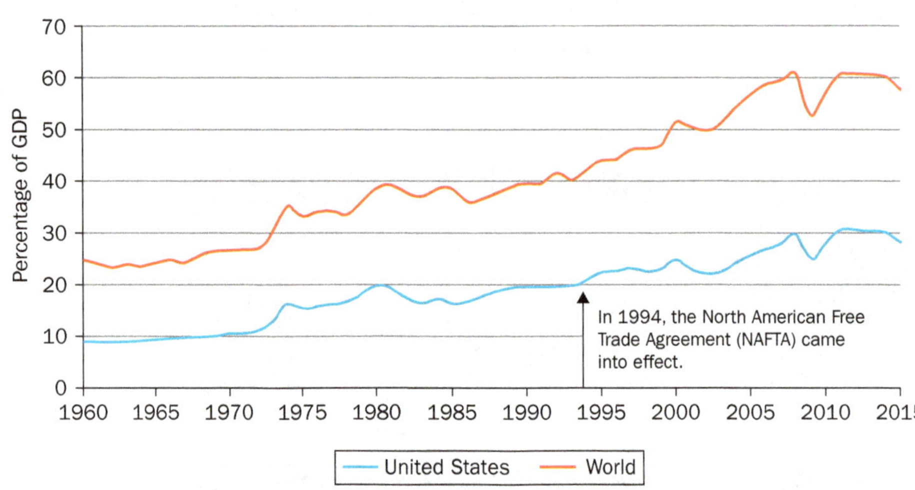

Sources: World Development Indicators, World Bank, 2016.

Liberalization in trade has occurred both multilaterally (i.e., between more than two countries) and bilaterally (between two countries) since the early 1950s. Consequently, there have been lower trade barriers in developed economies, and more recently by developing countries.[29] Along with lower trade barriers, technology-led declines in transportation costs also helped the division of production stages beyond national borders, which has permitted supply chains to become regional or even global.[29] **Global supply chains** refers to the managing of material and information outside of the factory walls, creating a network among different worldwide companies producing, handling, planning and forecasting, procuring, and distributing specific goods around the world. This growing role of global supply chains is accompanied by increased trade interconnectedness. The United States and the recent emergence of China represent important trading hubs.[29] This reflects the size of trade, the number of significant trading partners, and important overlaps between countries hosting both trade and financial centers.[29]

MONITORING AND PROMOTING TRADE: THE WTO

The World Trade Organization (WTO), which has 164 member countries, is a rules-based, member-driven international organization that deals with the rules of trade between its members. The WTO was established in 1995 and administers the WTO trade agreements, provides a forum for trade negotiations, handles trade disputes, monitors national trade policies, and administers technical assistance and training for developing countries.[31] The principles on which WTO agreements are established include a system of rules to make trade more open, predictable, and fair, while allowing flexibility for developing countries. Most of the WTO agreements are the result of the Uruguay Round of negotiations (1986–1994).[31] These agreements form the basis of the present WTO system and are designed to provide households around the world with benefits of trade.

North American Trade

Although China has been an increasingly important source of merchandise imports, the United States' neighbors, Canada and Mexico, have long been among its major trading partners. It is for this reason that NAFTA was negotiated and came into effect on January 1, 1994. NAFTA was signed by Canadian prime minister Brian Mulroney, Mexican president Carlos Salinas, and US president George H.W. Bush.[32] NAFTA strengthened the rules and procedures governing trade and investment, has set an example of the benefits of trade liberalization for the rest of the world, and was accompanied by net economic growth and rising standards of living for citizens in all three countries.[32]

PRESIDENT CLINTON AND PRESIDENT GEORGE H.W. BUSH TOGETHER AT NAFTA KICKOFF.

Source: *https://commons.wikimedia.org/wiki/File:North_American_Free_Trade_Agreement_(NAFTA)_Kickoff_01.jpg*

The Canada-United States Free Trade Agreement that preceded NAFTA was generally regarded as a successful trade agreement. For this reason, free trade was extended with NAFTA to include Mexico. Note that tariffs on covered goods traded between Canada and the United States became duty free on January 1, 1989. Under NAFTA, tariffs on all covered goods traded between Canada and Mexico, for example, were eliminated in 2008.[32] One of the unique principle elements of NAFTA is the establishment of a clear set of rules for dealing with the settlement of trade disputes. In fact, NAFTA was the first trade agreement to afford cross-border investors an impartial legal tribunal to address disagreements amicably through NAFTA's committees and working groups.[32] If no mutually acceptable solution is found, then NAFTA provides for dispute settlement procedures.[32]

It can be argued that the integration of the three North American economies has resulted in positive outcomes such that the three economies have become more innovative and competitive. In 1993, trilateral trade within the North American region was over US$288 billion.[33] In 2015, total trilateral merchandise trade amounted to over US$1.0 trillion. Although NAFTA partners have less than 7% of the world's population, they represent 28% of the world's GDP.

Canadian and Mexico now account for nearly 30% of total US trade (see figure 11.2). In particular, total merchandise trade between Canada and the United States more than doubled (i.e., over 100%) between 1993 and 2015, while trade between Canada and Mexico has increased more than 700% over the same period. Data for 2015 show that Canada is the second-largest market for US services exports, and the United States is the number one destination for Canadian merchandise exports.[32]

FIGURE 11.2 Top Purchasers of Goods from the United States and Suppliers of Goods to the United States, 2016

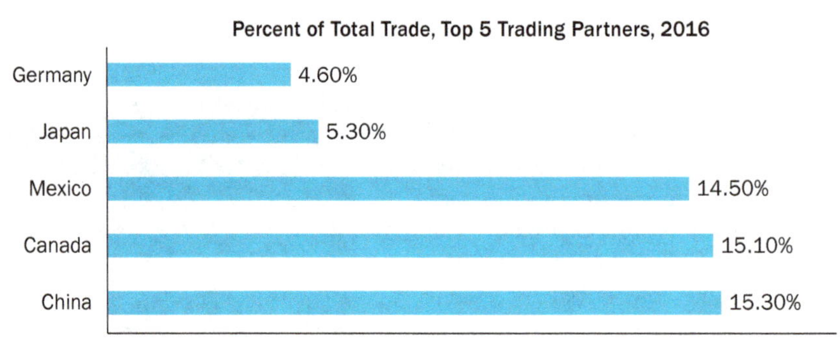

Source: U.S. Census Bureau, Foreign Trade Statistics, Top Trading Partners

According to the Bureau of Economic Analysis (BEA) and Statistics Canada, since the implementation of NAFTA, the North American economy has expanded, with the combined GDP for Canada, the United States, and Mexico reaching US$21 trillion in 2015.[32] In fact, according to the BEA (see figure 11.3), the first three quarters saw the United States exporting a combined value of US$330.2 billion to Canada and Mexico.

It should be noted that the United States has been experiencing a trade deficit or gap for about 40 years (see figure 11.4). This gap, measured as exports minus imports, has widened over the past decade mostly as a result of China's ascension as a major trader. In terms of goods, consumer goods and automobiles are the primary drivers of the trade deficit. In 2015, the United States imported nearly US$596 billion in consumer electronics, pharmaceuticals, apparel, and other household items.

FIGURE 11.3 Top Purchasers of Goods from the United States and Suppliers of Goods to the United States, January to September 2016

Exports (Jan.–Sept., 2016)			
Rank	**Country**	**Exports ($billions)**	**Percent of Total Exports**
—	Total, All Countries	950.4	100.00%
—	Total, Top 15 Countries	696.7	73.30%
1	Canada	178.0	18.70%
2	Mexico	152.2	16.00%
3	China	69.8	7.30%
4	Japan	40.8	4.30%
5	United Kingdom	36.9	3.90%
Imports (Jan.–Sept., 2016)			
Rank	**Country**	**Imports ($billions)**	**Percent of Total Imports**
—	Total, All Countries	1,435.50	100.00%
—	Total, Top 15 Countries	1,141.60	79.50%
1	China	295.0	20.50%
2	Mexico	193.8	13.50%
3	Canada	182.8	12.70%
4	Japan	86.6	6.00%
5	Germany	76.4	5.30%

Source: U.S. Census Bureau, Foreign Trade Statistics, Top Trading Partners

FIGURE 11.4 US Imports and Exports of Goods and Services, 1960–2012

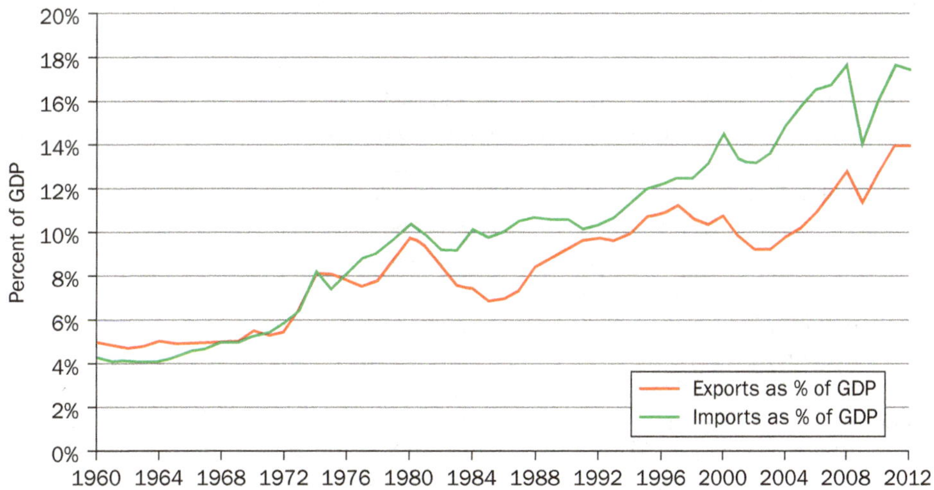

Source: Bureau of Economic Analysis, NIPA Tables 4.1 and 1.1.5

Not Everyone Wins With Free Trade: The Drawbacks of NAFTA

Will you lose your job because of free trade? Maybe. Will you gain a job because of free trade? Maybe. Although it is true that the winners from trade could compensate the losers, they are not always required to do so. The larger societal gains from free trade can mitigate job losses, so the net effect on jobs can be small. Let us take NAFTA as an example of winners and losers from free trade agreements.

It has been argued that a strong, modern, and flexible NAFTA is important for the United States, Canada, and Mexico to maintain their competitiveness in an increasingly complex and connected global marketplace. While cooperation through NAFTA has created a North American trade zone where Canadian, American, and Mexican firms increasingly produce goods and services in a dependent manner, it is this dependent manner in which things are made that makes NAFTA somewhat controversial. One would need to weight the pros and cons of the trade deal and determine whether there has been a net benefit.

We have already seen that trade between the three partners ballooned since NAFTA came into force. This has also helped consumers because prices for goods and services have been lowered. It has also made the United States less dependent on Middle Eastern oil because Mexican oil is imported into the United States at a lower price than it was before NAFTA. Although not very large, NAFTA has help increase annual US GDP growth more than it would have without NAFTA. And, yes, this has translated into job growth. Increased exports as a result of NAFTA resulted in about 5 million new US jobs, some in manufacturing. The sectors that have benefited most are health care services, agriculture, and financial services. The increased competition and lower costs in goods and services that resulted from NAFTA have also led to reduced government spending. Companies supplying the government with goods and services can now bid for contracts in all three NAFTA member countries.

One of the major drawbacks of NAFTA for the United States had been a loss of over half a million manufacturing jobs in various states, such as California, Michigan, and Texas, which were not able to compete with Mexico's cheaper labor costs. The industries most affected are motor vehicles, textiles, and electrical appliances. The migration of jobs from the United States to Mexico also resulted in suppressed wages in the US manufacturing industries affected by NAFTA because the remaining US workers in those industries could not bargain for higher wages. Furthermore, US unions lost bargaining leverage. NAFTA has also been a net negative for the environment as it allowed Canada to exploit the tar sands and led to deterioration of Mexico's environment.

According to the US-Mexico Border Health Commission, the vast majority of US investments into Mexico were in maquiladora factories. These factories are export-oriented manufacturing firms. The profits of these firms are captured by the United States without any direct economic development occurring within Mexico. Over 2,700 maquiladoras were constructed in the overpopulated border region between Mexico and the United States.[34] The towns in which these factories exist do not meet basic sewage and waste disposal needs, which has resulted in a hepatitis A infection rate more than double the Mexican average.[34]

It is clear that NAFTA's disadvantages are significant. However, from an economic perspective, the United States could not compete as effectively against the European Union or China and their trade agreements without NAFTA. While necessary, NAFTA could have been designed with better foresight in order to minimize these negative outcomes.

The Reason Countries Engage in Trade

We will work through an example in order to answer the question of why countries engage in trade. Suppose there are two countries, Italy and France, that are not currently engaged in trade and are self-sufficient in the production of the two goods that they need to survive. That is, both countries can produce baguettes and spaghetti, but they are not equally efficient at producing the two goods. We can illustrate the production of these two goods using a linear production possibility curve (PPC). This is the same PPC curve was introduced in chapter 1 and has all the same properties as those described in the first chapter. We will use a linear PPC instead of a concave PPC so that the math is more tractable. The results, however, are the same regardless of which type of PPC is used.

1. First, assume that Italy's daily PPC for baguettes and spaghetti is as illustrated in figure 11.5. If all of Italy's resources are employed in the production of baguettes, then Italy can produce 5 units of baguettes, but no units of spaghetti. If all of Italy's resources are employed in the production of spaghetti, then Italy can produce 10 units of spaghetti, but no units of baguettes. Of course, Italy can produce any combination of baguettes and spaghetti that lie on or below the PPC.
2. Now, assume that Italy has preferences that makes it want to consume 4 units of baguettes and 2 units of spaghetti (point I in figure 11.5).

FIGURE 11.5 Italy's Daily PPC for Baguettes and Spaghetti

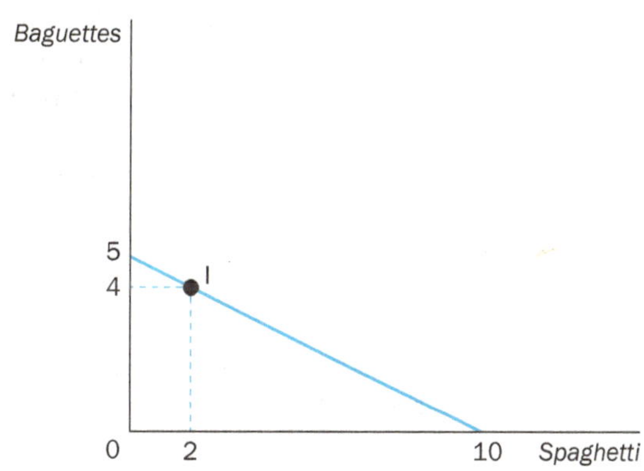

3. Furthermore, assume that France's daily PPC for baguettes and spaghetti is as illustrated in figure 11.6. If all of Frances's resources are employed in the production of baguettes, then France can produce 12 units of baguettes, but no units of spaghetti. If all of France's resources are employed in the production of spaghetti, then France can produce 12 units of spaghetti, but no units of baguettes. Of course, France can produce any combination of baguettes and spaghetti that lie on or below the PPC.
4. Assume that France has preferences that make it want to consume 7 baguettes and 5 units of spaghetti (point F in figure 11.6).

FIGURE 11.6 Frances's Daily PPC for Baguettes and Spaghetti

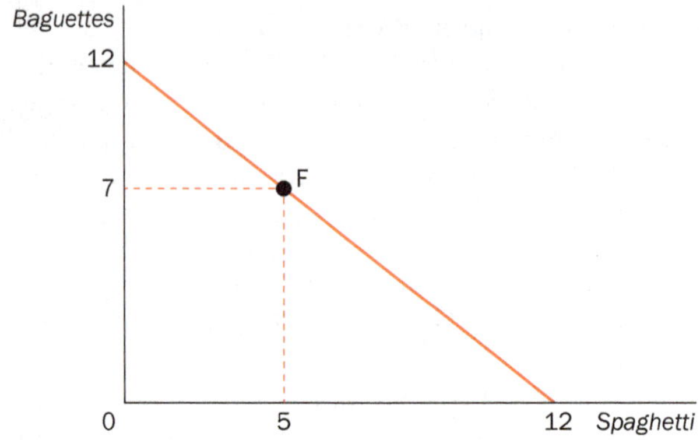

Without specialization and trade, here are the maximum output and consumption units of baguettes and spaghetti:

	Spaghetti	Baguettes
France	5	7
Italy	2	4
Total	7	11

The two PPCs can be placed on the same graph (see figure 11.7) for further examination. One can now ask the question of whether Italy or France has any advantage in the production of either good or both good. From figure 11.7 we see that France has an **absolute advantage** in the production of both spaghetti and baguettes. A country has an absolute advantage in the production of a good if it uses fewer inputs to produce a unit of the good. In addition to noting absolute advantages between countries, one must examine whether each nation has domestic opportunity costs that are either higher or lower than the domestic opportunity costs of other another country. Recall that an opportunity cost can be measured in forgone units of another good. To calculate the cost of the production of one more unit in terms of another unit, we need to first calculate the slope of each PPC.

FIGURE 11.7 Frances's Daily PPC for Baguettes and Spaghetti

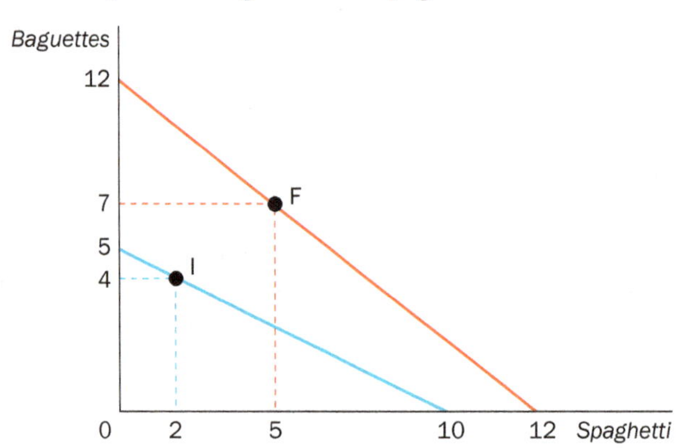

CALCULATING ITALY'S PPC SLOPE

In order to calculate the slope of Italy's PPC line, we need two points that fall on the line. The two endpoints, (10,0) and (0,5), will do just fine. Recall that slopes are calculated as follows:

$$\begin{aligned} slope &= \frac{rise}{run} = \frac{change\ in\ y}{change\ in\ x} = \frac{\Delta y}{\Delta x} = \frac{y_2 - y_1}{x_2 - x_1} = \frac{change\ in\ baguettes}{change\ in\ spaghetti} \\ slope(Italy) &= \frac{5-0}{0-10} = -0.5 = \frac{change\ in\ baguettes}{change\ in\ spaghetti} \end{aligned} \tag{11.1}$$

We can rearrange Italy's slope to read as −0.5(change in spaghetti) = change in baguettes.

Thus, for a 1-unit increase in spaghetti, Italy needs to give up 0.5 units of baguettes. In other words, Italy's opportunity cost is 0.5 units of baguettes for 1 unit of spaghetti.

Application Question

CALCULATING FRANCE'S PPC SLOPE

What is France's opportunity cost of baguettes in terms of spaghetti?

SOLUTION

Likewise, in order to calculate the slope of France's PPC line, we need two points that fall on the line. The two endpoints, (12,0) and (0,12), will again do just fine. Recall that slopes are calculated as follows:

$$slope(\text{France}) = \frac{12-0}{0-12} = -1.0 = \frac{change\ in\ baguettes}{change\ in\ spaghetti}$$

We can rearrange France's slope to read as −1.0(change in spaghetti) = change in baguettes. Thus, for a 1-unit increase in spaghetti, France needs to give up 1.0 unit of baguettes. In other words, France's opportunity cost is 1.0 unit of baguettes for 1 unit of spaghetti. Therefore, France has a higher opportunity cost than Italy in the production of spaghetti (i.e., it has to give up more baguettes for the same number of spaghetti).

This means that Italy has a **comparative advantage** in the production of spaghetti (although France still has an absolute advantage). A country has a **comparative advantage** in the production of a good if it can produce an extra unit of the good at lower opportunity cost. Given that Italy has a comparative advantage in the production of spaghetti and that France has a comparative advantage in the production of baguettes, then Italy should *specialize* completely in the production of spaghetti, and France should *specialize* completely in the production of baguettes. Countries may gain economies of scale from specialization, experiencing long-run average cost declines as output increases.

Let us examine the **gains from specialization** in figure 11.8. If France and Italy can arrange to specialize and then trade, both can be better off. There are more of both goods! In this case, the gains from specialization are 3 plates of spaghetti and 1 baguette.

FIGURE 11.8 Gains from Trade if Italy and France were to both Specialize in Production

	No Specialization		With Specialization	
	Spaghetti	Baguettes	Spaghetti	Baguettes
France	5	7	0	12
Italy	2	4	10	0
Total	7	11	10	12

The above analysis can imply to some readers that countries should always specialize in the production of goods in which they have a comparative advantage because it makes everyone better off. We must be careful about prescribing such a policy. It can be detrimental to a country's economic growth if countries simply limit themselves to producing a handful of commodities for which they have a comparative advantage. While it is true that trade and the gains from specialization help grow an economy, it is not a sufficient condition for economic growth. Rather, the implementation of a production policy based on comparative advantage needs to be carried out within the context of economic diversification. Diversification in exports and in domestic production has been conducive to faster economic growth for all countries, and it is especially true for low-income countries. Countries that are heavily dependent on a narrow range of primary products (i.e., low diversification), even if they hold a comparative advantage in the production of those products, historically have experienced higher output volatility and greater macroeconomic instability.

Five Arguments for Freer Trade

Here, we present five arguments that outline the benefits of international trading.

1. REDUCE THE COST OF LIVING

Countries that do not engage in trade tend to have much higher prices for the goods and services available in their economies. Trade lowers trade barriers through negotiation, and the result is reduced costs of production (because imports used in production are cheaper), reduced prices of finished goods and services, and more consumer choice.

2. IMPROVE RELATIONSHIPS BETWEEN COUNTRIES—POSSIBLY AVERT WARS

While trade relationships can cause friction, today, trade tensions are reduced because countries can turn to organizations, in particular the WTO, to settle their trade disputes. Before World War II, there was no venue for trade negotiations and no legal procedure for settling disputes.

3. INCREASE JOBS AND ECONOMIC GROWTH

Open economies tend to have higher growth rates of GDP. Higher growth rates usually translate into increased number of jobs created. The reason is that firms in open economies have access to a wider range of high-quality affordable inputs, including labor resources, than they would have otherwise. In addition, competition in the marketplace in open economies is a powerful incentive for firms to become more efficient in their production processes. Historically, countries that have taken more of a protectionist stance by blocking imports often have led their economies to stagnate.

4. INCREASE ECONOMIC DEVELOPMENT IN POOR COUNTRIES

More than three-quarters of WTO members are developing or underdeveloped countries. WTO agreements contain special provisions for developing countries, which include measures to increase their trading opportunities and support to help them build the necessary trade infrastructure and implement technical standards. Underdeveloped countries also receive special treatment to justify actions that might not normally be allowed under the agreements, such as government subsidies for certain industries.

5. PROTECT THE ENVIRONMENT

Numerous provisions in free-trade agreements between countries focus on environmental protections. For example, the United States provides (usually to developing nations) financial and technical assistance to aid its trade partners set up stronger regulatory and enforcement mechanisms to protect natural resources.

Five Arguments for Less Free Trade

1. THE JOBS ARGUMENT

A correct but myopic argument about trade is the jobs argument. When trade introduces lower costs from international competitors, it puts domestic producers out of business. While this argument is not technically incorrect, it may be short-sighted.[35] Free trade can reduce jobs in some industries, but it also creates jobs in other industries. It is the net job creation that is of concern (see case illustration 1, next section).

2. THE NATIONAL SECURITY ARGUMENT

A better, less myopic argument against free trade is the national security argument. It is risky to depend on potentially hostile countries for vital goods and services.[35] Under this argument, certain industries should be protected in the interests of national security.[35] Countries many not want to outsource vital communication networks, store private or sensitive information, or award military contracts to other countries that may have the lowest bidder.

3. THE INFANT-INDUSTRY ARGUMENT

In some industries, significant learning curves exist such that production efficiency increases rapidly as a company is able to stay in production longer and gets better at what it is doing.[35] "In these cases, companies often lobby for temporary protection from international competition so that they can become competitive."[35] A good example in favor of this argument is the Japanese automotive sector. Before World War II, Japan exported small-size passenger cars, but heavy procurement of trucks by the Japanese army in the late 1930s retarded the manufacturing capabilities for passenger cars. Protectionist policies were vital for the infant car manufacturing industry to acquire the skills and knowledge to manufacture automobiles and become competitive on the world market.

4. THE UNFAIR-COMPETITION ARGUMENT

Competition in a particular industry from another country sometimes is justly labeled as "unfair" because other countries do not have the same regulations, tax policies, and so forth and thus are not playing by the same rules. That is, "if another country is taking actions to keep its prices low," then "domestic consumers benefit from the existence of low-priced imports. Granted, this competition can put some domestic producers out of business."[35]

At times, the lack of fairness actually helps a domestic country rather than hurt it. If domestic consumers benefit more than domestic producers when other countries are not playing "fairly," then there might be a net gain (see case illustration 2, next section).

5. EFFECTS OF GLOBALIZATION DESTROY LOCAL CULTURES, ALLOW FOR EXTERNAL POLITICAL INFLUENCE, AND STRESS THE ENVIRONMENT

Trade can dilute local cultures, including religions, through the import of new ideas via trade in movies, books, tourism, clothes, music, immigration (movement of labor resources), and so forth. There is a strong desire, especially among nationalists, to protect culture from dilution or infringement of other values.

Trade can also create "banana republics," which are countries in which foreign corporations bully or blackmail weak local governments.

Furthermore, countries vary by the stringency of their environmental policies. Free trade can lead to greater pollution and resource depletion in countries with lax standards (called "pollution havens") because of an increase in demand for their less regulated resources (both human and natural) and the attractiveness of setting up cheap, dirty production (see case illustration 3, next section).

Case Studies in Freer Trade

CASE ILLUSTRATION 1: THE JOBS ARGUMENT AND THE US STEEL MARKET

Recall the "jobs argument": Free trade causes job losses domestically. As a result, governments impose a **tariff** on imports, which is a tax on an imported good or service.

In the United States, in the 1950s, steelmakers dominated the world steel market, producing about half of the world's steel. Since the 1960s, however, foreign steelmakers have increased their market share of the domestic US steel market. As a way to shield domestic producers from imported steel, the US government has consistently limited steel imports by imposing trade barriers to imported steel, such as tariffs or quotas. For example, in 2002, President George W. Bush imposed tariffs on imported steel. The tariffs were imposed for a two-year period, and the import tax ranged from 8% to 30%. Carbaugh and Olienyk (2004)[36] note that protecting steel placed a heavy burden on American steel-using industries, such as the car industry and the earth-moving equipment industry. All the tariffs temporarily saved 6,000 jobs, but the cost to US consumers and steel-using firms of saving these jobs was between $800,000 and $1.1 million per job. Moreover, the steel tariffs would cost as many as 13 jobs in steel-using industries for every single steel job protected.

Thought Question

Can you think of some reasons why, for years, US tomato growers have wanted higher prices for Mexican tomatoes?

The answer? See case illustration 2 below.

CASE ILLUSTRATION 2: THE UNFAIR-COMPETITION ARGUMENT AND MEXICAN TOMATOES

As a result of NAFTA, American producers of corn, soybeans, pork, and chicken have increased sales to Mexico greatly over the years as trade barriers have been dismantled.[37] Likewise, Mexico has become a growing supplier of produce to American supermarkets and restaurants.[36] Tomato exports, for example, have doubled since the mid-1990s and represent nearly half of the tomatoes consumed in the United States.[37] In fact, Mexicans have invested billions of dollars in greenhouses to grow tomatoes, while Florida tomatoes are largely picked green and treated with ethylene gas to help them ripen. It seems that Florida tomato growers cannot compete with Mexican growers because of lower labor costs, better weather conditions, and competitive investments in greenhouse technology.

While higher prices for Mexican tomatoes may help preserve American farm jobs, the tomato-using industry would lose out with higher prices. Many tomato importing, processing, and distribution centers in Arizona, for example, thrive on the lower-priced Mexican tomatoes. Many businesses and trade groups have lobbied the US Department of Commerce in favor of the current trade deals that keeps the price of tomatoes low. These companies argue that much of what is produced in Mexico ends up in the production plants in the United States, generating US jobs, and those goods are then consumed domestically.

CASE ILLUSTRATION 3: THE UNINTENDED CONSEQUENCES OF BANNING GOODS MADE WITH CHILD LABOR

In stitching centers, such as one located in a village outside Sialkot, Pakistan, girls and women, who have been making soccer balls for many years, are paid about $4 per day. Pressure from international groups, some of whom argue that free trade has resulted in child labor, have been pressuring companies to stop employing young children and adolescents. In response, these companies moved their manufacturing to countries like China, were machines do the bulk of the work. Thus, we can conclude that international trade is bad for impoverished children and women, and pressure on these companies is desirable. Well, let us first consider our first economic theme again—incentives—before arriving at any conclusion.

The wage rate of $4 per day is much higher than Pakistan's average wage. So, we can presuppose that the very fact that girls and women in these poor countries elect to work in such poor conditions implies that the work provided by these companies must be better than the next best alternative available to them. Recall the notion of opportunity cost. If there were a better alternative, then they would have chosen it if it were available to them. These girls and women would otherwise be employed in some farm-related job, which in these regions carries high risk of exposure to malaria. Worse still, when anti-sweatshop protesters led firms such as Nike to close down soccer-ball and other similar manufacturing plants in Pakistan, average family income dropped considerably.[38] University of Colorado economist Keith Maskus found that many of the out-of-work child laborers were later found begging or being bought and sold in international prostitution rings.[38]

It is important to note that sweatshops are only a symptom of poverty, not a cause, and banning them may actually impose a barrier to escaping the cycle of poverty.[38] One needs to tread carefully when using strict labor standards as a pretext to argue against trade and for protectionism.

Chapter Summary

In this chapter, we examined the growth of global and regional trade. Since World War II, trade liberalization and the specialization in production have awarded many with the benefits of freer trade. This trade liberalization that has occurred in the past 30 to 40 years is manifested in free trade deals such as the North American Free Trade Agreement. Moreover, the World Trade Organization now exists as an international rules-based institution with 164 member countries that deal with trade rules among its members. Countries engage in trade because the production of goods and services is higher under free trade than under protectionism, which tends to restrict specialization. However, it is fallacious to argue that because free trade maximizes production capacity and income via specialization, it will also, by extension, maximize the income of every individual of every country engaged in free trade.

Free trade will create many winners, but it will also create losers. The extent to which free trade is successful is based on the net amount of winners. It is also equally true that fallacious protectionist arguments against free trade exist. One such fallacious argument is that it is impossible to achieve mutually advantageous trade because one country's gain must be the other country's loss.

Countries that have succeeded in expanding trade over the past several decades have seen improvements in their standard of living for most of their citizens. Yet, despite the gains to the overall economy, free trade remains controversial because some groups within a free-trading economy or country do lose from free trade. Therefore, a government engaged in free trade must balance opposing interests. That is, it must successfully protect firms and workers from foreign competition while simultaneously promoting trade so that it fosters economic growth and increases the average standard of living.

SECTION 3: Testing Your Comprehensive Knowledge

Instructions

- After a thorough study of section 3, proceed with test 3.
- A well-prepared student should be able to complete this test within 75 minutes.
- Solutions to the questions follow the test.

Part 1: Multiple Choice (Please select the best answer.)

1. A producer's comparative advantage occurs when
   a. the producer has a lower opportunity cost than another producer.
   b. the producer has a higher opportunity cost than another producer.
   c. the producer can produce less units of the good than another producer.
   d. the producer can generate a bigger revenue than another producer.
2. A producer's absolute advantage occurs when
   a. the producer has a lower opportunity cost than another producer.
   b. the producer has a higher opportunity cost than another producer.
   c. the producer can produce more goods or services per unit of time than another producer.
   d. the producer can generate a bigger revenue than another producer.

Scenario: Assume that there are two countries: Phoenicia and Samaria. Each Phoenician citizen can produce 1,000 pounds of grapes annually or 500 pounds of firewood. Each Samarian citizen can grow 400 pounds of grapes or 1,200 pounds of firewood annually.

3. Refer to the scenario above. The opportunity cost of producing one pound of grapes in Phoenicia is
   a. 1.0 pound of firewood.
   b. 0.5 pounds of firewood.
   c. 2.0 pounds of firewood.
   d. 2.5 pounds of firewood.
4. Refer to the scenario above. The opportunity cost of producing one pound of firewood in Phoenicia is
   a. 2.5 pounds of grapes.
   b. 2 pounds of apples.
   c. 1.5 pounds of grapes.
   d. 1.2 pounds of grapes.
5. The CPI for Samaria was 129 and 133 in years 1 and 2, respectively. Thus, the inflation rate of Samaria between the two years is approximately
   a. 4.5%.
   b. 3.1%.
   c. 2.7%.
   d. 3.9%.

6. Which of the following is incorrect about the difference between the GDP deflator and the CPI?
   a. The GDP basket includes things that households do not purchase, like coal-fired power plants, locomotives, subway stations, city buses, aircraft carriers, and nuclear submarines.
   b. Even if a product is included in both the GDP basket and the consumer basket, it is likely to have a different weight in the two baskets.
   c. The CPI and GDP would both include housing-related expenditures.
   d. Cost-of-living adjustments such as Social Security payments depend on accurate GDP deflator calculations.
7. The standard of living in the United States is best measured by the
   a. nominal GDP.
   b. nominal GDP per capita.
   c. real GDP.
   d. real GDP per capita.
8. The value of the concrete purchased by a contractor to build your new home's foundation is not counted in GDP because
   a. spending of any type of housing is excluded from GDP.
   b. it would be double counting.
   c. the contractor cannot possibly know the value of every material used.
   d. all of the above.
9. The GDP equation is
   a. GDP = C + I + G + (M – X)
   b. GDP = C – I – G – (X – M)
   c. GDP = C + I + G + (X + M)
   d. GDP = C + I + G + (X – M)
10. The calculation of 2019's GDP would include
    a. the purchase of a new helicopter.
    b. the purchase of a 1978 Mustang convertible.
    c. the gift Tony receives from his parents to help pay his mortgage.
    d. the cleaning services Tony provides to himself.
11. NAFTA is intended to foster trade in/among
    a. North America.
    b. Africa.
    c. Allied Forces.
    d. the world.

12. Economists generally view trade as a _______ proposition for the trading partners.
    a. zero-sum
    b. win-win
    c. win-lose
    d. lose-lose
13. Free trade between countries does not occur with a formal trade agreement. One reason formal agreements are necessary is because countries may limit trade for internal political reasons.
    a. True
    b. False
14. NAFTA was
    a. envisioned, negotiated, and passed under President Reagan.
    b. envisioned by President Reagan but negotiated and passed under President George H.W. Bush.
    c. envisioned by President Reagan, negotiated by President George H.W. Bush, and passed under President Clinton.
    d. envisioned, negotiated, and passed under President Clinton.
15. Economists generally view NAFTA as
    a. the worst trade deal ever made.
    b. neither good nor bad.
    c. a qualified success; trade is greater than it would otherwise have been.
    d. the best trade deal ever made.
16. Deflation refers to decreasing average prices.
    a. True
    b. False
17. Banks create money through lending.
    a. True
    b. False
18. Hyperinflation refers to high rates of inflation such as Germany experienced in the 1920s and Zimbabwe experienced in the 2000s.
    a. True
    b. False
19. Assume that in your online reading of economic news over the past few months, the Fed increased the interest rate thrice. You conclude that the Fed is likely trying to
    a. decrease the rate of inflation in the economy.
    b. increase the rate of inflation in the economy.
    c. decrease its fiscal stimulus.
    d. increase the level of employment.

20. Suppose that in Phoenicia, 140 million adults are employed, 10 million are unemployed, 5 million are not in the labor force, and 10 million are part-time workers looking for full-time jobs. As the country's statistician, you calculate the Phoenician unemployment rate to be

    a. 3.44%.

    b. 5.50% .

    c. 6.67%.

    d. 7.70%.

Part 2: Short Answer

1. The US food supply provides 2000 calories per person per day above that which is required for a moderately active male. In terms of GDP calculations, describe two negative economic consequences that may or have arisen from this excess energy production.
2. Explain how each of the following changes the money supply.

    a. The Fed buys bonds.

    b. The Fed raises the bank rate.

    c. The Fed raises the reserve requirement.

Part 3: Analytical Reasoning

1. For the ancient Greeks, lunch was considered a midday snack. So, it was common for the Greeks to dine on relatively light things like figs, salted fish, and olives. A rise in these prices would therefore be of concern. The table below presents the average prices per pound for three items for selected periods.

    a. Calculate the simple price index for figs for the years 15 and 18 using year 2 as the base year. Prices are in denarii, ⁎.

    b. Interpret the 2 index numbers calculated in a) above. (Be specific and write in complete sentences.)

	Year (A.D.)		
Food	2	15	18
Figs	⁎5	⁎9	⁎15
Salted fish	⁎34	⁎44	⁎68
Olives	⁎12	⁎17	⁎22

2. Consider an economy that produces and consumes only three goods. The following table shows the prices and quantities of each good consumed in 2006, 2007, and 2008.

Year	Price of Fish	Quantity of Fish	Price of Pork	Quantity of Pork	Price of Beef	Quantity of Beef
2006	$7	400	$8	225	$10	175
2007	8	550	7	250	12	275
2008	9	900	6	275	15	275

Calculate real GDP for 2008. Use 2007 as the base year.

Solutions to Test 3

Part 1: Multiple Choice

1A	11A
2C	12B
3B	13A
4B	14C
5B	15C
6D	16A
7D	17A
8B	18A
9D	19A
10A	20C

Part 2: Short Answer

1. Possible answers:
   - One can elaborate on the costs to the health care system in terms of treatment for obesity-related diseases, which are negative externalities not subtracted from GDP.
   - One can elaborate on the costs of environmental damage caused by increased energy inputs to produce excess food, which are negative externalities not subtracted from GDP.
   - One can elaborate on the costs of environmental damage caused by excess waste of nonconsumption of food, which are negative externalities not subtracted from GDP.

2. a. The Fed buys bonds … leads to more money circulating. INCREASES money supply.
   b. The Fed raises the bank rate … less borrowing. DECREASES money supply.
   c. The Fed raises the reserve requirement … less money to loan by commercial banks. DECREASES money supply.

Part 3: Analytical Reasoning

1a. $I_{15} = \frac{P_{15}}{P_2} \times 100 = \frac{(9)}{(5)} \times 100 = 180$

$$I_{18} = \frac{P_{18}}{P_2} \times 100 = \frac{(15)}{(5)} \times 100 = 300$$

1b. The price for figs increased by 80% from year 2 to year 15. The price for figs increased by 200% from year 2 to year 18.

2. We need to use 2007 prices and 2008 quantities.

   Real GDP for 2008 is therefore:

   $Y_{2007} = \$8 \times 900 + \$7 \times 275 + \$12 \times 275 = \$12{,}425.$

References/Endnotes

1. Boundless. "Incentive Theory of Motivation and Intrinsic vs. Extrinsic Motivation." Boundless Psychology, 2016.
2. Scott Horton, "The Economics of Terrorism," Antiwar.com, June 22, 2005, http://original.antiwar.com/scott/2005/06/22/the-economics-of-terrorism.
3. Alfred McCoy, "Tomgram: Alfred McCoy, Washington's Twenty-First-Century Opium Wars," TomDispatch.com, February 21, 2016, http://www.tomdispatch.com/post/176106/tomgram%3A_alfred_mccoy,_washington%27s_twenty-first-century_opium_wars.
4. Samuel Bowles, "When Economic Incentives Backfire," *Harvard Business Review*, March 2009, https://hbr.org/2009/03/when-economic-incentives-backfire.
5. Steven E. Landsburg, *The Armchair Economist: Economics and Everyday Life* (New York: Free Press, 1995).
6. Thomas F. Homer-Dixon, "Environmental Scarcities and Violent Conflict: Evidence from Cases," *International Security* 19, no. 1 (Summer 1994): 5–40, http://magnus1.prv.pl/FILES/TSM/HomerDixon.pdf.
7. Avert, "HIV and AIDS in India," last modified December 5, 2017, https://www.avert.org/professionals/hiv-around-world/asia-pacific/india#footnote27_9deqq8h.
8. Thor Benson, "Stop Calling Bernie Sanders a Socialist," *New Republic*, April 30, 2015, https://newrepublic.com/article/121680/bernie-sanders-democratic-socialist-not-just-socialist.
9. William Easterly, *The White Man's Burden: Why the West's Efforts to Aid the Rest Have Done So Much Ill and So Little Good* (Oxford: Oxford University Press, 2006).
10. Questions adapted from Neva Goodwin, Julie A. Nelson, and Jonathan M. Harris, "Useful Economic Tools and Concepts," Global Development and Environment Institute, Tufts University, 2008, http://www.ase.tufts.edu/gdae/education_materials/modules/Useful_Macroeconomic_Tools_and_Concepts.pdf.
11. Robert H. Nelson, "Economics and Environmentalism: Belief Systems at Odds," *Independent Review* 17, no. 1 (Summer 2012): 5–17.
12. "The Sustainable Coffee Program," http://www.sustainablecoffeeprogram.com.
13. "Government Cheese," *Wikipedia*, last modified January 6, 2018, https://en.wikipedia.org/wiki/Government_cheese.
14. Tatiana Andreyeva, Michael W. Long, and Kelly D. Brownwell, "The Impact of Food Prices on Consumption: A Systematic Review of Research on the Price Elasticity of Demand for Food," *American Journal of Public Health* 100, no. 2 (2010): 216–22, http://www.ncbi.nlm.nih.gov/pmc/articles/PMC2804646.
15. F. Kuchler, A. Tegene, and J. Harris, *Taxing Snack Foods: What to Expect for Diet and Tax Revenues* (Washington, DC: US Department of Agriculture, 2004).
16. Lizzie Dearden, "Martin Shkreli: Pharmaceuticals CEO Who Raised HIV Drug Price by 5000% 'Also Hiked Cost of Pill Taken by Children with Incurable Kidney Disease,'" *Independent* (London), September 23, 2015, http://www.independent.co.uk/news/people/martin-shkreli-pharmaceuticals-ceo-who-raised-hiv-drug-price-by-5000-also-hiked-cost-of-pill-taken-10513645.html.
17. Office of Advocacy, "Frequently Asked Questions," Small Business Administration, September 2012, https://www.sba.gov/sites/default/files/FINAL%20FAQ%202012%20Sept%202012%20web.pdf.
18. D. Arindrajit and K. Jacobs, "Hidden Cost of Wal-Mart Jobs, Use of Safety Net Programs by Wal-Mart Workers in California," UC Berkeley Center for Labor Research and Education, 2004.

19. Leah Douglas, "Monsanto-Bayer Mega-deal a Nightmare for America?," CNN, May 23, 2016, http://edition.cnn.com/2016/05/23/opinions/monsanto-bayer-douglas.
20. Jonathan Levin and Paul Milgrom, "Introduction to Choice Theory," 2004, https://web.stanford.edu/~jdlevin/Econ%20202/Choice%20Theory.pdf.
21. E. Shafir and R. A. LeBoeuf, "Rationality," *Annual Review of Psychology* 53 (2002): 491–517.
22. I. P. Levin, S. L. Schneider, and G. J. Gaeth, "All Frames Are Not Created Equal: A Typology and Critical Analysis of Framing Effects," *Organizational Behavior and Human Decision Processes* 76 (1998): 149–88.
23. *Economist*, "The Trouble with GDP," April 30, 2016, https://www.economist.com/news/briefing/21697845-gross-domestic-product-gdp-increasingly-poor-measure-prosperity-it-not-even.
24. National Bureau of Economic Research, "The NBER's Business Cycle Dating Procedure: Frequently Asked Questions," http://www.nber.org/cycles/recessions_faq.html.
25. Michael McLeay, Amar Radia, and Ryland Thomas, "Money Creation in the Modern Economy," Bank of England, 2014. https://www.monetary.org/wp-content/uploads/2016/03/money-creation-in-the-modern-economy.pdf.
26. Board of Governors of the Federal Reserve System, "About the FOMC," last modified January 5, 2018, https://www.federalreserve.gov/monetarypolicy/fomc.htm.
27. Board of Governors of the Federal Reserve System, "Reserve Requirements," last modified November 3, 2017. https://www.federalreserve.gov/monetarypolicy/reservereq.htm.
28. Federal Reserve Bank of Dallas, "Hyperinflation in Zimbabwe," Globalization and Monetary Policy Institute Annual Report, 2011, https://www.dallasfed.org/assets/documents/institute/annual/2011/annual11b.pdf.
29. Strategy, Policy, and Review Department, "Changing Patterns of Global Trade," International Monetary Fund, June 15, 2011, https://www.imf.org/external/np/pp/eng/2011/061511.pdf.
30. World Development Indicators.
31. World Trade Organization, "The WTO," https://www.wto.org/english/thewto_e/thewto_e.htm.
32. Government of Canada, "North American Free Trade Agreement (NAFTA)—Fast Facts," last modified June 8, 2017. http://www.international.gc.ca/trade-commerce/trade-agreements-accords-commerciaux/agr-acc/nafta-alena/fta-ale/facts.aspx?lang=eng&_ga=2.22396155.1758154451.1513974894-51046992.1513974894.
33. Export Council of Australia, "Advancing Trade Development: A Study into International Trade Promotion: Understanding International Best Practice in Trade Promotion," 2015.
34. Sierra Club, "NAFTA's Impact on Mexico," http://vault.sierraclub.org/trade/downloads/nafta-and-mexico.pdf.
35. Jodi Beggs, "The Arguments against Free Trade," ThoughtCo, March 27, 2017, http://thoughtco.com/arguments-against-free-trade-1147626.
36. Robert Carbaugh and John Olienyk, "U.S. Steelmakers in Continuing Crisis," *Challenge* 47, no. 1 (January–February 2004): 86–106.
37. Elisabeth Malkin, "Mexico Finds Unlikely Allies in Trade Fight," *New York Times*, December 24, 2012, http://www.nytimes.com/2012/12/25/business/global/mexico-finds-some-us-allies-in-trade-dispute.html.
38. Tomas Larsson, "The Race to the Top: The Real Story of Globalization," Cato Institute, 2001.

Index

G

H

I

K

L

M

N

O

P

CPSIA information can be obtained
at www.ICGtesting.com
Printed in the USA
BVHW050708250719
554341BV00001B/7/P

9 781516 534753